Other books by Paul Hogarth

Artist As Reporter
Artists on Horseback
Arthur Boyd Houghton
Drawing Architecture
Drawing People
London à la Mode *(with Malcolm Muggeridge)*
Looking at China
Majorca Observed *(with Robert Graves)*
A Russian Journey *(with Alaric Jacob)*
Travels in America
Walking Tours of Old Philadelphia

Walking Tours of Old Boston

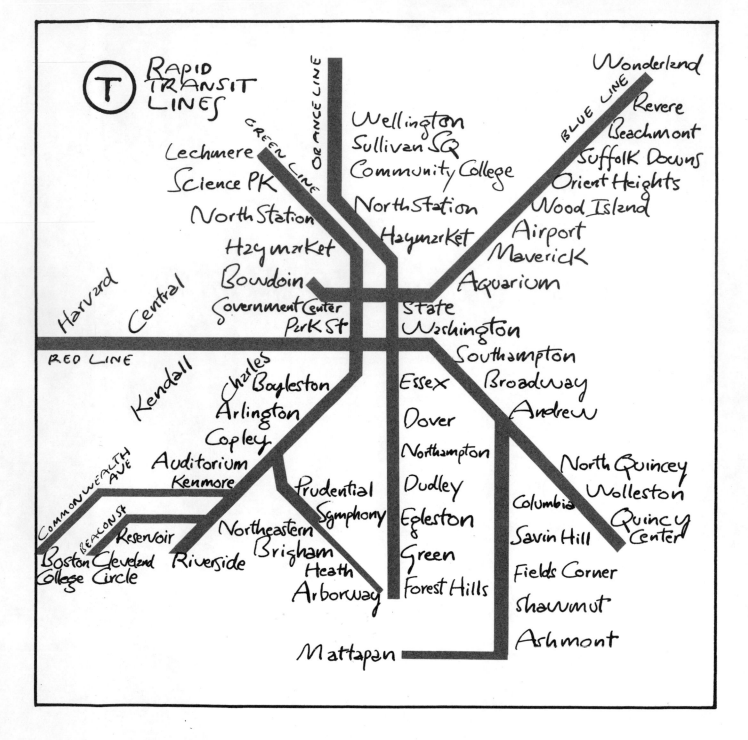

PAUL HOGARTH'S

Walking Tours of Old Boston

Through North End, Downtown, Beacon Hill, Charlestown, Cambridge, and Back Bay

With Forewords by Peter Blake and Sinclair Hitchings

A BRANDYWINE PRESS BOOK
E. P. DUTTON
NEW YORK

This book was edited and produced by
THE BRANDYWINE PRESS, INC.
Clarkson N. Potter, President

Designed by Helga Maass
Margaret M. Madigan, Editor
Typography by David E. Seham Associates, Inc.

Published, 1978, in the United States by E. P. Dutton,
a Division of Sequoia-Elsevier Publishing Company, Inc.,
New York and simultaneously in Canada by Clarke, Irwin & Company
Ltd., Toronto and Vancouver

Hogarth, Paul, 1917–
    Walking tours of old Boston.

    "A Brandywine Press book."
    Bibliography
    Includes index.
        Boston—Description—1951–   —Tours.
I. Title.
F73.18.H63   1978   917.44'61'044   77-18258
ISBN: Cloth 0-87690-282-4; Paper 0-87690-295-6

Contents

Acknowledgments

For my text I have drawn on previous books, notably such authoritative sources as Cleveland Amory's *The Proper Bostonians* (1947), Ray Bearse's *Massachusetts: A Guide to the Pilgrim State* (1971), Bainbridge Bunting's *Houses of Boston's Back Bay* (1975), Susan Okie and Donna Yee's *Boston: The Official Bicentennial Guidebook* (1975), and Walter Muir Whitehill's definitive *Boston: A Topographical Guide* (1975). To these authors' researches and comments I am indebted.

I should also like to thank the convivial spirits of the Club of Odd Volumes. Surely there can be no place in America at which one can find a more gregariously clever circle of fellows. They are too numerous to cite individually, but, collectively, they sustained the lone artist at regular intervals during long sessions of exploration; to the Boston Athenaeum and David McKibbin for their valuable assistance; to Sinclair Hitchings for his own unique orientation program as well as reading the manuscript; to the Boston Landmark Commission and Judy McDonough for their helpful cooperation; to the Massachusetts Historical Commission whose extensive files provided so much information; to the Massachusetts Historical Society for research facilities; to Whitney Haley and Crosby Forbes for much friendly advice and hospitality; to illustrator Amy Myers who introduced me to Boston's young preservationists and planners; and last, but certainly not least, to Edward Riley, who as always was a source of strength in helping me complete the book.

. . . If I had known what it was like,
I wouldn't have been content with
a mere visit. I'd have been born here.

—Stephen Leacock

Forewords

Paul Hogarth is not exactly a recorder of architecture, he is a lover of buildings. He idealizes them, romanticizes them, makes fun of them, and ultimately identifies with them. His drawings and watercolor washes are like love letters to buildings; and, like all love letters, they exaggerate. They are cartoons; they make you smile. Not many artists know how to get a building to make you smile. Hogarth knows. He is absolutely shameless in the ways in which he manipulates his audience.

Can Boston really be that pretty? Of course not—the *real* Boston is rained in, fogged in, sleeted in, hailed in, or snowed in, roughly nine months out of twelve; whereas Hogarth's Boston is a phantom of delights, the kind of town that we, who live here, imagine it to be; the kind of town our friends, who live elsewhere, are sure it is.

Hogarth clearly owes a debt or two to other artists: to Paul Klee, who provided the range of color and some of the wit—but who drew very few buildings; to Gordon Cullen, the British delineator of architecture and of townscapes, whose unrestrained calligraphy described an urban fabric previously unrecognized—but who does not quite possess Hogarth's mastery of color; and, above all, to Saul Steinberg, who probably invented architectural criticism—but gave it an edge too tart for Hogarth's taste.

So Paul Hogarth is a highly innovative artist—an artist who combines some of the wittiest insights of contemporary draftsmanship with some of its most charming imagery. He is also, and by no means incidentally, a very fine writer and a dependable historian. His writing style is as sober and as precise as his draftsmanship is romantic and loose; and, these two accomplishments, in juxtaposition, make for a very nice book.

Paul Hogarth is (need I mention it?) British by birth. To date he has turned his charm on Philadelphia—and, now, on Boston. Those are the only American cities to date; but it would be interesting to see what Paul Hogarth might do with Chicago, San Francisco, and New Orleans. Many of the very best portraits of American towns and cities have been drawn or painted by British types: Rudyard Kipling, Evelyn Waugh, Aldous Huxley, Reyner Banham, and Ian Nairn. Paul Hogarth has joined this illustrious band.

Peter Blake, Director of the Boston Architecture Center

In each age, there are only a few masters of the art of travel. Paul Hogarth is one of these. Wherever he goes, he carries with him talents and skills which most of us do not possess. He is that rarest of species in the twentieth century, and itinerant draftsman, who earns his bread by means of very portable tools: pencil, pen, watercolor brushes, and a modern pocketful of felt-tipped markers which vary the ways he can apply color to big sheets of watercolor paper. Among his many books are a number of manuals that tell how he does it.

He is part topographical draftsman and part portraitist. He has an intense feeling for the endless grace, character, and variety of the human figure, a feeling that is especially evident in *People Like Us* (London: Dennis Dobson, 1958), which was published in 1960 in the United States by Thomas Nelson & Sons under the title *Sons of Adam*. In this journal of his travels in South Africa and Rhodesia, Hogarth unites his pictorial art with his professional skills as a writer.

He is blessed with a sense of humor, and many of his drawings show a keen eye for the quirks and quiddities of humankind. Hogarth is, fully in keeping with these other attributes, a pictorial journalist, an on-the-spot reporter who can say, "I was there." Of course, he says it in a way that is entirely his own, evolved from many different experiences in drawing, from an incredible capacity for work, and from the ability, as well, to identify himself with his subjects, be they people, buildings, or landscapes. (He has, I notice, a great love of old burying grounds where tall trees spread a canopy of green shade above weathered and canted gravestones.)

As a traveler, he benefits from the knowledge that caricaturists and reporters share. Sometimes it is as a stranger that you see most clearly and most objectively and with a flash of immediacy. His inventory of Boston landmarks in pictures and text is second to none, provided you share, as many of us do, pleasure in the survival of elements of the old town of Boston in the changing city of today.

A traveler such as Hogarth does not come with a fanfare of publicity. He comes to see, explore, walk, read, understand, and to learn, as he works with paper, pencil, pen, and watercolor. When his work is done, he moves on to other places and projects. His current series of "watercolor notebooks" embraces volumes on Philadelphia and Boston, and he is working on one of Washington, D.C. How I wish I were his publisher! I would use all the arts of persuasion to encourage him onward to New Orleans, San Antonio, and San Francisco. Then I would suggest a well-earned vacation in Boston.

Sinclair Hitchings, Curator of Prints and Drawings,
Boston Public Library

Preface

My first visit to Boston took place during the spring of 1969. I drove up from Bucks County, Pennsylvania, to visit the Museum of Fine Arts, the Peabody Museum, and the Houghton Library. I stayed at the Parker House and delighted in Charles Bulfinch's mellowed façades and the democratic elegance of Old Harvard Yard. I found Boston unique, perhaps even more than Charles Dickens did when, more than a century ago, in 1842, he began a celebrated tour with an equally celebrated stay in the Hub. Boston was then a town of 125,000 and it was the great man's first glimpse of the young, lusty republic. Before I walked Boston's streets, I had drawn the cities of the United States for a decade. Boston had become a metropolis of 700,000. Yet so much remained; and Boston where it all began, with its historic architecture, its Puritan reserve, its institutions of learning, its clubs and coteries, immeasurably deepened my understanding of America.

I was delighted to be back again in 1972 to draw hippies and hardhats arguing the political toss on the Common for *Smithsonian Magazine;* and again in 1973 to depict night baseball at Fenway Park for *Sports Illustrated.* The big discoveries on this trip were again architectural (the new City Hall) but also gastronomic (Locke-Ober's), which I depicted and described for *Pastimes,* Eastern Airlines' inflight magazine.

I remained a little longer on a fourth visit in 1975. Boston was my starting point for a London *Daily Telegraph Magazine* story to depict the battlefields of the Revolutionary War. Yet after drawing Paul Revere House, Old State House, and Faneuil Hall, I felt Boston remained unrecognized for what it essentially remains. The opportunity to do so presented itself sooner than expected. After the modest success of *Walking Tours of Old Philadelphia* (1976) I felt encouraged to go ahead.

I was back for three months during the spring and fall of 1976 to explore the city in much greater depth. I grew as fond of Beacon Hill as any Bostonian. I likewise became attached to Back Bay and the North End, whose streets had become so familiar to both my eyes *and* feet.

Inevitably, there are omissions. I have restricted my Boston to six walks, resisting the temptation to include South End, Brookline, Bay Village, and other neighborhoods. Time was always short. So I have selected the more important and most interesting places to see and visit, beginning with Colonial North End and ending with Victorian Back Bay.

I have not attempted to list theaters, museums, and hotels, or events of interest to visitors, although I have cited outstanding restaurants.

Each walk will provide you with the general historic background, using outstanding or unusual examples of architecture to bring alive the unique past of Boston. For this reason, too, I have included an appendix dealing with related subjects such as footscrapers, grave-rubbing, and a glossary of architectural terms.

Boston has always aroused the greatest affection in the hearts of its visitors. The way America was, much of Boston still is.

Author's Note

Boston (including Cambridge) is divided into some twenty sections. Here, we are concerned only with North End, Downtown, Beacon Hill, Cambridge, Charlestown, and Back Bay: six sections which enable us to best appreciate the one city that is, more than any other, the birthplace of the United States of America.

Finding your way around is much easier if you travel in downtown Boston by subway or on foot. The city's characteristic features—a colonial past amidst a thrusting present—belong to the walker. Winding one-way streets, formerly lanes, are a delight to stroll in but frustrating to drive in. It is also difficult to park. Buses are scarce in the center of the city. Most Bostonians prefer to use the T (Transit) subway or their feet. A subway ride costs 25 cents, which you must deposit in the turnstile upon entering. If foot-sore, or in an emergency, taxicabs are numerous, but as there are few stands you have to hail one on the fly.

Boston's weather is far from being ideal. If you don't like it, wait five minutes and it'll change, the saying goes. Winters are, of course, cold, very cold indeed, with much snow. A midsummer visit in July and August is not recommended either. Temperatures soar into the nineties with extreme humidity, although air conditioning will bring relief in museums and some historic buildings. Spring is sometimes mild and sometimes not. The best time of all is in the autumn. Early fall between mid-September and late October is usually a fine period.

Unless you plan to stay at least a week, you won't have time to do all six walks. So I suggest you first browse through my book to find the Boston that especially appeals to you.

Each of the six walking tours in this book begins with a map showing all the buildings I have drawn, with numbers keyed to the text. Museums or places of interest not illustrated are indicated in the text and on the maps by a star (*). The arrows indicate the direction in which I walked (which could be reversed should you wish to begin your walk at the opposite end). The top of the page is north.

Much of the factual information in my book has been, and is, subject to change. Visitors to historical sites should check on opening and closing times and on admission charges. In some cases, too, continuing restoration on sites may have altered them since they were drawn or described here.

Walk One

NORTH END TO WATERFRONT PARK

Distance: approximately 5 miles. Time: 5 to 6 hours, at least one whole day. May be done in 2 to 3 hours, depending on how many historic buildings are visited. The North End is the oldest residential neighborhood of Boston, with much to remind us of the city's turbulent and colorful past. Rich in historical associations, it can claim a precious nucleus of historic sites from the seventeenth, eighteenth, and nineteenth centuries, with many narrow streets and crooked lanes surviving in the midst of the bounding Fitzgerald Expressway. Paul Revere House, Old North Church, Copp's Hill Burying Ground, the Moses Pierce-Hichborn House, the Ebenezer Hancock House, and Bulfinch's New North Street Church (now St. Stephen's Roman Catholic Church) take us right back to those days.

Much of Old Boston—in colonial and Federal times—was concentrated here and in the Downtown neighborhood (see Walk Two page 20), comprising the commercial center of a seaport, "alive," in Sinclair Hitching's words, "with smells and shouts and echoing hammers and mallets [and] the drinking, whoring, and brawling of sailors." Even today, although the character of the Waterfront has changed radically, it's not difficult to imagine thickets of masts, riding above the wharves and warehouses, of the ships that brought both luxuries and necessities from the mother country, mingling with those that carried the furs, cod, and lumber of New England in exchange.

Here, merchants and shipbuilders built houses, yards, and warehouses, enlarging the North End by converting the marshy shore of a small, wide peninsula into wooden piers: "wharfing out" has gone on without pause ever since, each time Boston's trade outgrew its berths.

During the nineteenth century, the population jumped from 33,787 in 1810; 136,881 in 1850; to 341,919 in 1875; at the end of the century Boston had become a cosmopolitan city of 560,892 inhabitants. The North End, close to the point of debarkation as well as jobs, burst at the seams as tens of thousands of Irish, Jewish, and Italian immigrants arrived between 1840 and 1890 to make it their home.

The walk is based on the North End loop of the Freedom Trail which includes all the major historic sites. Marked by a line of red brick set into the sidewalk, you will have little difficulty finding it in the midst of the Italian district, a safe colorful neighborhood with pastry shops, restaurants, and street markets to both tempt and enliven your progress.

2

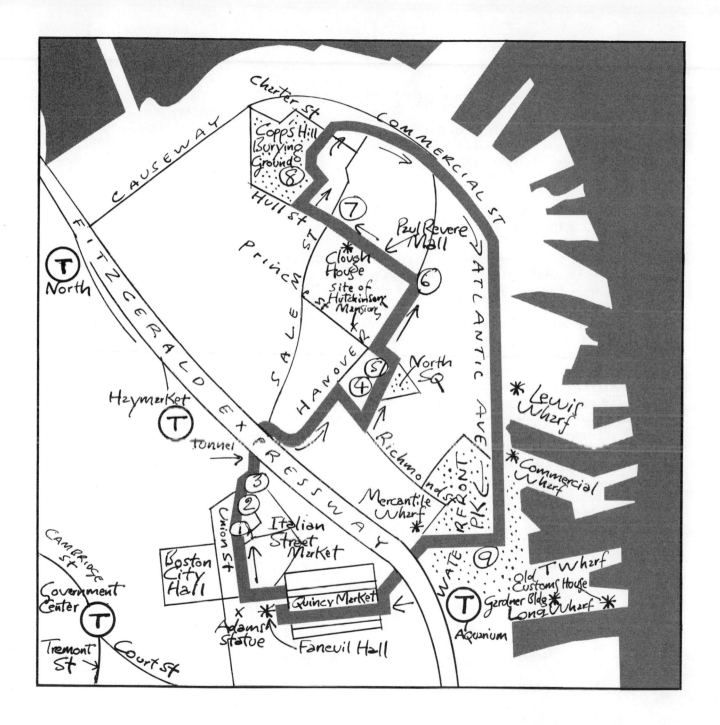

The Capen House

41 Union Street. Open daily. Lunch 11:00–3:00. Dinner: 3:00–9:00 (10:00 Saturday). Reservations unnecessary. Telephone CA 7-8600.

Starting at the statue of Samuel Adams in front of Faneuil Hall, walk north along Union Street, passing through what was Boston's oldest commercial district and the only one that retains the original seventeenth-century street "plan." On Union, which was laid out in 1636, is the **Capen House (1),** a three-story brick house with a gambrel roof, built between 1713 and 1717. Here in 1742 Hopestill Capen opened a dry-goods store which during the Revolution became the headquarters of Ebenezer Hancock, first paymaster of the Continental Army. From 1771 to 1775, the upper part served as the editorial and printing offices of Isaiah Thomas, America's first newspaper tycoon, publisher of the *Royal American Review* and the radical *Massachusetts Spy.* Some years later, the Duc de Chartres, afterwards Louis Phillipe (the "Citizen King" of France), while he was an impoverished exile during the French Revolution, lived on the second floor and gave French lessons to Boston's merchant princes and their daughters. Since 1826, the building has served as the Union Oyster House, Boston's oldest restaurant.

Immediately to your left as you enter is the crescent-shaped oyster bar, Daniel Webster's favorite fleshpot, where he is said to have imbibed many a toddy with a dozen plates of oysters on the half-shell. Legend has it that the quaint old wooden settles or stalls were used by the wives of the Adamses, the Hancocks, and the Quincys, who sat there with their friends, making bandages and repairing clothes for the ragged patriot army. Unashamedly a seafood stronghold, Union Oyster is proud of its eighteen different lobster dinners.

Continue on the Freedom Trail to Creek Square. At 10 Marshall Street is the **Ebenezer Hancock House (2)** (behind Union Oyster House in my illustration), built about 1760. Not open to the public. John Hancock owned the house from 1764 to 1785, during which time it was occupied by his youngest brother Ebenezer. In the basement were stored two million silver crowns sent by France to help pay the revolutionary troops.

Across from the Hancock House is the curious **Boston Stone (3),** originally a millstone for grinding powder color into paint, imported from England by the painter, Thomas Child. Like its counterpart, the famous London Stone, it was, and remains, the official centerpoint from which distances from Boston are measured. As a child, Benjamin Franklin lived nearby, at the corner of Hanover and Union Streets. His father, Josiah Franklin, had his house and candlemaker's shop here in 1712. His sign, a blue ball hanging from an iron bracket, may be seen at the Old State House (see page 29).

The Old Boston Stone

The Capen House

Paul Accardi
Moses Pierce-Hichborn
House

Moses Pierce-Hichborn House

29 North Square. Owned by Paul Revere Memorial Association. Telephone 227-0972. T stop: Haymarket on Green or Orange lines. Five minute walk. Open Monday through Saturday 9:00–4:00. Closed Sundays. Winter: by appointment only, call director, Paul Revere House. Free guided tours. Adults 50 cents, children (6–18) 25 cents; under 6 free. School groups with advance reservation 10 cents per person. Time: 20 minutes.

The trail leads us across Blackstone Street, on through a pedestrian tunnel under the Fitzgerald Expressway; leaving on our right the **Haymarket***, an Italian-style open-air market. On the other side of the pedestrian tunnel turn right on Cross Street and, after walking a block, turn left on Hanover Street. We are now in the North End proper; old, crowded, and full of vitality. Before the Revolution, Hanover Street was lined with the mansions of Boston's Tory aristocracy. With the defeat of the British, they fled to Canada. The fine houses were taken over by merchants who converted them into shops.

A turn right on Richmond Street brings us to North Street and the site of several taverns, gathering places of merchants, artisans, and the Sons of Liberty. Turning left on North Street, we enter North Square, once the site of a colonial market place. Close by, at Garden Court and Prince Street, is the site of the great mansion of Thomas Hutchinson (1711–1780), last Royal Governor of Massachusetts and leader of the Loyalist party. The mansion was ransacked by a mob after the Stamp Act of 1765 and finally demolished in 1834.

On the northwest side of the square is the **Moses Pierce-Hichborn House (4),** a three-story brick house with characteristic belts and paneled chimneys, built in 1711 by Moses Pierce, a glazier and one of the founders of the original New North (wooden) Church. Pierce sold the house in 1747 to William Shepard, a gentleman who in 1781 conveyed it to Nathaniel Hichborn, boatbuilder and son of Deacon Thomas and Isannah Hichborn. His son (and also cousin of Paul Revere) Samuel Hichborn, a sailmaker, lived here from 1805 for many years.

After 1850, the house passed through many hands. The North End became a teeming immigrant ghetto; for many years the house was a rooming house-*cum*-barbershop. Miraculously, many of its original features survive intact, notably, the fine Jacobean-style staircase with balusters and pendant drops. The house has been restored and furnished by Carleton R. Richmond, with additional furniture on loan from the New York Metropolitan Museum of Art.

Boston: Paul Revere's House

Paul Revere House

19–21 North Square. A National Historic Landmark owned by the Paul Revere Memorial Association. Telephone 227-0972. T stop: Haymarket on Green or Orange lines. Open Monday through Saturday 9:00–3:45. Closed Sundays and holidays except April 19. Winter: 10:00–4:00. Closed Thanksgiving and Christmas Day. Adults 50 cents; children (6–18) 25 cents; under 6 free. School groups with advance reservation 10 cents per person. Free guided tours. Time: allow at least 30 minutes.

Next door to the Moses Pierce-Hichborn House is the **Paul Revere House (5).** Built in 1677 on the site of a house once occupied by Increase and Cotton Mather, this is the oldest frame building in Boston. Revere bought the house in 1770 and lived here until 1800 with his first wife Sara, his mother, and his many children. In his day, however, it had been enlarged to a three-story house; in no way like the little gray wooden house that we see today. The house was restored to its original seventeenth-century appearance in 1908. Be that as it may, the house and its contents enable us to pause and think about Revere, his long life, and the events which combined to lift him to the rank of folk hero.

Paul Revere (1734–1818) was born and bred in the North End. His father, Apolloa Rivoire, was of French Huguenot origin, and was sent to Boston as a boy of thirteen to escape persecution in the land of his parents, changing his name to Paul Revere after serving an apprenticeship to goldsmith John Coney. His mother, Deborah Hichborn, was a native Bostonian descended from English mariner-artisans who had helped pioneer the earliest New England settlements.

It was here on March 5, 1771, on the occasion of the first anniversary of the Boston Massacre that Revere staged the celebrated shadow-figure enactment on oiled-paper stretched across his front windows. The drama depicted the whole sequence of events, from the line-up of British soldiers and the subsequent death of five patriots, to the appearance of the ghosts of the victims, demanding retribution.

It was from here also that Revere set out on his famous midnight ride. The British expedition that marched out of Boston on the night of April 18, 1775, had the special objective of seeking out hidden military stores in Lexington and Concord as well as the radical leaders, John Hancock and Samuel Adams. Suspecting British intentions, the patriots set up an alarm system and Revere rode out to pass the word of warning. "A hurry of hoofs . . ." as Longfellow wrote, "a shape in the moonlight, a bulk in the dark. . . ."

The little house is a typical example of a colonial version of the medieval English or Tudor style of home which Boston's earliest settlers built in the North End and elsewhere in New England. Two storys high, with the second story projecting above the first, a steep roof, paneled shutters, and leaded casement windows. The interior is furnished with a fine collection of authentic pieces, including Mrs. Rachel Revere's favorite chair and her kitchen crane. You can also see Paul Revere's saddlebags and pistols.

Leave North Square by way of Prince Street and walk a block left to Hanover Street. We proceed north on Hanover, passing colorful shops offering pasta, salami, artichokes, olives, and cheese. Espresso cafes and pastry shops are everywhere.

Pump in the courtyard of the Revere House: a reconstruction of a type in use during the seventeenth century.

Hanover Street w. R. St. Stephen's

St. Stephen's Church

401 Hanover Street. T stop: Haymarket on Orange or Green lines. Ten minute walk. Open daily 10:00–4:00. Visitors welcome. Time: allow 15 minutes.

At the corner of Hanover and Clark Streets is **St. Stephen's Church (6),** Boston's only remaining church designed by the great Charles Bulfinch (1763–1844); restored to its original site and appearance in 1964–1965 through the efforts of Cardinal Cushing.

Built in 1804 as the New North Meeting House, St. Stephen's has undergone changes of denomination which reflect the changing social and ethnic character of the neighborhood. Originally Congregational, the church was Unitarian from 1813 through 1849 and had Francis Parkman, father of the historian, as its minister. By 1850, the North End had become primarily populated by Irish immigrants who were replaced at the turn of the century by the Italians who predominate today. The church was renamed and became a Roman Catholic Church in 1862.

Although some changes have been made, it remains a fine example of Bulfinch's restrained Neoclassical style which so strongly influenced the Federal architectural era. The design reflects the traditional New England Meeting House with characteristic Bulfinch touches. White wooden paired pilasters enliven a red brick façade, and, below an ornate cornice, a recessed arch holds a lunette. Above the cornice are pairs of consoles and urns, and a tower which supports a belfry and domed cupola. The interior is no less impressive, its main feature being a superb gallery with lower and upper arcades supported by Doric and Corinthian columns.

Christ Church (Old North)

193 Salem Street between Charter and Hull Streets. A National Historic Landmark. Telephone 523-6676. T stop: Haymarket on Orange or Green lines. Ten minute walk. Open daily October 1–May 31 10:00–5:00; June 1–September 30 9:30–4:30. Sunday service 9:30 and 11:00. Visitors welcome. Advance notice required for groups. Clough House is not open to the public. Time: free guided tours last 10 to 20 minutes—more if you saunter among its treasures.

Walk across Hanover Street to the **Paul Revere Mall*** or Prado, a small neighborhood park dominated by Cyrus Dallin's statue of Revere on horseback. Notice the many bronze tablets on the flanking walls—interesting reading for an outline history of old Boston. One is dedicated to the Salutation Tavern which stood at the corner of Salutation and North Streets and was the rendezvous of the famous North End caucus, the instigators of the celebrated Boston Tea Party.

As you leave the Mall and walk towards Christ Church, you cross Unity Street, laid out in 1710–1711 by Ebenezer Clough, Solomon Townsend, and Mathew Butler. Clough, a mason, was a Son of Liberty and took part in the Boston Tea Party. His house at 21 Unity Street, the **Clough House*** was erected in 1715. The second of the North End's two surviving eighteenth-century homes, it was built by Ebenezer Kimball of brick laid in the English bond. The windows are wide with square panes. As was usual with the homes of patriots, the British took possession at the outbreak of the Revolution and occupied it throughout the siege. The house was restored in 1968 by the Corporation of Christ Church.

Next door, at No. 19, stood the house (unfortunately demolished during the building of the Mall) owned by Benjamin Franklin, which he inherited from Richard Dowse, second husband of his sister Elizabeth. Franklin allowed his two sisters to live here but they did not do so happily, which prompted the great man to write a famous letter urging the younger sister to practice the virtue of forbearance.

A few steps past the Clough House, through a tiny courtyard, is the front of **Christ Church (7),** formerly Christs, now affectionately known as "Old North," the most famous church in Boston, if not in the entire United States.

"Old North" won its special place in American history on April 18, 1775, when sexton Robert Newman climbed into the belfry and hung two lanterns as a signal that a British force under General Gage was moving up the Charles River to Cambridge to begin their march to Lexington and Concord. At that very moment Paul Revere was being rowed across the Charles under the guns of the British frigate *Somerset* to Charlestown, where he began his famous ride. The incident of the lantern hanging is reenacted every year on the eve of April 19, Patriots' Day.

This historic church was built in 1723 by masons James Varney and Ebenezer Clough (our old friend). The architect was the Boston draftsman and printseller, William Price, who adapted various designs Christopher Wren had made for the churches of the city of London.

Its tall, slim tower, surmounted by a thin wooden spire—obscured today by Boston's

207
A De STEFANO
TAILOR & CLEANER
1-DAY SERVICE

Salem St with 'Old North'

skyline—made Christ Church an ideal landmark for guiding ships into the harbor. This also made it vulnerable to hurricanes, and in 1804 and 1954, the steeple came toppling down. The present restoration of the colonial spire with its Shem Drowne weathervane was completed in 1974 by Kenneth Lynch.

The interior is simple yet intimate, with its freshly painted white walls and white woodwork. High-sided box pews carry small brass nameplates of North End's wealthy merchant families. The superb wine-glass pulpit is situated on the left of the sanctuary high above the floor to give the congregation an unobstructed view of the preacher. Notice the two brass English chandeliers hanging above the central aisle of the church. These were the gift of Captain William Maxwell and were first lit on Christmas Day, 1724. Each bears twelve candle holders and is topped by a dove of peace, and each is still used for afternoon and evening services. In keeping with the Anglican or Episcopal custom, 1,100 of the early members of the church are buried in crypts, and with them, much legendary lore.

Among the historic persons is Major John Pitcairn, who led the detachment that exchanged the first shots of the Revolution at Lexington, and who died at Bunker Hill. And thereby hangs another tale. Some time after the Revolution, when passions had subsided, Pitcairn's descendants sent for his body but another was shipped by mistake; it is said that the monument tomb in Westminster Abbey contains the remains of a man who died from inflammation of the brain and not as the result of bullet wounds.

We leave Christ Church by way of Hull Street directly opposite the front entrance to the Church. A short walk up the street brings us to our next stop, Copp's Hill Burying Ground.

Copps Hill Burying

Copp's Hill Burying Ground

Between Hull and Charter Streets. Open daily 8:00–4:00. Ten minute walk. T stop: North on Green or Orange lines. Time: 25 minutes; add another 50 if you are an epitaph or gravestone buff.

Originally the North Burying Ground, **Copp's Hill Burying Ground (8)** was Boston's second cemetery in colonial days. Established in 1660, thirty years after King's Chapel Burying Ground (see page 52), it was known as Snowhill or Mill Field. The original plot belonged to one William Copp, a shoemaker from Stratford-on-Avon, England, who had his house here. Today, the historic old graveyard is a quiet and picturesque backwater in the bustling city.

My illustration show's Copp's Hill from Charter Street, itself almost as historic, named for the original charter of the Massachusetts Bay Colony brought over from England in 1692 by Sir William Phips, whose house stood on the corner of Charter and Salem Streets. On the Southwest corner of Charter and Hanover Streets stood the house of Paul Revere, who

lived there during the last twenty years of his life.

Many early settlers and founders of Boston lie on Copp's Hill. The most famous are those indomitable Puritan divines, the Mathers—Increase, Cotton, and Samuel—who occupy a modest family tomb. Increase (1639–1723), an able and influential minister and early president of Harvard; Cotton (1663–1728), author of 444 books and witch-hunter extraordinary; and Samuel (1706–1785), who unlike his father and grandfather did not venture so boldly into the outside world. There's hardly a name among the old Boston families that isn't here, including those of members of former Tory families, such as Clark, Goodrich, Gee, Greenwood, Hutchinson, Martyn, Mountfort, and Watts. These are identified by their family crests or armorial devices and, as was customary, bear no inscription or epitaph. Rich and poor, black and white, merchant-artisan and scholar, lie together in some 227 tombs and nearly 2,000 graves.

Here lies Robert Newman, who placed the lanterns for Revere and Edmund Hartt, builder

of the *Constitution* ("*Old Ironsides*"); Shem Drowne, maker of weathervanes, who died in 1774 at the ripe old age of ninety; and Prince Hall, founder of the first ever African Masonic Grand Lodge of Massachusetts, commemorated, if one may be forgiven the pun, by an equally princely marble monument. The Snowhill Street side of the cemetery was originally laid out for slaves and freedmen, of whom over a thousand are buried here, Boston's blacks having arrived as early as 1638.

The oldest markers sink and tilt with age, and are gradually disappearing with vandalism and the severe New England winters. Most are of fieldstone, or a flinty slate that offered the most sympathetic surface for the stonecutter's chisel. The earliest stones date from 1660 and up to the Revolution strongly reflect the Puritan concern to honor the dead as well as warn the living. Carved on the early stones are such symbolic images as the hourglass, reminding us that the sands of time are running out; skeleton and skull, with and without crossbones; shafts of light, rising suns, and cherubic faces, which, striking a cheerful note, remind us of the day of resurrection when man shall be happier in the kingdom to come.

Those of the eighteenth century reveal the growing influence of Methodism and Unitarianism and continue to remind us of death, but with much less intensity, and bear the Neoclassical funerary motifs of wrens, broken columns, willow branches, spheres, cylinders, and lyres. Those of the nineteenth century seem positively pompous by comparison.

During the Revolution, Copp's Hill was of great military importance: On it the British established a battery of cannon and earthworks from which Burgoyne and Clinton directed the bombardment of Bunker Hill and its aftermath, the burning of Charlestown. During the Battle of Bunker Hill itself, the houses along Charter Street were crowded with spectators. Look across the Charles River and see why; off to the far left you will see the Bunker Hill Monument.

At this point we leave the Freedom Trail. Descend the stairs that lead down to Commercial Street. Turn right on Commercial and walk south on Atlantic Avenue. A few minutes later we enter Waterfront Park, our next stop.

Waterfront Park

Atlantic Avenue Between Mercantile Street and Long Wharf. T stop: Aquarium on Blue Line. Time: 25 minutes.

Waterfront Park (9) is the centerpiece of the bold Waterfront Urban Renewal Project completed in 1976 by the Boston Redevelopment Authority. Some half a dozen years ago, the waterfront was a dilapidated scene of rusting fish shacks, fruit warehouses, and rotting wharves. Today, the new park looks out on to the harbor and is thronged with lovers, lunchers, and strollers. It is the city's most remarkable example of urban renewal. Some historic buildings had to go, but most of the great wharves and warehouses from the heyday of Boston's great maritime past remain, recycled as luxury apartments, trendy boutiques, and chain restaurants.

To savor something of those days of canvas, spars, and rigging, of Yankee clippers racing the seven seas, begin by walking along the waterfront to **Long Wharf** (1710), which once went back as far as the Old State House. Many splendid brick warehouses lined this historic wharf. Miraculously, one of these survives as the **Gardner Building*** (*circa* 1830), now the Chart House Restaurant.

A little farther along is the immense granite **Customs House*** (1845), designed by Isaiah Rogers. Nathanial Hawthorne worked here as an inspector. Surprisingly, with such close sight of far voyages to exotic places, he did not, like his young friend, Herman Melville, make use of tall tales overheard.

18

Retrace your steps along the waterfront. Face north. On your left is the Italianate granite **Mercantile Wharf*** (1857), designed by Gridley, Bryant, and Veux. Here ship's chandlers, sailmakers, and riggers supplied and maintained every type of sailing vessel.

Look now to your right at **Commercial Wharf*** (*circa* 1833), attributed to Isaiah Rogers and built as Granite Wharf. Farther on, immediately behind, is **Lewis Wharf*** (1836–1840), attributed to Richard Bond.

Leaving Waterfront Park, we proceed west on Mercantile Street under the Fitzgerald Expressway to view **Quincy Market** (see page 26) before returning to Faneuil Hall, our starting point.

Waterfront Park

Walk Two

DOWNTOWN

Distance: 4 miles. Time: 3 to 5 hours, depending on how many buildings are visited. If you have only a strictly limited amount of time, it would be best to make Walk One—the North End Freedom Trail—in the morning and then, after a half-hour break for a sandwich lunch or a plate of oysters and a mug of beer at the Union Oyster House (halfway between the two trails), pick up the Downtown Freedom Trail at the new City Hall. You will cover the more important historic sites in one day.

Downtown, together with the North End, has a history that goes back to William Blackstone, or Blaxton (1595–1675), scholarly hermit and former Anglican clergyman, who in 1625 settled on what is now Beacon Hill, the highest point of the Shawmut (an Indian word meaning living or sweet waters) peninsula.

Blackstone's desire for solitude gave way to concern for fellow colonists in 1630 when he sold the leader of the Puritan flight to the New World, John Winthrop (1588–1649), all but six acres of Shawmut for £30. Their first settlement at Charlestown on the mainland lacked fresh water and many had died. Nine hundred Puritans settled along what is now Washington Street and Spring Lane. Shawmut was renamed Boston on September 7, 1630.

Downtown has long been the nerve center of the city. From earliest times, public life centered on and around the site now occupied by the Old State House where Great Street (later King, now State Street) led from the harbor to join what is today Washington Street, the road leading to the mainland. Here, strangers, sailors, and townspeople jostled each other for years, and still do, in a maze of streets and lanes.

Here can be found some of America's major landmarks, where dramatic historical events took place. The Downtown loop of the Freedom Trail takes us to the site of the Boston Massacre of 1770 on King (now State) Street, which occurred in front of the Old State House, then the seat of the Royal Government of Massachusetts. Faneuil Hall, marketplace and forum which resounded with the orations of the Revolution's leaders. Venerable Old South Meeting House, where patriots dressed as Mohawks in war paint dumped chests of fine but taxable tea into the harbor. Old Corner Bookstore, a famous literary meeting place where Longfellow, Emerson, and Holmes hobnobbed. Granary Burying Ground, where Paul Revere, Samuel Adams, and John Hancock repose. King's Chapel and the adjacent Puritan Cemetery, last resting-place of John Winthrop. Park Street Church, where William Lloyd Garrison preached the first public attack on slavery in 1829. And the golden-domed Massachusetts State House whose Archives Museum displays documents relating to both Pilgrim and Puritan fathers.

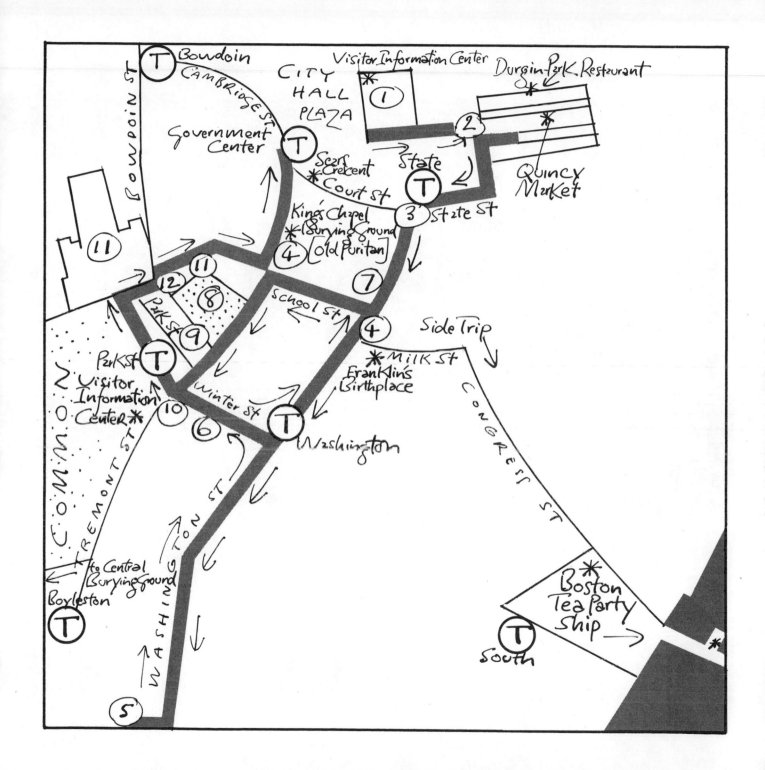

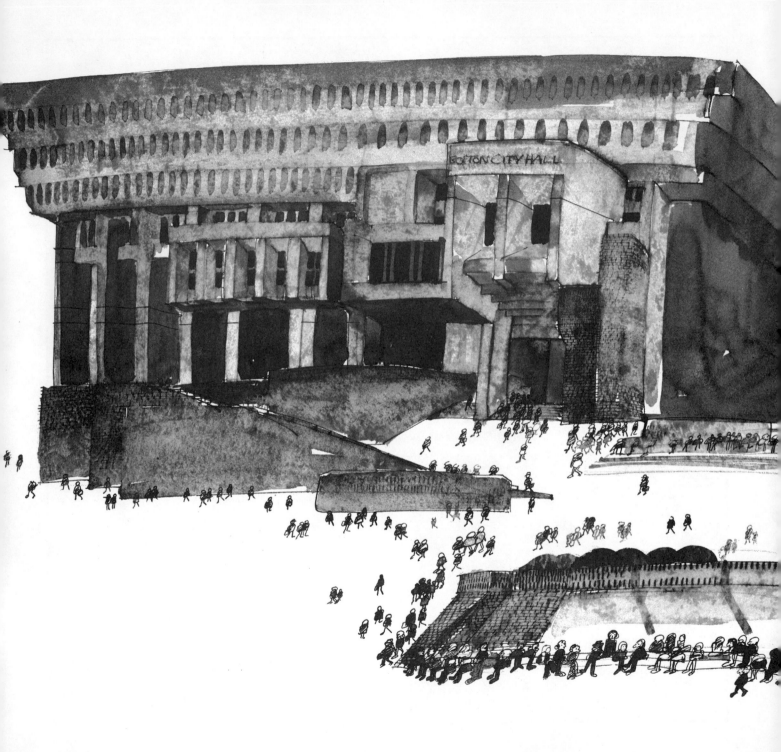

New City Hall

Boston: City Hall Plaza

On City Hall Plaza, Government Center. Telephone 722-4100. T stop: Government Center on Green line. Free guided tours, year round, Monday through Friday 10:00–4:00 starting every half hour. Visitor Information Center open daily 10:00–6:00. Art gallery on fifth floor has changing exhibits by major artists. Time: 25 minutes.

We begin our tour of the Downtown historic area with a quick look at the Government Center complex built between 1968 and 1975 to replace the colorful but rundown Scollay Square section where the famous Old Howard burlesque theater once stood.

After emerging from the subway, face City Hall to identify the more interesting buildings which surround the vast eight-acre plaza. On your left are the twin towers of the John F. Kennedy Federal Building. Just behind is the massive State Service Center. On your right is **Sears Crescent*** (1841), a Federal commercial block altered in Victorian times and restored in 1969. Once part of Cornhill, it was both publishers' row and the center for Boston's second-hand books.

The centerpiece of Government Center and certainly its finest building is the new **City Hall (1),** designed by Kallman, McKinnell, and Knowles. Completed in 1969, its low-slung, massive, box-like bulk, reminiscent of the ancient Zapotec city of Monte Albán, enlivens the vast concourse—a much-needed asset for a big American city. The terraces of open-air cafes and restaurants by the Sears Crescent building

23

make it a pleasant place to have coffee, lunch, or dinner. During summer and fall, the plaza also serves as a venue for open-air plays and concerts.

Just ahead of us, to the right and behind City Hall, is Faneuil Hall (pronounced Fan'l), historic marketplace and our next stop on the Freedom Trail.

Faneuil Hall

Dock Square. T stop: Haymarket on Orange or Green lines. Open Monday through Friday 9:00–5:00, Saturdays 9:00–12:00, Sundays 10:00–5:00. Closed Thanksgiving, Christmas, and New Year's Day. Free. Time: 25 minutes. Armory (Third Floor). Open Monday through Friday 10:00–4:00. Advance notice required for groups. Call curator: Sydney M. Abbott. Telephone 227-1638. Free. Time: 20 minutes.

Much of downtown Boston was torn down to make way for the monstrous Fitzgerald Expressway and Government Center. Fortunately the city is still rich in single historic buildings. One of the most impressive is **Faneuil Hall (2),** marketplace and political forum in one. Long called the "Cradle of Liberty," this is where revolutionary leaders mounted their attacks on George III and Parliament. The Huguenot merchant prince, Peter Faneuil (1700–1743), had Edinburgh painter John Smibert (1688–1751) design the building; he then gave it to the town after completion. Faneuil himself was a genial man about Boston, fond of display and good living. He loved Madeira wine, and once wrote to his shipper that they should make sure that "I have the best. I am not fond of the strongest."

Faneuil Hall

Paul WASCARLA
Boston: July 4 Faneuil Hall

Enlarged in 1805 by Bulfinch, it still preserves much of its original character. Along its street level is a flower market always thronged with carefree young local residents and out-of-town visitors. My illustration shows the Hall on July 4, 1975, just after the citizens of Boston had heard a reading of the Declaration of Independence from Old State House balcony, and after following Shea's Military Band (beating out "Yankee Doodle" "as played in 1776") for the annual reading of the famous pledge of that year—"For the support of his Declaration, with a firm reliance on the divine Providence, we mutually pledge to each other our lives, our fortune, and our sacred honor." Outside, Sam Adams, leader of the anti-British patriot underground, looked well-satisfied, or so it seemed.

The interior is gracious and impressive. Confronting us is George Healey's monumental canvas of Daniel Webster, in the stance of a classical orator, replying to Senator Robert Y. Hayne (South Carolina). It is January 26, 1830, and the issue, states' rights. Webster intones the immortal words: "Liberty and the Union, now and forever. . . ." On each side are portraits of celebrated citizens, including a full-length one of Peter Faneuil, himself, by Henry Sargent.

The stiff climb upstairs to the Armory of the Ancient and Honorable Artillery Company of Massachusetts is an anticlimax. Chartered in 1638 to protect early settlers, the Company maintains a Military Museum and Library of considerable interest and importance, but *professional* display of the conglomeration of weaponry is needed.

As you leave Faneuil Hall glance upwards to view the celebrated grasshopper weathervane designed by Shem Drowne (see page 17). Peter, whose father Andrew, immigrated from England to establish a flourishing family business in the New World, may have been given refuge in England by Sir Thomas Gresham (c.1519–1579), merchant, financier extraordinary, and protector of Huguenots. Sir Thomas, who founded the London Royal Exchange, topped its central tower with a grasshopper, his family emblem (Gresham derives from the medieval English *Greshop* meaning cricket or grasshopper). Perhaps Faneuil commissioned the vane not only as a symbol of commerce but also as a tribute to the memory of that remarkable Englishman.

Continue to our next stop, **Quincy Market***, designed by Alexander Parris (1780–1852), and recently restored to all its former glory. The market was named for Josiah Quincy, a Boston mayor whose idea it was and

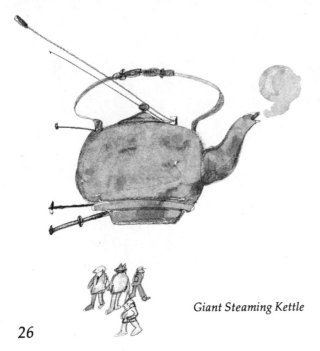

Giant Steaming Kettle

26

who built it as a revenue-earning investment. The handsome granite and copper building, 535 feet long and 50 feet wide, flanked by the North and South markets, is the centerpiece of a Greek Revival ensemble of major historic importance. Note the Yankee Bull weathervane. The upper floor is reserved for public events and meetings, as in its earlier days.

On the left as you face the Fitzgerald Expressway, at 30 North Market, is another landmark of a different kind, the famous **Durgin-Park Restaurant***, surely America's most unique eating place. You will not see its duplicate *anywhere*, I guarantee. Its bustling ambience of convivial conversation and sharp-witted waitresses reminded me of the one or two Victorian chophouses left in the City of London. Portions are enormous and perfectly prepared, too. Roast beef rare, in big thick slabs, chowders, the Baked Indian Pudding, the Old-Fashioned Apple Pie, not to mention Bear Steaks in winter, are justly celebrated. No one has ever succeeded in reserving a table in this citadel of Yankee cuisine. Menus aren't easy to come by either. But Theodore Roosevelt didn't bother. Neither did Jim Farley, Groucho Marx, or Paul Hogarth. You tend to stick firmly to a favorite dish because you cannot bring yourself to believe you will ever taste its like again. Lunch 11:30–2:30, dinner 4:00–9:00. Closed Sundays and holidays. A good tip: if you can't make it at least a half-hour before the posted times of serving, then stop at the Gaslight Pub downstairs. Have a drink to join a shorter line ascending the back stairs. Show your receipt. Immediate seating results!

And while on this subject of the inner person. You may have wondered at a huge steaming kettle outside the Oriental Tea Company's coffee shop on the corner of Court and Tremont Streets and City Hall Plaza. (It can also be seen from the Old State House). Long a Boston sight, it was made by the coppersmiths Hicks and Badger in 1873 and has a capacity of 227 gallons, 2 quarts, 1 pint, and 3 gills and once accommodated eight boys and a tall man inside. Together with the mammoth pipe above Ehrlich's pipe and tobacco shop at 32 Tremont Street (2 minutes walk), it reminds us that Boston is one of the few cities that can still boast of colorful street signs, so very much a characteristic of Victorian America.

As you come out of Quincy Market into Dock Square follow the Freedom Trail to the next historic site, the Old State House.

Ehrlich Pipe Sign

27

Old State House

Corner of State and Washington Streets. A National Historic Landmark owned by the City of Boston and administered by the Bostonian Society. T stop: State on Blue or Orange lines. Open daily Monday through Sunday 9:00–5:00. Closed New Year's Day, Christmas, Thanksgiving, and Mondays during the winter. Group tours by appointment only. Call or write curator: Thomas Wendell Parker. Telephone 523-7033.

A short walk brings us to the corner of State and Washington Streets where one finds at the busy intersection of five streets, dwarfed by the skyscrapers of investment banks and insurance companies, the **Old State House (3),** or colonial Town House.

As early as 1634, the site was established as a location for town meetings. Here, the Puritan fathers set up their stocks, whipping posts, pillories, and a marketplace. These were moved to the Common and the first Town Hall built in 1657. This burned down in 1711 and was replaced by the present building (Old State House) in 1713. Here, various legislative bodies of the young thriving colony met to discuss matters of moment. The council chamber was occupied by the colonists' governors and by royal governors sent from England. From the balcony, edicts and proclamations were read to the populace. Everyone gathered to hear the latest news, adjourning to conveniently sited taverns before returning to the square to protest. Here, just in front of the East Gable (a circle of cobblestones marks the spot) on March 5,

1770, a patrol of British soldiers panicked when provoked, firing on a mob of rioting youths led by a former slave, Crispus Attucks. Three of the rioters were killed and six wounded, two fatally. Astute politician as he was, Samuel Adams made the most of the situation, spreading the story far and wide that the citizens of Boston were being shot down in their own streets.

The architect of Old State House is unknown, but the design is of Georgian style, embellished with many beautiful and evocative details. The Lion and Unicorn, symbols of British power, still flank the stepped pediment of the East Gable, although they are replicas. The originals were pulled down and burnt by the jubilant citizenry when the British Army evacuated Boston on March 17, 1776. Note the handsome sundial set in the wall between them. Below is the historic balcony gripped by the famous and celebrated on so many patriotic occasions. It was here on July 18, 1776, that the Declaration of Independence was read by Sheriff William Greenleaf; here Washington reviewed a parade in his honor in 1789.

After the Revolution, Old State House became the meeting place of the new Commonwealth Legislature until Bulfinch's new State House was ready. Later, it was used as commercial office space, a bank, and a post office before being saved from demolition and restored in 1881 as the museum and library of the Bostonian Society.

In the Royal Council Chamber (restored to include the portraits of George III and Queen Anne) John Hancock was sworn in as first governor of Massachusetts. Today, the spacious and lovely interior houses the Bostonian Society's unique collections. These include a superb collection of portraits of those associated with

Boston's political and cultural life. Another depicts life at sea, the sailor's art of scrimshaw, and instruments for navigation. My personal favorite is that devoted to Boston merchant shop signs. Many of these have a maritime association, such as *The Little Admiral*, thought by Nathaniel Hawthorne to be a portrait of Admiral ("Old Grog") Vernon, carved by Shem Drowne for the Admiral Vernon Tavern, which stood on the lower corner of State and Row Streets. Note also the wooden ship's figurehead, *Lady with Scarf*, by Isaac Fowle, one of the master shipcarvers of the Atlantic seaboard.

Old South Meeting House

Washington Street between School and Milk Streets. A national Historic Landmark. Preserved by the Old South Association of Boston. Curator: Gaile Seybold. Telephone 482-6439. T stop: State on Orange or Blue lines. Open Monday through Saturday April 1–August 30 10:00–6:00; September 1–October 31 10:00–5:00; November 1–March 30 10:00–4:00.Closed Sundays, Thanksgiving, Christmas, and New Year's Day. Admission: 50 cents. Free for children under 12 with adult, and school groups with leaders. Time: 15 minutes. Guided tour: 10 minutes.

Continue on the Trail down Devonshire Street to Milk Street. Take a right turn on Milk and walk to the end of the street. Look up to view the bust of Benjamin Franklin on the second floor ledge of 17 Milk Street and the plaque inscribed **Birthplace of Franklin***. The great man was born here in 1706 in a modest little house long since demolished. Even at the age of three hours he was tough. His father, anxious to comply with tradition, bundled him up and rushed him to Old South Church to have him christened. Turn right on Washington Street to the next official site, the **Old South Meeting House (4)**.

"Old South" is even more imposing than "Old North" and is a red-brick Colonial church of great architectural and historic interest. It was built in 1729 to replace an earlier wooden meeting house erected in 1669. The architect was Robert Twelve, and his design, enhanced by a magnificent white wooden spire and a clock by Gawen Brown, again reflects the influence of Wren's London churches.

The interior is equally handsome with its great gallery and gilded clock that is topped by a spread eagle bearing in his beak twin strings of gilded balls. The clock is a reproduction of the original by the master Boston clockmaker, Simon Willard (1753–1848).

Like many Congregational churches, it had more than its share of involvement with the struggle for independence, and suffered accordingly. Whenever Faneuil Hall burst at the seams with angry colonists, they marched to the much more spacious South Church. Among the meetings held here was the one which commemorated the Boston Massacre, with Sam Adams, Joseph Warren, and other rebel leaders in the pulpit, much to the anger of a group of British officers who nearly lynched them. But the officers had their revenge. During the Siege of Boston in 1775, they ripped out the pews and the pulpit, burning them as firewood, and the church was used as a stable and riding hall for the cavalry. The pews and the pulpit were restored after the war but many valuable books and precious manuscripts (part of the library of the assistant pastor, Thomas Prince) stored in the tower also burned. One of the more important manuscripts, however, Governor William Bradford's *Of Plimouth Plantation*, was rediscovered in the Library of the Bishop of London at Fulham in 1855 (now in the Archives Museum, Massachusetts State House).

Old South Meeting House

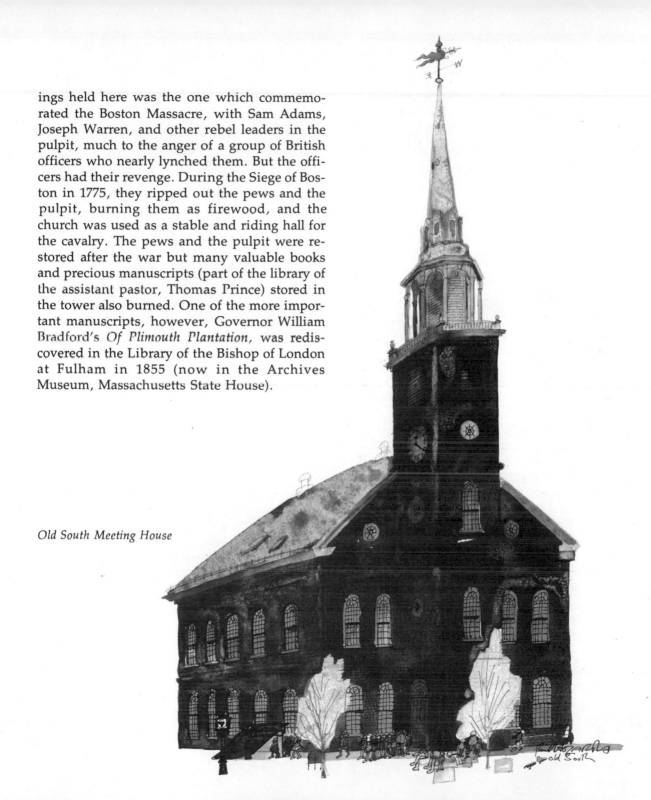

The most famous of all meetings held here was the one which took place on December 16, 1773 when 7,000 citizens assembled to decide what to do about the three tea ships anchored at Griffin's Wharf. Parliament had reconsidered the Townshend Acts of 1767 which had imposed new taxes on glass, lead, paint, paper, and tea, dropping them all except the tax on tea. Prime Minister Lord North seemed to have outfoxed Sam Adams, until the East India Company unexpectedly furnished an opportunity for the colonists to turn the tables.

In 1773, the East India Company, near bankruptcy, asked the British Government for financial assistance. To save the company it was allowed to export tea, wholesale and free of duty, to the British colonies and there to auction the tea in direct competition with the traders in smuggled teas from Dutch ports. The American duty on tea thus remained. But the Government's hope was that the scheme would eliminate traditional American smuggling while keeping the right to tax the colonies. The point was not lost on Boston's merchants, whose business interests merged with defense of principle when they realized that the East India Company would ruin them by obtaining a virtual monopoly of the tea trade in America if they did not oppose the Tea Act.

The meeting at Old South sent a message to the Royal Governor at his Milton house demanding that he give permission for the tea ships to leave Boston and return to England. Governor Hutchinson refused and Sam Adams signaled activists in the meeting house to slip away and put an alternative plan into action. Shortly thereafter, the meeting saw, in the words of eyewitness Samuel Cooper, "two or three hundred Persons in Dress and appearance like Indians gave a War Hoop."

Outside Old South, the "Indians" gave a few more war whoops, and, brandishing tomahawks, ran down Milk Street to Griffin's Wharf shouting "Boston harbor a teapot tonight!" At Griffin's Wharf, the Tea Party boarded the brigantines, *Dartmouth*, *Eleanor* and *Beaver*, cracked open their cargo of 342 tea chests, and emptied 105,000 pounds of tea into Boston harbor, estimated to be worth between £11,000 and £18,000. Parliament was incensed and retaliated by closing the port of Boston to further trade. To implement this and to discourage further acts of defiance by reorganizing the government of Massachusetts along authoritarian lines, a military Governor, Thomas Gage, was appointed to replace the unfortunate Hutchinson. Thus the break with England was brought another step closer by an incident which historians have described as the most important single event leading to the American Revolution.

You can follow the path of the Tea Party from Old South yourself (10–15 minutes). Turn left onto Milk Street, continue to Post Office Square, and then turn right down Congress Street. From here you will see the **Boston Tea Party Ship and Museum***. The ship is a full-size working replica of the *Beaver*, one of the three original East India Company ships. The museum even has one of the original chests thrown overboard that night. (You will have seen some of the original tea leaves in Old South.)

Boston Tea Party Ship and Museum is located near Congress Street bridge on the Tea Party Path. T stop: South on Red Line. Audiovisual presentations and historical documents. Visitors may explore the entire ship and enact their own Boston Tea Party. Open daily year-round: 9:00–5:00 winter, 9:00–8:00 summer. Adults $1.50, children 14 or under, 75 cents. Time: 20 minutes.

Retrace your steps along the Tea Party Path to Old South. You may, at this point, want to make another side trip before continuing on the Freedom Trail. We are roughly halfway and, with the additional visit to the Boston Tea Party Ship and Museum, you may need sustenance. And, if happily the time of day has now brought us to lunch, what better than to sample one of Boston's most famous restaurants in the Downtown section. If not, proceed to the Old Corner Bookstore (see page 37).

Jacob Wirth's Restaurant

33–37 Stuart Street. Telephone 338-7194 and 8586. T stop: Boyleston on Green Line. Five-minute walk. Open Monday through Saturday. Lunch served 11:00–2:00, dinner 2:00–10:00. No credit cards. No reservations.

A five minute walk from Old South. Turn left and walk six blocks south to Stuart Street. Turn right on Stuart and shortly you'll see the large black clock sign proclaiming a Boston institution almost as celebrated as any of the historic sites we have visited. This is **Jacob Wirth's German Restaurant (5),** famous since 1868 for its beer and hearty food, and still going strong.

If you like, as I do, to make the most of an opportunity to eat and drink in a completely authentic ambience, then you will like Jacob Wirth's. It is one of those rare places, the literary haunt, and the antithesis of both the modern fashionable restaurant and Howard Johnson's. And it is inexpensive. Lunches from $2.50 to $3.50. I had, on my first visit, the Fancy Brisket of Beef, seidel (mug) of excellent Light beer, Apple Strudel, coffee, and a cigar, all for

black ties, jackets, and long white aprons and scurry about bearing platters of pig's knuckles, knockwurst, or double-thick slabs of broiled beef, or seidels of Wirth's healthful Special Dark, said to be most like Münchner Hofbrau in all Boston.

This is a good place to take your girl or your wife and children. But it can also be appreciated by those who have no one to lunch or dine with, but who respond to warm and friendly service.

Wirth's can also be visited on Walk Six, the Victorian Back Bay Trail, as it is five minutes from the First Cadet Corps Armory, Arlington and Stuart Streets.

Locke-Ober Café

3–4 Winter Place, Winter Street. Telephone 542-1340. T stop: Park Street on Red or Green lines. Five minute walk. Reservations advisable. Jacket and tie for men required. Luncheon 11:00–3:00. Dinner served 6:00–9:00 Sunday through Thursday; 6:00–10:00 Friday and Saturday.

under $7.00. Not overcrowded either, but peopled with an interesting assortment of Bostonians of all ages and varieties—Harvard, Hard Hat, and Beacon Hill—mingling happily within the high-ceilinged, bentwood and brass interior. Note the organ-like overmantel above the long mahogany bar with its circular medallion of Jacob Wirth, Sr., with his magnificent handlebar moustaches and the wise motto: *Suum Cuique* (To each his own). Waiters wear

As you emerge from the Park Street subway, cross over Tremont Street and walk south to Winter Street. Turn left on Winter. Winter Place is the first alley on your right. Up ahead you'll see the big lock sign I've drawn.

The second of Boston's two most famous traditional restaurants Downtown, the legendary **Locke-Ober Café (6)** is a unique survival of the Gilded Age. It is unashamedly a temple of

Locke-Ober Café

35

gastronomy. Unlike Jacob Wirth's, however, it *is* expensive. Yet for the superb quality of its cuisine it *is* reasonable. I would have eaten a fuller meal if I hadn't been thinking of the drawings I had to make. So I had a simple traditional repast. Sirloin steak, a bottle of vintage Châteauneuf du Pape, some cheese, brandy, plus a cigar from Ehrlich's of Tremont Street. This all came to little more than $20. The service is impeccable.

Since its early origins in the 1880s, Locke-Ober's has passed through several owners and managers, yet hardly a detail of the main dining room on the ground floor has been touched, including the vast L-shaped, ornately carved, mahogany bar with its wondrous silver dish-covers suspended from the ceiling with pulleys and counterweights. Drinks are still hoisted to the private rooms upstairs on a dumbwaiter embellished with gleaming brass rods. Note the

Old Corner Bookstore

large rosy nude above the bar by Tommaso Juglaris. She is draped in black when Harvard loses to Yale.

Locke-Ober's clientele consists largely of businessmen from Downtown's banks and offices during luncheon, and largely from Harvard and Beacon Hill at dinner. Ladies are welcome if accompanied in the Men's Bar and main dining room. But if you are a girl alone you may have to be content with just a lingering look and have your meal in the adjacent Camus Room.

Old Corner Bookstore

Northwest corner of Washington and School Streets. Massachusetts Historic Landmark. Owned by Historic Boston, Inc., and the Boston Globe. T stop: Washington on Red or Orange lines. Open daily except Sundays 9:00–5:00. Visitors welcome. Time: 10 minutes.

Back at Old South Meeting House, cross Washington Street to the next Freedom Trail site, the **Old Corner Bookstore (7),** the only eighteenth-century house remaining in this part of the city.

Old Corner Bookstore served as a residence for over one hundred years before conversion for use as a bookstore. Built soon after the Great Boston Fire of October 2, 1711, by Thomas Crease, an apothecary, the house passed through several hands until 1828, when the ground floor was converted into a bookstore for the firm of Carter and Hendee, the first of a long line of booksellers and publishers to occupy the premises.

The most famous of these was undoubtedly Ticknor and Fields. From 1833 to 1864, under the guidance of the able William D. Ticknor (1810–1864) and James T. Fields (1817–1881), publishing in America came of age with Boston as its epicenter. The store became the lounge and resort of the *literati* of Boston and Harvard. Here, Longfellow looked in to have a chat. Here, Louis Agassiz showed his genial and benevolent face. Here, Oliver Wendell Holmes came in to give or receive the news of the day. Here, poets, lecturers, preachers, professors, and newspapermen combined, without premeditation, to establish a literary exchange where they learned what new books were forthcoming, looked at them even if they did not buy them, and talked together about literature and life. Little wonder that Old Corner was dubbed "Parnassus Corner" after the mountain in Greece sacred to the Muses.

Much of this success was due to Fields, who firmly believed that the interests of authors and publishers were identical. To make doubly sure he got the best, he offered generous royalties. And instead of pirating, a common practice on both sides of the Atlantic (at this time there was no international copyright agreement), Fields either paid his British authors a flat sum or placed them on the same royalty scale as his American authors.

By the 1850s, this enlightened code of business practice made Fields both publisher and friend of almost every great British and American author of the nineteenth century. Among his British men of letters were Dickens, Thackeray, Tennyson, Browning, Matthew Arnold, and Leigh Hunt. His American writers were just as celebrated, and included Hawthorne, Emerson, Thoreau, Longfellow, Howe, Holmes, Whittier, Stowe, and Lowell.

In 1859, he persuaded Ticknor to buy the *Atlantic Monthly*, the voice of liberal Boston. With Fields as its editor (his office was a tiny back room behind the second window on School Street), it also became the most famous. And in 1864 he acquired the *North American Review*, Boston's answer to the great Scotch quarterly, the *Edinburgh Review*. After the death of Ticknor that same year, Fields moved the flourishing enterprise from Old Corner to much larger quarters in Tremont Street.

Other booksellers and publishers followed Ticknor and Fields at the Old Corner until 1903. After that time the building fell to less distinguished use and was for years hidden from view by huge billboards and garish signs. That it was saved from further deterioration and demolition is due to the nonprofit corporation, Historic Boston, Inc. The Old Corner Bookstore, restored in 1964 to its 1828 appearance, now functions as the office of the Boston *Globe*.

From here continue up School Street to our next site, the Granary Burying Ground.

Here, beneath the linden and oak, lie the famous and infamous: patriots and loyalists in seventeen hundred graves and two hundred tombs. The central path leads us to the most distinctive feature, the granite obelisk over the tomb of Franklin's parents, designed by Solomon Willard (1783–1861), who also designed the public entrance gates. Other monuments include those to Samuel Adams, John Hancock, James Otis, Robert Treat Paine, and, of course, the victims of the Boston Massacre. Here lie Peter Faneuil (the inscription was cut "Funel"), Paul Revere, and a host of famous old Bostonians including Governors Bellingham, Bowdoin, Cushing, Eustis, Sullivan, and Sumner,

Old Granary Burying Ground

83–115 Tremont Street (next to Park Street Church). T stop: Park Street on Red or Green lines. Open daily 8:00–4:00. Free. Time: 25 minutes; add another 25 if you are a tombstone buff.

Continue along School Street, past the Parker House Hotel. Turn left on Tremont, and soon you will spot the Egyptian Revival pylon gateway of **Old Granary Burying Ground (8).**

as well as distinguished eccentrics like Dr. John Jeffries, who had served with the British at Bunker Hill and became an exile, but didn't like England and returned to Boston when peace was restored.

Old Granary was the scene of many elaborate funerals. One of the most dramatic, that of the victims of the Boston Massacre, was conducted with great ceremony one wintry day in March, 1770, and attended by a crowd of 10,000. The funeral of Hancock was no less impressive. His remains were brought here by an immense crowd of mourners. The aged Sam Adams followed the bier until fatigue compelled him to retire; he himself was buried here with similar pomp in 1803.

Like Copp's Hill, Granary contains a rich variety of designs carved on slate or fieldstone markers. Again, the Puritan prohibition of imagery accounts for the stark simplicity of the early stones. But by the eighteenth century, when the distinction was made between images for gravestones and those in churches, symbols like death's-heads, hourglasses, and crossbones became common.

Park Street Church

Corner of Tremont and Park Streets. Telephone 523-3383. T stop: Park Street on Red or Green lines. Open Monday through Friday 9:00–4:30, Saturdays 9:00–12:00, Sundays 9:00–1:00. Closed July 4 and Labor Day. Sunday services: 10:30 A.M. and 7:30 P.M. Visitors welcome. Time: 15 minutes.

Park Street Church (9), built in 1809 on the site of the town Granary, is an outstanding example of a large Congregational church of the Federal era. Its architect was Peter Banner, an Englishman who worked in Boston between 1806 and 1828. The great Wren telescopic steeple towered above the neighboring houses until the late nineteenth century, but after a severe gale caused it to sway, it was rebuilt with modifications. Yet even today, surrounded as it is by inappropriate commercial premises, the great tall church remains an impressive spectacle. The chimes (a Schulmerich electronic carillon), installed in 1961, ring out familiar hymns like "Rock of Ages" several times daily, and provide a poignant score to the swirling scene below.

The walls are of brick laid in Flemish bond, and the windows of the main structure are arranged in two tiers. The windows in the north and side walls are in two-story-high arches and the immensely tall windows in the upper level have semicircular heads. A square three-and-a-half story brick tower topped by a superb four-stage wooden tower and spire rises to a height of 217 feet. An unusual feature is the semicircular, deeply recessed, two-story arcades within which are set the main entrance and, above, a Palladian window. Both the main entrance and this window are framed by elaborately carved pairs of columns, the work of Willard.

The stiff two-story climb takes you inside to the huge auditorium, with galleries extending around on three sides; unexpectedly, however, the interior woodwork has a distinct Victorian flavor.

During the War of 1812, the church was dubbed "Brimstone Corner" because brimstone, or sulphur, used in making gunpowder, was stored in the basement. Some Bostonians, however, attributed the name to the fiery sermons preached upstairs. The church has long been associated with important social issues. It was here in 1829 that the youthful William Lloyd Garrison (1805–1879) launched his attack on the dragon of slavery, with dramatic results. Two years later, the Nat Turner slave revolt broke out in Virginia, causing the deaths of many whites and blacks. Although such protests were not new, the whole South blamed Garrison. Georgia put up a reward for him dead or alive. Thus the movement that plunged America into civil war was launched here.

Here, also, "America" was first sung in public, by Sunday school children on July 4, 1831. Written by Samuel Francis Smith, a Baptist clergyman, it was set to a tune he found in a book of German school songs. Only later did he

Park Street Church

find out that he had inadvertently used the tune of the British national anthem "God Save the Queen," also derived from the same source!

At this point, you are halfway through the Trail. So, if you wish, you can take a break and eat your sandwich lunch on the Common. Otherwise continue to the next stop, St. Paul's Cathedral.

St. Paul's Cathedral

Tremont Street and Boston Common. Telephone 542-8674. T stop: Park Street on Red or Green lines. Open Sunday through Friday 8:00–5:00. Visitors welcome. Time: 15 minutes.

Although not an official Freedom Trail site, or even a Massachusetts Historic Landmark, Episcopal **St. Paul's Cathedral (10)** is as firmly Old Boston as is Faneuil Hall or Locke-Ober's. Overshadowed by Park Street Church and adjacent commercial buildings, its somewhat gloomy Ionic-columned façade has an unfinished look. But don't be deceived by outward appearances. It is one of the finest examples of Greek Revival in the city.

Actually, the building *is* unfinished. The pediment was intended to be richly ornamented with a bas-relief of Paul before Herod Agrippa II, which would have added much to its appearance, but lack of funds is said to have prevented execution. Built in 1819, St. Paul's initiated a new style in Boston church architecture, and again involved the collaboration of Parris and Willard. The two also collaborated on the design of Quincy Market, which we looked at earlier, and Willard was the designer of the Egyptian Revival entrance gates to the Old Granary Burying Ground.

Despite the somewhat forbidding façade, the interior is intimate and discreetly sumptuous with warm, light gray walls, dark green Venetian-style shuttered windows, and symmetrically arranged box pews. The ceiling is a cylindrical vault, with panels spanning the entire width of the church.

The list of its original founders invokes the elitist spirit of Federal Boston and glows with such Boston First Family names as Amory, Winthrop, Bowdoin, Greene, and Hancock. The members of the Building Committee were George Sullivan, Daniel Webster, John and George Odin, William Appleton, David Sears, Francis Wilby, and Henry Codman. Among the earliest members were Dr. John Warren, a leading surgeon; Isaac Hull, a Captain of "*Old Ironsides*"; and Harrison Gray Otis, Senator, Mayor of Boston, and political boss of the Old Federalist party machine. Its clergy included many outstanding men, notably Phillips Brooks, Boston's greatest preacher, and Bishop William Lawrence, its greatest patriarch.

Almost opposite St. Paul's, a little farther down Tremont, is the Boston Common Visitor Information Center. Open daily 9:00–5:00 to deal with your enquiries.

Retrace your steps to where we left the Freedom Trail at Park Street Church. Follow the Trail up through the Common to the next Freedom Trail site, the Massachusetts State House.

St. Paul's Cathedral

43

Massachusetts State House

The Massachusetts State House

Beacon Street. Telephone 727-3676. Archives Museum: Telephone 727-2816. T stop: Park Street on Red or Green lines. Five minute walk. Open Monday through Friday 9:00–5:00. Visitors may sit in gallery to observe state legislature in session. Call 727-2356 for schedule of sessions. Free guided tours year round: 30–45 minutes. Group tours by appointment only. Call 727-3676 or write Room 275, State House, Boston 02133. Time: 1–2 hours, depending on your interest.

Walk through the Common along the avenue of huge, old English elms. Here we enter the Boston of Charles Bulfinch with its classic façades and tree-shaded streets. On our right is Park Street, once lined with fine Federal town houses occupied by affluent and influential citizens. Only the Amory-Ticknor house survives from the original development designed by Bulfinch. But because the later buildings are the same height as the original Federal structures they replaced, Park Street maintains something of its original flavor.

The Amory-Ticknor House*, at the corner of Park and Beacon Streets, was designed by Bulfinch for Thomas Amory, a wealthy Boston merchant. This great and handsome mansion received many distinguished guests, among them Lafayette, who stayed here in 1825 when he came to Boston to take part in the dedication of the Bunker Hill Monument. The house was called "Amory's Folly" because of its great size. Later it was divided into two. At 9 Park Street lived the famous literary historian, George Ticknor (1791–1871). Greatly honored were those invited to the Ticknor salon. In the celebrated library upstairs, kindred spirits like Thackeray were favored with quiet cordiality. The less distinguished, however, were confined to the downstairs parlor.

On the left, as we exit the Common and enter Beacon Street, is the high-relief bronze memorial to the 54th Massachusetts, the first regiment of Negro volunteers organized during the Civil War. The sculptor was Augustus St. Gaudens (1848–1907).

Turn now to view the magnificent **Massachusetts State House (11),** with its warm red-brick walls, white marble trim, and great golden dome. The dome, originally shingled and whitewashed, was covered in copper by our old friend, Paul Revere, in 1802. Painted gold in 1861, gilded in 1874, it immediately found a place in the hearts of all New Englanders. Visiting Boston in 1870, the English artist, Arthur Boyd Houghton, gave another version of the Hub story when he quoted one Yankee farmer—in Boston for the first time—thinking it "so like a big hub, that it had to be the hub of the Universe." Even Brahmin novelist Henry James, not so inclined to superlatives, raved about it looking "as fresh as a Christmas toy."

Bulfinch designed the State House in 1787, but it wasn't until 1795 that construction began. It is without doubt his greatest public building. The influence of Sir William Chambers (architect of London's new Somerset House), for the facades, and Robert Adam, for the interiors, is said to predominate. But to me the general ensemble seems posessed by a new and vigorous spirit. The slender proportions, a robust delicacy expecially suited to wood and plaster in countless exquisite devices and emblems, are essentially American elements which enrich the bold classical form. President Monroe, visiting Boston in 1817, was so impressed that Bulfinch was appointed architect of the reconstruction of the Capitol in Washington, D.C. where he duly repeated his rotunda and dome motif, adapting it to the original design by William Thornton.

Massachusetts grew so fast that a series of additions to the State House was begun as early as 1831 to provide more space for records and papers. A second addition, built in 1853–1856, provided more space for the growing State Library and other departments. Bulfinch's design looked essentially the same as these portions were added on behind. But later additions, the Brigham extension to the north across Mt. Vernon Street, 1889–1895, and the east and west wings built in 1914–1917, engulfed Bulfinch's State House, making it much less essentially his.

Many of these later additions can be viewed on the guided tour. These include the **Memorial Hall,** or Hall of Flags, which displays an impressive collection of regimental flags of the Civil War, the Spanish-American War, and both World Wars; the **State Library** at the north end of the Brigham annex; the **State Archives and Museum** with its priceless source materials of colonial American history; and the palatial **House of Representatives** where hangs the historic Sacred Cod symbol of early wealth, brought from the Old State House in 1798. A solid piece of pine, it is a unique example of American folk art.

Ideally, these should be seen if you *have* the time, but for those with less time, or those who feel disinclined to suffer mental indigestion, stay with Bulfinch's State House. We will therefore only visit the Doric Hall, the Senate Reception Room, the Senate Chamber, and if he isn't there, the Governor's office.

Enter the State House by the side door in the right or east wing. Proceed to the Doric Hall on the first floor, where you can either join the guided tour or pick up the self-guided-tour leaflet.

Doric Hall takes its name from the double row of columns with Doric capitals which run from one end of the room to the other. It is the only room on the ground floor which retains, to a large extent, Bulfinch's original design. Arched niches and panels frame busts, memorials, statues, and paintings of famous Americans. Among them you will find portraits of provincial Royal Governors, including John Winthrop, John Leverett, and William Shirley; Thomas Ball's marble figure of Governor John A. Andrew and, unexpectedly, a statue of Washington by British sculptor Sir Francis Chantrey.

On the second floor the Bulfinch interiors also remain substantially much as they were, especially the superb blue and white **Senate Chamber,** which lies directly below the gilded dome of the State House itself. Originally designed as the House of Representatives, this beautiful room fulfilled this function for almost a century.

Again, Bulfinch is revealed as a master of the Palladian interior. His decorations, beginning at the very center of the dome itself, descend in circle after circle of exquisitely balanced ornament. The four emblems at each of the four corners of the chamber symbolize commerce, agriculture, war, and peace. Each is gracefully embellished with swags of classical drapery. In niches are dignified busts of the great: Franklin, Washington, Lafayette, Lincoln, and many others. I especially liked the robustly carved eagle above the North Gallery, holding in its beak a banderole bearing the words, "God Save the Commonwealth of Massachusetts."

We next enter the **Senate Reception Room,** which from 1798 to 1896 was the original Senate Chamber. It is barrel-roofed, with a small gallery at the west end. Bulfinch's decorations on walls and ceiling again display great virtuosity. Among the portraits is that of Elbridge Gerry, who changed the shape of the district he represented to that resembling a salamander. Hence the term, "Gerrymander."

The last remaining room of the Bulfinch State House, the **Governor's Office,** was originally the Council Chamber. Well-proportioned, superbly decorated with Corinthian pilasters, festoons, and sunbursts, the room ranks with the Senate Chamber and the Senate Reception Room as a gem of Federal interior design. A pewter chandelier, made by Paul Revere, hangs from the ceiling. The gold star on the east wall signifies that Massachusetts was one of the original thirteen states.

Exit from the State House from the Archives Museum (reached by elevator to the basement) on Beacon Street. As you leave pause to look at **Boston Common,** the oldest public park in the United States, providing much-appreciated green space and shaded walking paths following those established by grazing cattle in the days of Governor Winthrop. Here stood stocks and pillories, as well as a compound for holding those who desecrated the Sabbath. Free speech is now the law on the Common, and, down by the Park Street subway, the babble of argument is heard on every kind of problem, on every day of the week.

Dotted about the State House grounds below the central promenade are statues of the once-famous or infamous: Horace Mann (1796–1859), great spokesman for public education, and Daniel Webster, spellbinding orator and leader of New England's Whigs. Overlooking Beacon Street is the equestrian statue of Civil War General Joseph Hooker by Daniel Chester French. Handsome "Fighting Joe" Hooker, who was said to do more sulking than fighting, distinguished himself in the Peninsular and Antietam Campaigns but frequently failed to live up to his nickname. As a young officer, he had asked for the hand of a pretty young Beacon Hiller but was rejected. In later life, that pretty young thing, now a silver-haired old lady, occupied the Amory-Ticknor House, from where the statue was visible at all times. "The irony of it," she told Jack Frost, "my old suitor looking in at my bedroom night and day!" Other statues include those of Mary Dyer, a martyr to her Quaker faith, hanged on the Common in 1660, and Anne Hutchinson, banished by Winthrop in 1637 for eighty-two heretical opinions, "some blasphemous, others erroneous, and all unsafe."

From here, turn left and continue along the Freedom Trail down Beacon Street, to our next stop, the Chester Harding House.

Chester Harding House

16 Beacon Street. A National Historic Landmark restored in 1962. Headquarters of the Boston Bar Association. T stop: Park Street on Red or Green lines. Five minute walk. Visitors welcome to view Federal reception room on ground floor. Press buzzer for entry. Time: allow 10 minutes.

On the east side of Beacon, opposite Bowdoin Street, stands the elegant **Chester Harding House (12).** Built by Thomas Fletcher in 1808, the architect is unknown. What makes the house especially interesting is that from 1827 to 1829 it was the first studio-residence of portrait-painter, Chester Harding (1792–1866). At this point, you may ask, *who* is Chester Harding?

Because his art doesn't rate so highly as that of his idol, Gilbert Stuart (1755–1828), Harding's extraordinary career has not been so well publicized. He had little formal schooling and began work at twelve, yet rose to become not only the painter of Boston Brahmin society but also of the English aristocracy. The Whig Duke of Sussex (son of George III), the Dukes of Gloucester and Norfolk, Thomas Coke, and Robert Owen sat for him. Note the characteristic portrait of the saturnine Daniel Webster above the fireplace in the reception room.

The artist's own account of his life in Regency England from 1823 to 1826 and again from 1846 to 1847 made his biographer wonder how an American with a backwoods background could possibly have obtained patrons of such standing. The secret lay in his Paul Bunyan-like personality and appearance. He was "the finest specimen of manly beauty," over six feet tall. His strength was prodigious. While helping his father clear land, he would himself drag away the fallen timber instead of using oxen. His hands and feet were so large he was obliged to have his gloves and shoes specially made. To cap it all, he was also a rare talker; a teller of tall frontier tales.

After a colorful beginning as a drummer boy in the War of 1812, he opened a sign-painter's shop in Pittsburgh. Business was good, but he aspired to portrait-painting. After watching an itinerant limner paint a picture of himself and Caroline, his wife, he decided that he, too, would have a go. Since pre-Revolutionary times, such artisan-painters had produced some of the most vigorous portraits to meet the demand of those doctors, lawyers, and shopkeepers who wished to commission family pictures as marks of status in the local community. After making a portrait of Caroline himself, Chester discovered he had the knack of making a likeness. When the local baker offered him five dollars for a portrait, he was launched on his long career.

Meanwhile, Chester's chairmaker brother Horace had established himself at Paris, Kentucky. Chester was invited to join him. To save money the young artist moved wife and child down the Ohio on a raft, and opened a studio next door to Horace's shop. He did so well that he was able to take two months off in Philadelphia to study at the Academy of Fine Arts—the only professional instruction he ever received.

His biggest break was painting Daniel Boone. The old pathfinder urged him to "go West" to booming St. Louis, and gave him a vital letter of introduction to Governor George

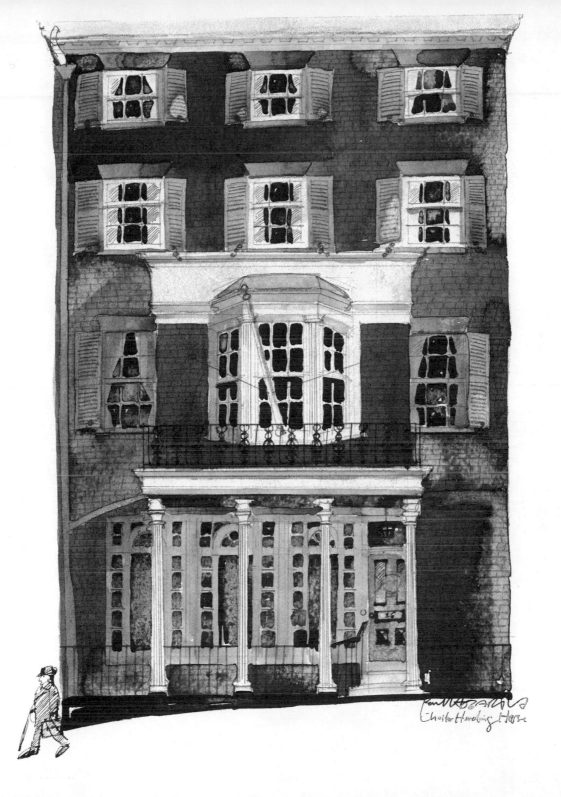

Chester Harding House

Rogers Clark. Success quickly followed. By now Harding had become a legend, the physical embodiment of the energetic age of Jacksonian democracy, and enthusiastic patrons urged him on to Boston, the Federal portrait-painter's happy hunting ground. Thus began the famous "Harding fever," a term coined by the less fortunate Stuart, whom Harding inadvertently caused to die in poverty after having emptied the older artist's studio of eighty sitters in six months.

Boston Athenaeum

10½ Beacon Street. A National Historic Landmark. T stop: Park Street. Five minute walk. Members only, but visiting scholars and researchers can obtain guest card at front desk. Free guided tours, Tuesdays and Thursdays. Call 227-0270. Open daily 9:00–5:30. Summer: weekdays only. Closed holidays. Time: about 30 minutes.

Continue down Beacon Street to the Palladian brownstone façade of the **Boston Athenaeum (13),** built 1847–1849 to the designs of Edward C. Cabot, and enlarged in 1913 to those of Henry Forbes Bigelow. As one enters to view its five floors of booklined, high-ceilinged rooms, one is transported to some strange and elegant palace devoted not only to literature but to all the arts of life-enhancement. Here, indeed, in the words of Walter Muir Whitehill, it's Director Emeritus, "the crush of city life is quickly left behind."

The Athenaeum, one of the world's most famous private libraries, is a descendant of the Anthology Club, founded in 1807 by William Emerson, Ralph Waldo's father. It was the first to be built in the United States and is, with the Philadelphia Athenaeum, the only surviving example of a unique Victorian institution; an association of persons of literary, scientific, and artistic attainment, practitioners *and* patrons, established in the context of a luxurious clubhouse. It is managed by trustees elected by shareholders or "proprietors," who have always made sure of acquiring important collections of rare books and manuscripts. Among the half-million volumes are special collections of rare source material such as the King's Chapel library, sent by William III of England to King's Chapel in 1698; a large portion of Washington's personal library; and newspapers, books, and pamphlets published in the Confederate States during the Civil War.

In 1827 an art gallery was established, and for almost fifty years, the Athenaeum functioned as both Louvre and Salon, showing seminal exhibitions of European painting and sculpture, as well as the work of American artists. During 1858, one such exhibition featured the work of the then controversial English Pre-Raphaelites—Ford Maddox Brown, John Everett Millais, Holman Hunt, and Dante Gabriel Rossetti—a formative influence on one of Boston's (and America's) most famous artists, Winslow Homer (1836–1910).

The Athenaeum's own collection is celebrated and includes a large and important group of portraits of Federal political leaders and merchant princes; those of George and Martha Washington by Gilbert Stuart are now housed in the Museum of Fine Arts on Huntington Avenue but many remain, at the

Athenaeum, where you can see them on the tour. These are concentrated in the Gallery on the second floor and form a congenial background to the Art Reference Department.

Despite its illustrious past, the Athenaeum has (surprisingly) aroused differences of opinion as to its purpose. Some join Henry James, who (naturally) thought it "an honored haunt of all the most civilized." Others, like Cleveland Amory, dismiss it as a shrine "whose primary purpose is to preside over the last rites of Brahminism." Unruffled by such criticism, the Athenaeum remains what it essentially is, a unique working library open to scholars, professional authors, and unmotivated amateurs whoever they may be.

Cross Beacon and follow the Freedom Trail down to Tremont Street. At the corner of Tremont and School Streets is King's Chapel and adjacent burying grounds, our next official site.

King's Chapel

Corner of Tremont and School Streets. A National Historic Landmark. T stop: Park Street on Red or Green lines. Five minute walk. Open Monday through Friday 10:00–4:00; Saturday 10:00–11:45 and 12:45–4:00; Sunday 10:00–4:00. Sunday services at 11:00. Free guided tours year-round. Advance notice of group visits required. Concerts are a regular feature. Call 523-1749 for program. Time: 15–20 minutes; more if you saunter among the markers and tombstones of the Burying Ground.

52

This brownstone chapel is one of America's most historic churches. It was built between 1749 and circa 1754 over part of the adjacent Puritan cemetery, appropriated by Governor Andros to establish the first Anglican or Episcopal Church in Puritan New England. The architect was Englishman Peter Harrison (1716–1775), the Newport merchant who designed some of the finest public buildings of the colonial period. The low, massive base was intended to support a tower but this was never built.

King's Chapel (14), Unitarian since 1785, is not only a rare example of colonial church architecture, but also a welcome oasis in busy downtown Boston. The interior, sparkling with freshly painted white walls and white woodwork takes us back in time to those years before the Revolution. King's Chapel was then Boston's most fashionable parish. Here worshipped the Royal Governors and their retinue of officials and officers. The large canopied Governor's Pew, dismantled in 1826 as "an undemocratic reminder of a bygone era" was restored in 1926. Royalty favored the chapel with gifts. William III and his queen, Mary, gave the Communion table in the Chancery; George III and his queen, Anne, donated the Communion plate, still in use, and plush red cushions and vestments.

The adjacent Old Puritan Burying Ground, or as it is now called, **King's Chapel Burying Ground***, was established in 1630 and is the oldest in the city. Open daily 8:00–4:00. Here are many old markers and tombstones of celebrated colonists and patriots. Among them, the indomitable John Winthrop and his family, including his son and grandson, both governors of Connecticut colony; Governor William Shirley; William Dawes, who was Paul Revere's companion on the famous ride to Lexington; Robert Keayne, founder of the Ancient and Honorable Artillery Company; and Mary Chilton, first woman pilgrim in the Plymouth colony. Less celebrated but perhaps more human is the stone of Elizabeth Pain, a young Puritan woman who was branded with an 'A' for adultery because she gave birth to a child by a minister. Captain Kidd, the pirate, is supposed to be buried here, too, but the location of his stone isn't known.

Return to Tremont Street and turn right. This will take you back to Government Center, our starting point.

King's Chapel

Walk Three

THE BEACON HILL HISTORIC DISTRICT

Distance: 3 miles. Time: one whole day of 5 to 6 hours including a half-hour break for a sandwich lunch on Charles Street. If not possible, 2 to 3 hours, concentrating on the South Slope (Beacon to Pinckney Street).

Directly west of the Downtown area lies the Beacon Hill Historic District, with its fine old homes and tree-shaded streets, one of the finest examples of urban planning in the United States, or, for that matter, anywhere. Many of its handsome Adamesque residences were built by wealthy merchant princes of the Federal Period, when Boston prospered from its booming trade with China, the Far East, and Europe. Many famous statesmen and celebrated thinkers and writers lived here, and it has long been the habitat of the *First Family Beacon Hiller*, the *Proper Bostonian*, and the *Boston Brahmin*.

Beacon Hill was originally known as Tri-mountain, the sole remnant of three peaks or mounts (Pemberton, Beacon, and Vernon) cut down to make development possible and fill in Boston's shoreline. The Hill takes its name from a steep and rugged eminence where a warning beacon stood from 1634 to 1789.

Development of the Hill started in 1795 with the building of the new State House on the site where the old beacon stood. The South Slope with its panoramic view of the common and to the west over the Charles River made it an ideal location for the establishment of a fashionable residential area. The largest project of its kind in Boston, it involved the transformation of a wilderness of rocks, brambles, and hilly pasture (twice the present height) and was financed by a syndicate of prominent Bostonians known as the Mount Vernon Proprietors (Harrison Gray Otis, Jonathan Mason, Charles Bulfinch, Benjamin Joy, and Mrs. James Swan). Building began in 1789 but the Hill was not completely built up until 1848, hence the rich variety of Late Colonial, Federal, and Greek Revival styles.

The North Slope, or "Back of the Hill," which sprawls down behind the shadow of the State House from Pinckney Street to Cambridge Street, was once a part of the Old West End, demolished to make way for Government Center and the new City Hall. Although not lacking in historical interest (for example, it abounds with Black Heritage Trail Sites), it possesses little of the elegance of the South Slope. Successively a neighborhood of tradesmen, mariners, and small businessmen; a red light district; and after the Civil War, a black community, it now houses a mixture of middle-class professionals, students, and working people. Much that was of interest, including early wooden or brick houses dating back to the

54

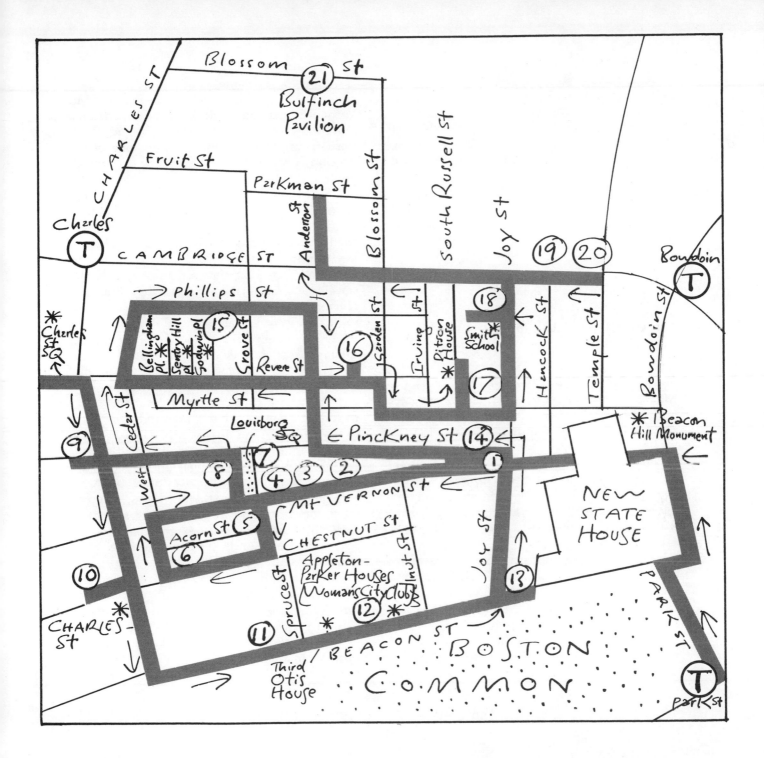

Colonial Period, was demolished and replaced by Late Federal and Victorian apartment buildings and rooming houses.

South Slope, North Slope, or West of Charles Street, Beacon Hill's brick row houses, hugging steep streets with brick sidewalks and old-style street lighting, are remarkably intact. They will remain so, too; all form part of the Beacon Hill Historic District, designated in 1963 by the National Park Service as a National Historic Landmark.

Nichols House

55 Mt. Vernon Street. Owned by Nichols House Museum Trust. Open year-round, Wednesdays and Saturdays, 1:00–5:00. Closed Holidays. Guided tour: 15–20 minutes. Admission $1.00.

Begin the Beacon Hill walk at Park Street subway. Walk up Park Street to Beacon. Turn right on Beacon Street. Cross the street and turn left on Bowdoin. Another left turn brings you to Mt. Vernon Street (Michael J. Delehanty Square).

As you thread your way through the many automobiles parked in and around the State House annex, look right to view the Roman-Doric memorial pillar, a restoration of the original **Beacon Hill Monument*** designed by Bulfinch to commemorate the original colonial beacon and train of events which led to the American Revolution.

Proceed under the wing of the State House annex to Mt. Vernon Street. It was here the Mt. Vernon Proprietors built their early mansions. Our first stop: the Mason Houses, 55 and 57 Mt. Vernon, built by Jonathan Mason, one of the original proprietors. The architect of both houses was Bulfinch.

55 Mt. Vernon, known as the **Nichols House (1),** is one of the three remaining houses Bulfinch designed for Mason. It has been changed least and is largely in its original state. It was purchased in 1885 by Dr. Nichols and remained in the family until the death of the traveler and landscape architect, Rose Standish Nichols. The handsome Federal mansion with its magnificent spiral staircase is now, under the terms of her will, a private museum of great interest. As such, it is the only private house on the Hill which enables us to savor a gracious lifestyle that was, and still is, enjoyed here.

The house contains its original furniture, including a console table that once belonged to John Hancock and many rare Chippendale pieces from the eighteenth century.

57 Mt. Vernon, the house on the left of my picture, was originally occupied by Mrs. Samuel Parkman, a daughter of Mason. Apparently she didn't like it and in 1838 sold it to Cornelius Coolidge, who extended the house several feet and built the Greek Revival front entrance to Mt. Vernon Street.

Several famous Bostonians have lived here. Webster was a tenant from 1817 to 1819. For forty years it was also the Boston residence of Charles Francis Adams, Sr. (1807–1886) the son of President John Quincy Adams. As U.S. Minister to England during the difficult years of the Civil War, he is remembered for his re-

Paul Hogarth
The Mason Houses

57

Beacon Hill

58

markable diplomatic achievement in keeping England from backing the Confederacy. In this house was born his son, Henry Adams (1838–1918), author of the classic *Education of Henry Adams.*

Note the next house, 59 Mt. Vernon, probably the most distinguished Greek Revival house on Beacon Hill, built in 1837 from the designs of Edward Shaw. At the end of the last century it was the home of Thomas Bailey Aldrich (1836–1907), editor of *Atlantic Monthly,* and is still the residence of that family.

Mansion Block, Mount Vernon Street

The early houses we have just seen at 55 and 57 Mt. Vernon were built by the Mt. Vernon Proprietors as free-standing mansions with large gardens and stables. We will be looking at more such houses at 85 and 87 Mt. Vernon. By 1803, land on the Hill was in much greater demand. Blocks of tall row houses without gardens or stables were built after the street was laid out in 1832. My illustration shows a portion of one such mansion block, **75–83 Mt. Vernon Street (2)**, *circa* 1836–1837.

Walk down the street, starting from left to right. Note the profusion of Greek Revival cast-iron balconies, elaborate newel-posted entrance gates, and heavy, ornate railings and fences. Almost all the houses are now privately owned apartments; others are used as premises for clubs and institutions. All have rich historical associations. Those of interest include:

77: Club of Odd Volumes. Founded in 1887 as a literary dining club. Since 1936, this engagingly gregarious coterie of poets, scholars, and bibliomaniacs has gathered here to entertain the distinguished stranger at convivial weekly luncheons.

79: Here lived Horace Gray (1828–1902), a celebrated justice of the Supreme Court, descendant of the merchant prince, William Gray, and described by Cleveland Amory as the "founder of the bluest of Boston's many blue-blood law firms."

83: Once the house of William Ellery Channing (1740–1842), the great reformer and Unitarian leader, whose writings on slavery paved the way for emancipation. It was here that Charles Dickens and his wife, Catherine, joined Channing for breakfast on February 2, 1842, shortly before his death.

Second Harrison Gray Otis House

85 Mt. Vernon Street. Private residence. Not open to the public.

Adjacent to the Channing home, is the superb **Second Harrison Gray Otis House (3),** designed by Bulfinch and built in 1802. Otis lived here for only six years before moving to an even larger house on more prestigious Beacon Street.

Tall, strikingly handsome, and wealthy, patrician Harrison Gray Otis (1765–1848) knew how to live. Descended from a long line of lawyers, he was unable to go on to London to complete his law studies after graduating from Harvard, as the Revolutionary War had bankrupted his father. London couldn't have taught him anything. By the time he was 35, he was not only a successful lawyer, but had also made a fortune in real estate, and was a leading light of the Federalist Party. His day, it is said, usually began with a breakfast of *pâté de foie gras*.

Otis built three homes, all designed by Bulfinch, his friend and business associate (see pages 60 and 91). But without doubt, this second house is the finest. The free-standing mansion is a masterful exercise in stately, classical dignity. Yet the details themselves are simple enough. Four long windows set in arched recesses open onto wrought-iron balconies of Chinese fret design. White wooden Corinthian pilasters provide a finishing touch. All the windows have sandstone lintels and slat shutters called "jalousies," highly fashionable at the time. Above a great box cornice is a balustrade, and on the roof itself, a glazed, octagonal cupola.

This splendid house has been occupied by a succession of old First Family Bostonians. So much so that it has become a living symbol of Beacon Hill and of Proper Boston. It was a joy to paint it.

AQVA
an Street. Second Otis House

87 Mt. Vernon Street

Headquarters of the Colonial Society of Massachusetts. Not open to the public.

We now come to a second free-standing mansion, **87 Mt. Vernon Street (4),** built in 1805 by Bulfinch for himself and his family. But before completion, financial troubles compelled him to sell it to Stephen Higginson, Sr., a wealthy merchant and former sea captain. Set back high above the street with stables in the rear, the fine old house is approached by a picturesque cobblestoned carriageway that is still in use.

Higginson lived here until 1811. Then, following the example of Otis, he moved on to Beacon Street. Again like Otis, he was a prominent Federalist, the descendant of Francis Higginson, the Puritan minister of Salem. He moved to Boston in 1778 to found another of Boston's indomitable First Families. He traveled abroad a great deal and filled the house with fine furniture, paintings, and *objets d'art*.

For many years, the house was the home of Charles Jackson Paine (1833–1916), great-grandson of Robert Treat Paine, signer of the Declaration of Independence. A Civil War general and railroad tycoon, Charles Paine was best known as a famous yachtsman who financed the building of several successful defenders of the America Cup; repeatedly dashing British hopes of winning that much-coveted trophy.

Note the bearded and benign gentleman striding briskly down Mt. Vernon Street in my illustration. I am always on the lookout for people passing by who seem to be a part of the scene or subject I have chosen to depict. This time, however, I had inadvertently included the celebrated Walter Muir Whitehill, Brahmin high priest and preservationist extraordinary, on his way to join a friend or colleague for tea, or more probably an *aperitif*.

Continue down Mt. Vernon Street. Turn left on Willow until you come to Acorn Street, a cobblestoned lane on your right, our next stop.

Acorn Street

Hidden behind the great tall mansions lining Mt. Vernon is little **Acorn Street (5),** the last surviving cobblestoned lane on the Hill. Time seemed to stand still as I drew its deeply rutted slope, lined on one side with a cliff-like row of houses. Designed and built by Cornelius Coolidge for coachmen in 1828–1829, they were later occupied by servants and tradesmen who worked in the great mansions nearby.

Retrace your steps to Willow. Turn right and stroll down to **Chestnut Street (6),** laid out in 1800 and perhaps the most beautiful street on the Hill. Look up the street for a perspective of mellowed façades, gas lamps, cast-iron fences and chimney pots, leading the eye up to the glistening golden dome of the State House. You may, at this point, wish to walk up the street and take a closer look at the many fine old houses. Among those with historic associations (not open to the public, unfortunately,) are:

13-15-17: Built in 1806 by Mrs. Swan (the only woman to be a Mt. Vernon Proprietor) for her three lucky daughters. Bulfinch was the architect. Later, Julia Ward Howe (1819–1910), Boston's grand literary dame and author of "Battle Hymn of the Republic," lived at 17. For many years the house was the meeting place of the Radical Club that followed the celebrated Transcendental Club. Emerson, Whittier, and Longfellow were regular visitors.

29a: The first house built by the Mt. Vernon Proprietors in 1789. Bulfinch was again the architect. For many years it was the home of Edwin Booth, famous actor and father of John Wilkes Booth, Lincoln's assassin.

43: The home of Richard Henry Dana (1815–1882), author of *Two Years Before the Mast*.

50: Francis Parkman (1823–1893), the greatest of Brahmin historians and author of the classic, *The Oregon Trail*, lived here for many years, battling with migraine, insomnia, and semi-blindness to complete his series of volumes on the epic theme of France versus England in the New World.

82: Phillip de Lazlo, fashionable Hungarian portrait painter of the Twenties, rented a studio here to execute his portraits of the Larz Andersons and other Boston notables.

Walk down Chestnut to West Cedar Street. Continue along West Cedar and turn right on Mt. Vernon until you come to Louisburg Square, the *pièce de résistance* of Beacon Hill-dom.

Eagle head hitching post, 33 Chestnut Street.
Cast iron, 1870.

87 Mt. Vernon Street

Chestnut Street Beacon Hill

Louisburg Square

20 Louisburg Square

Louisburg Square

Louisburg Square (7) is an elegant residential enclave of great charm and character. It was planned by the Mt. Vernon Proprietors in 1820 and probably named to commemorate the capture of Fort Louisburg from the French in 1745 by an expedition of New England troops led by William Pepperell, the Maine lumber baron. The Greek Revival and Late Federal houses were built and designed by various architects and housewrights between 1834 and 1848. Their bow fronts, reminiscent of Regency Brighton and Bath, make the old square one of the places which most poignantly recalls the English heritage of Old Boston.

Early in the seventeenth century, the site was part of the estate of William Blackstone, who settled in 1625 near a spring of fresh water on the northern side of what is now Louisburg Square. Indeed, "Blackstone's Spring" still makes its presence felt in certain Pinckney Street basements whenever unusual weather conditions prevail.

The square has a small fenced park, pleasantly shaded with great elms, but its use is reserved for residents. At both ends are statues; Aristides faces Mt. Vernon and Columbus faces Pinckney. They were presented to the Proprietors of Louisburg Square in 1850 by Joseph Iasigi, wealthy merchant and one-time resident of 3 Louisburg Square. Here, cats of every kind gather; not the homeless variety, but well-fed cats who, between stalking birds and exchanging opinions of masters and mistresses, check out strangers like me before spreading themselves contentedly on steps and doorways.

The well-proportioned, soft-toned, rose-red brick townhouses create an enviable ambience of cultivated domesticity, heightened by a wide variety of cast-iron fences, stair rails, balconies, and footscrapers. Richly decorated high-ceilinged interiors are both warm and intimate, especially on Christmas Eve when the old English customs of placing lighted candles in the windows, carol-singing, and open-house (now invited guests only) take place. Occasionally, some houses are open for visits. Check with the Visitor Information Center at City Hall or Tremont Street for details.

If you're not in Boston over Christmas and New Year's you may have to console yourselves with thinking about all the famous people who have lived here. Start your tour on the left side, facing north.

4: Built in 1842 by housewright Jesse Shaw. William Dean Howells (1837–1920), a great editor of *Atlantic Monthly*, lived here from 1883 to 1884, devoting his mornings to writing his masterpiece, *The Rise of Silas Lapham*.

10: Louisa May Alcott (1832–1888) celebrated author of the immensely popular bestseller, *Little Women*, lived here during her most successful years. Her father, Amos Bronson Alcott, the famous Transcendentalist philosopher, died here in 1888. Her own death followed the day of his funeral.

16: William Dean Howells lived here for the first six months of 1882.

20: Jennie Lind, "the Swedish Nightingale," was married here, while performing in Boston, to her accompanist, Otto Goldschmidt, in 1852. The house **(8)** was then the home of Samuel G. Ward, banker and Boston representative of the Baring Brothers, the *prima donna's* London bankers.

13-19: On the east side at the corner of Pinckney Street is St. Margaret's Convent (Episcopal) with its motto, *Per Augusta Ad Augusta* (through trials to triumph), emblazoned on its entrance portal. Once four separate houses, 19 was the residence of Frederick Lincoln, mayor of Boston at the time the Prince of Wales visited Boston in 1860. Then 19, the future Edward VII was, according to McIntyre, "more Boston-feted than Lafayette."

Charles Street Meeting House

Corner of Mt. Vernon and Charles Streets. A Black Heritage Trail Site. T stop: Charles on Red line. Five minute walk. Coffee house open Monday through Friday 12:00–2:00, and Sunday 3:00–12:00. Visitors welcome in main hall if and when guides are available. Time: 10 minutes. Free.

Turn left down Pinckney, then left again on Charles Street. Just ahead of you across the street is **Charles Street Meeting House (9)** built in 1807 as the home of the Third Baptist Church. The site chosen was by the Charles River, which in those days came up to the foot of Beacon Hill. River Street, from where I made my picture, was the shoreline.

In those days, too, the Charles River was cleaner. Many baptismal immersions took place. But the church's chief claim to fame is that it was a forum of antislavery activity. Here abolitionists such as Garrison, Wendell Phillips, and Charles Sumner, joined by the celebrated black leaders Harriet Tubman, Frederick Douglass, and Sojourner Truth, spoke out in the days preceding the Civil War.

Its architect was Asher Benjamin (1773–1845), another well-known figure of this early Federal period. Like Bulfinch, he was influenced by the Palladian classicism of the Adam brothers. The most interesting part of the exterior is the great clock tower with a belfry, dome with pennant weathervane, and a clock which still tells the time. Sadly, its once handsome interior has not survived. The box pews and gallery supported by slender Greek columns were torn out in the 1850s and replaced with Victorian slip pews and pseudo-Gothic columns.

Between 1876 and 1939 the building became the center of black religious activities and was owned by the African Methodist Episcopal Church.

Nowadays, it is run by the Unitarian-Universalists as a social center.

Charles Street Meeting House

Charles Street Meeting House

Antique store, Chestnut Street

Charles to Beacon Street

Before leaving Charles Street Meeting House you can take a short side-trip down Charles to Cambridge Street to learn a little more about Beacon Hill, and browse in bookstores and antique shops at the same time.

Charles Street is the only local business street in the Historic District. Once a prestigious residential thoroughfare, it was widened in the 1920s, changing much of its character, especially the west side. Some buildings were sliced off and given new façades; others were built anew. On the east side, two groups of Greek Revival rowhouses survive between Revere and Cambridge Streets.

131: Here, as a young man in the 1860s, lived the great novelist Henry James (1843–1916), and later, Aldrich who succeeded Howell as editor of *Atlantic*.

On the side now occupied by the Volkswagen Service garage, once stood the residence of publisher James Ticknor Fields (see page 37), long the scene of Boston's most famous literary *salon*. Here, beautiful, intelligent Annie Adams Fields (1834–1915) gathered the famous and the gifted in what Henry James called "the Charles Street Waterside Museum" indulging her addiction to hospitality and talk. Regrettably, the house, after standing empty for many years, was demolished in the 1920s. One can only take comfort that so historic a landmark would not be razed today.

Retrace your steps on the right side of Charles. Turn right on Revere. A few more

Charles Street street sign

steps brings you to the entrance arch to **Charles Street Square***, built on what was once the garden of the Fields house; the trees were planted by Longfellow. The architect of this pleasant backwater, reminiscent of demolished Pemberton Square, and built in the 1920s, was Frank Bourne.

Back at Charles Street Meeting House, you may at this point wish to take a break for lunch. We are about halfway through the entire trail and almost through with the south slope loop. Otherwise, continue to Beacon Street via a short detour.

75

Turn left on River Street, then left on Lime to view the picturesque street of artists' studios. Before turning left on Brimmer, pause to look at 44 Brimmer Street, long the home of the late Samuel Eliot Morison (1887–1976), one of America's greatest and most distinguished historians. The homes of many residents of this short, quaint street once served as houses and stables for the carriages and horses of the wealthy residents of Mt. Vernon and Chestnut Streets.

Continue on Brimmer to Beacon, pausing to look up Chestnut to note more antique shops. Lower Chestnut together with Charles Street comprise Beacon Hill's Antique Row. Here, you will find many shops dealing in a wide variety of American and British antique furniture, pictures, bric-a-brac, weathervanes, and pewter. Some are specialty shops of the do-not-handle kind. **Louis Prince (10)** on Chestnut Street is more tolerant and has a large general collection. Like most antique shops, there is no agreed opening or closing time. Some open early at 9:00, most by 10:00, and usually closing is between 5:00 and 5:30.

Turn left on Beacon and commence ascent of the street, the last leg of the south slope loop of the trail.

William Hickling Prescott House

55 Beacon Street. Headquarters of Massachusetts Chapter of the Society of Colonial Dames. Not open to the public.

Continue up Beacon. Above Charles Street begins a delightful row of Greek Revival and Federal dwellings, though with some later insertions. Many of the houses retain their original cast-iron gates, railings, and balconies. Start with 63–64, distinguished Greek Revival houses of 1820, now King's Chapel Parish House and Rectory. You can see a few panes of the celebrated Beacon Hill purple glass here. Some residents installed imported glass from England between 1818 and 1824, only to see their windows become a rosy mauve color after exposure to the sun. After the manufacturers eliminated the impurities which caused this phenomenon, residents of Beacon Hill refused to install the new glass, or so the story goes!

The next house of note is 55, the **William Hickling Prescott House (11),** the second along in my picture. It is one of a pair of handsome bow-fronted residences built in 1808 for a wealthy young merchant, James Smith Colburn. 55 was for himself and his family; 54 for his sister's family, the Gills. The architect was Asher Benjamin. The Colburns lived in great style and the elegant oval dining rooms, drawing rooms, and bedchambers still survive.

In 1844, the house became the home of William Hickling Prescott (1796–1859), another

76

Beacon Street

great historian dogged by partial blindness. Here he wrote *The Conquest of Peru*. In the middle of the third volume of the epic, *Philip the Second, King of Spain*, he suffered a stroke and died here. Dickens and his wife, Catherine, were his guests during the first week of their visit to America in 1843, as were Thackerary and his secretary cousin, the English painter, Eyre Crowe, who dined here in 1853. Crowe was intrigued that Prescott's secretary had labeled all the great man's overcoats as suitable for certain degrees of temperature and were "donned" accordingly when he sallied forth.

Crowe also noted the Prescott-Linzee swords (Collection, Massachusetts Historical Society) that had been carried by two relatives of Prescott, fighting on opposite sides during the struggle for Charlestown, one of them Loyalist, Captain John Linzee, grandfather of his wife, Susan Amory Prescott; the other his opponent, Colonel William Prescott, grandfather of the historian. Thackeray, much moved, used the family conflict in his novel, *The Virginians*, in which one Esmond fights for George III and the other Esmond for Washington.

Pause at Spruce to note the tablet to William Blackstone. This, apparently, is the site of his original settlement.

Continue to 45, the third **Harrison Gray Otis House***, built in 1806. Otis died here in 1846. Once again Bulfinch was the architect. The house and its lavish furnishings were the talk of Boston in their day. Every day, servants replenished a giant blue and white Lowestoft punch bowl with ten gallons of punch to sustain guests on their climb up to the second floor drawing room. Although the once fabulous interior is no more, the exterior is well cared for

78

The Somerset Club

The Somerset Club

54 Bower Street

by the present owners, the American Meteorological Society. Not open to the public.

From the Otis house, continue up the street to 42, the David Sears House, now the **Somerset Club (12),** built in (1819–1821) on the site of a house owned by John Singleton Copley (1738–1815), America's first great painter. Here Copley painted his American portraits, noted for their vitality and realism; among them those of Samuel Adams, John Quincy Adams, Hancock, Thomas Boyleston, Revere, and many others. Some of these can be seen in the Museum of Fine Arts. With the decline of work during the political upheavals of the 1770s, Copley left his native city for London, never to return.

Copley had bought land in 1764 on the south slope of Beacon Hill: some eleven acres bounded today by Beacon to Pinckney Streets, thence by Walnut down to Charles Street. He sold them to Mt. Vernon Proprietors in a much-regretted transaction in (1795–1796) for much less than the land was worth.

Somerset Club

41–42 Beacon Street. Not open to the public.

You can't pass this massive, somewhat baronial three-story granite mansion without wondering what it is. Originally the Sears home, it is said to have formally introduced the Greek Revival style to Beacon Hill. The architect was Parris, again assisted by his *alter ego*, Willard. David Sears was a wealthy merchant with a downright code of behavior that enabled him to amass great wealth. Today the David Sears Charity dispenses money "for the support of citizens or families who may have seen better days."

In 1872 the Somerset Club, of which Sears was a member, acquired 41–42 Beacon Street. A third floor was added, and much else, notably the brooding frontage. A banded rusticated wall is broken at the sides by the front entrance on the right and a tradesmen's entrance on the left; and in the middle by a sinister portal with an iron-studded door, lion-head knockers, and clawlike decorated hinges. If you wonder where this might lead to, it's only the kitchen.

The Somerset Club, founded in 1851, is one of the two leading men's clubs of Boston; the other is the Union Club, founded in 1861 by members who broke away from those of the Somerset Club, whose members were Southern sympathizers. Within, it seems more like an elegantly appointed private residence than one of the world's finest clubs, which pioneered such innovations as guest membership for visiting strangers as well as having bedrooms where wives can spend the night with their husbands—an unheard-of concession in London!

Our next stop is 39–40, the **Appleton-Parker Houses*,** since 1913 the Women's City Club. Built *circa* 1818 and designed in Bulfinch's office by the young Parris for Nathan Appleton, a textile manufacturer, and Daniel Parker, a shipping merchant. Guided tour available 10:00–4:00. Winter: open Wednesday only. Summer: open Monday, Wednesday and Friday except holidays. Admission $1.50, children under 12, 50 cents. Time: 20 minutes. Do take advantage of this opportunity to see what a

Beacon Street home looked like. There are handsome fireplaces and chandeliers, elegant furniture, and of course, the room where Longfellow married Fanny Appleton, with its fine view of the Common through purple glass.

34 Beacon Street (13), once a family residence of that remarkable and legendary First Family that speaks only to God, the Cabots. It now houses Little, Brown, one of Boston's distinguished publishing companies and the New York Graphic Society. This superb mansion was acquired in 1909 and like its neighbor the **Parkman House*** at 33, was designed and built in 1825 by Coolidge. Note the fine cast-iron veranda with fluted roof. Not open to the public.

33, the Parkman House, was for many years, from 1853 to 1908, the home of George Francis Parkman who, with his mother and sister, Harriet, lived here in distinguished seclusion after his father, a prominent and wealthy Bostonian, Dr. George Parkman, was murdered in 1849 by John White Webster, Professor of the Harvard Medical School. It was an extraordinary case which long fascinated students of less-than-ordinary crime, from Dickens, who, revisiting Boston in 1867, asked to be shown the Cambridge laboratory where Dr. Parkman was murdered, to Cleveland Amory, who devoted an entire chapter of *Proper Bostonians* to the macabre incident.

The house itself was left to the City of Boston (together with 5 million dollars for the maintenance of Boston Common) and is now used by Mayor Kevin White as a retreat from City Hall to receive distinguished visitors. Not open to the public.

At this point we are between the two parts of the trail. So, you can either call it a day, or have a break, eat your sandwich lunch

Pinckney Street

Pinckney Street

(cafeterias and restaurants are in the lower reaches of Beacon Street) and continue.

Begin your tour of the North Slope at Mt. Vernon and Joy Streets. Turn right on Joy. Pinckney is the first street on the left. Named for Charles Cotesworth Pinckney, the man who refused to give the French a sixpence, the street is the dividing line between the two slopes of the Hill. Laid out in 1803, Mt. Vernon Proprietors used Pinckney as a barrier against an increasingly disreputable "combat zone" north of Louisburg Square.

Pinckney Street (14) exudes the more relaxed ambience of Greenwich Village. Many of the fine houses are now apartments or used as boarding houses for students. Some are single-family houses, the homes of academics and especially men (and women) of letters. Among the numerous houses of historic interest are:

5: This small clapboard house is one of the oldest in Boston. Built in 1795, its original owners were George Middleton, a black horse-breaker, and Lewis Clapion, a black barber. Middleton is best remembered as Colonel Middleton, who led the all-black company known as the Bucks of America, which distinguished itself in the Battle of Bunker Hill.

11: Edwin Whipple, a well-known literary critic during the decades following the Civil War, lived here.

20: As a child, Louisa May Alcott lived here in rented rooms. The unconventional Alcott family, individualists all, were kept together by her strong-minded mother, Abba May Alcott, a city missionary and pioneer social worker. The Alcott apartment was part of the Boston literary scene, and, during the decades before the Civil War, Louisa's father, Amos, held court here with Emerson, Channing, and Garrison. The Alcotts moved to 10 Louisburg Square in the 1880s following the success of her novel, *Little Women*.

54: Built in the 1830s. George Hillard, transcendentalist lawyer, publisher, and man-of-letters, lived here in the 1840s. Hawthorne lived here after his brief stay at the transcendentalist commune at Brook Farm and before marrying Sophia Peabody in 1842. Later Hillard moved to 62. By now he had become a U.S. Commissioner whose job it was to issue warrants for the arrest of fugitive slaves. His wife, however, was an abolitionist who hid slaves in the house, supposedly without his knowledge—activities later confirmed when, at the turn of the century, a hidden trapdoor in the ceiling fell on a workman's head. A cubbyhole was discovered, large enough to hold several people. Plates and spoons were found on the floor. Note the splendid ornamental cast-iron stair rails.

65: A Federal dwelling built *circa* 1807 as a boarding house (it still is) to accommodate sailors (on the extreme right of my picture). Note the windowed cupola topping its five storys, which offered a fine view of the harbor and ships riding at anchor. Boston was a big home port and it was the practice of ships' masters to keep the highly skilled and unmarried clipper crews together between voyages by providing good accommodations.

Pause on the west corner of Anderson for the only view of the Charles River before turning right to view the Greek Revival structure, built in 1920 as Beacon Hill's first High School. The school, now the Carnegie Institute, was primarily for boys "intending to become merchants and mechanics."

Proceed along Anderson Street and turn

Lewis Hayden House

left on Revere. As you walk down Revere Street, note the three small private courts or alleys built *circa* 1845, and lined with red-brick houses, originally the homes of artisans and tradesmen. These are: **Goodwin Place*, Sentry Hill Place*,** and **Bellingham Place*.**

Turn right on West Cedar and then right again on Phillips Street. At 66 is the **Lewis Hayden House (15),** formerly the home of Lewis and Harriet Hayden, intrepid leaders of the celebrated "Underground Railroad."

Lewis Hayden (1816–1889) himself was born a slave in Kentucky. After escaping to Detroit over the "Railroad," he became a leader of the Abolitionist Movement in Boston while operating a store on Cambridge Street. When the Fugitive Slave Law was passed in 1850 and slaveowners were given legal rights to recapture slaves, Boston became a risky place for runaways. Undaunted, the Haydens used their Phillips Street house as a station on the "Railroad" to Canada, and reputedly kept two kegs of gunpowder in the basement, saying that they would rather blow themselves up than surrender the slaves they were hiding. But the house was never searched.

Later, Hayden worked for the desegregation of Boston's school and transportation systems. He became a member of the Prince Hall Grand Lodge of Masons and worked as a messenger to the Massachusetts Secretary of State. In 1873, he was elected one of two black Representatives in the Massachusetts Legislature. After his death, Harriet Hayden established a scholarship in his name at Harvard.

Walk now along Phillips. Pause briefly on the corner of Phillips and Anderson to view the monumental Victorian hotel before turning right. Continue up Anderson and turn left on Revere. A few more steps on your left is **Rollins Place (16),** a quaint, picturesque, tree-shaded private court lined with red-brick houses. Built in 1843 by John W. Rollins to house artisans and tradesmen, it is now one of the most sought-after locations to live on the Hill. Note what looks like a white and green Greek Revival villa at the end. This is a decoration, framing the end like a stage set, to prevent the absentminded from dropping off the precipitous cliff behind!

Take a right at the end of Revere, then a left on Myrtle. Turn now down South Russell Street. At 43 is the **Ditson House*,** one of the oldest houses on the hill, built *circa* 1697 by the merchant, Joseph Ditson. Not open to the public. Retrace your steps and look for the arched tunnel on your left. This is **Holmes Alley (17)** leading to basements of various houses which hid runaway slaves.

Continue up South Russell. Turn left on Myrtle. Then left again on Joy Street. At 46 Joy is the **Abiel Smith School*,** built in 1834. Now an American Legion post (not open to the public), it once served as Boston's first black school (from 1834 to 1855), built with a legacy left by a wealthy white Boston merchant, Abiel Smith.

Smith Court itself is a reminder of the days when this section of the North Slope was a neighborhood of blacks who either worked as servants in the big houses of the South Slope, or for themselves as carpenters, masons, coachmen, and barbers.

3: Built *circa* 1800, was from 1851 to 1856 the home of William Neil, a black historian and activist who initiated the movement to persuade the Massachusetts Legislature to integrate Boston's public schools.

7-10: Typical of the clapboard frame houses occupied by nineteenth-century Afro-American families up to 1900.

Rollins Place

African Meeting House

8 Smith Court, Joy Street. Check for opening date with Visitor Information Center or present Museum of Afro-American History, 719 Tremont Street. Telephone 445-7400.

Directly opposite the houses of Smith Court is the simple Federal red-brick **African Meeting House (18).** Sometimes called the Abolitionist Church, it was the place where Garrison founded the New England Anti-Slavery Society in 1832. "We have met tonight in this obscure school house," he said. "Our numbers are few and our influence limited, but . . . we shall shake the nation by their mighty influence."

At the moment the meeting house is being restored. When work is completed, the two upper stories will have their old pews back again with balconies on either side. The building will house meetings of Boston's black groups and, occasionally, religious services. The ground floor will be the Museum of Afro-American History.

Holmes Alley

Old African Meeting House

First Harrison Gray Otis House

First Harrison Gray Otis House

141 Cambridge Street. Telephone 227-3960. Headquarters Society for the Preservation of New England Antiquities. T stop: Bowdoin on Blue line or Charles on Red line. Five minute walk. Open Monday through Friday 10:00–4:00. Guided tour every hour on the hour. Closed holidays. Admission: $1.00; children under 12, 50 cents. Special reductions for groups. Time: 30 minutes.

Located in a district unhappily obliterated by the misguided urban renewal project of 1957, the **First Harrison Gray Otis House (19)** is one of the few surviving reminders of the once fashionable residential neighborhood centered on Bowdoin Square, or what is now Bowdoin T stop. It was built in 1795 for Harrison Gray Otis, lawyer and statesman, entrepreneur, and future king of Boston society in the Federal era. Six years later, Otis sold the house to John Osbourn, paint merchant, and moved his wife Sally and their four small children into the even grander 85 Mt. Vernon Street (see page 60).

From that time on, the house had a varied history before restoration to its former glory.

In 1820, the house was occupied by Stillman Lothrop, the mirror-glass manufacturer; but by 1834, it was being rented by a succession of dubious enterprises including Dr. and Mrs. Motts's "Select Establishment for invalid ladies and gentlemen with their wives"; a Turkish bath for women; a Chinese laundry; and finally a rooming house. It was purchased in 1916 by the Society for the Preservation of New England Antiquities.

The house was the first of the three magnificent homes designed for Otis by Bulfinch, his friend and business associate. It represents the architect's earlier, more severe style–of redbrick with a Palladian window above the entrance with a lunette window on the floor above. The windows are rectangular sash, except on the third floor where they are almost square. On the roof are a pair of shed dormers. The semi-circular entrance porch dates from *circa* 1810.

Since 1970, the inside has been restored and furnished to recall the house as it was during the Otis family occupancy. No pains have been spared to ensure accuracy. Samples of several original wallpapers were found under subsequent layers, and reproduced to match the originals wherever possible.

The house has the usual plan of the period. On the ground floor is the front parlor, the dining room with kitchen in the rear. Above is the drawingroom (or withdrawing room, as it was then called), the master bedchamber, and other bedchambers. The servants' rooms are on the top floor.

Everything about this beautiful old house reflects the early lifestyle of an extravagant, calculating patrician who entertained everyone of substance and importance in the city. The furniture and fixtures are of the period. Some are original family heirlooms, for example, the superb portrait of Otis himself by Gilbert Stuart in the dining room; the exquisite miniature of Mrs. Otis by Edward Greene Malbone (1777–1836); and the porcelain tea set which belonged to Otis's half-sister, Mary.

Old West Church

131 Cambridge Street. Telephone 227-5088. T stop: Bowdoin on Blue line or Charles on Red line. Five minute walk. Open Monday through Friday 9:00–4:30. Sunday Services: 11:00. Visitors welcome. Free. Time: 15 minutes.

Next door to the Harrison Gray Otis House is **Old West Church (20),** built in 1806 as a Congregational meeting house.

The first church building suffered as a casualty of the struggle for independence. After Old North Church had been so successfully used as a signal station by the Americans, the British decided to take no chances and ordered the demolition of the tower. Pews were ripped out and the interior used as a barracks.

The present building was built in a handsome Federal style with Adamesque overtones. Its architect was Asher Benjamin.

The church has a stylish clocktower with flanking windows and a belfry terminating in a gilded dome topped by a weathervane. White rectangular panels and pilasters enrich the graceful façade with its recessed windows. The interior is spacious, with a beautiful ceiling. The highly ornamental galleries are original, as are the supporting Corinthian columns. Pulpit and pews were restored in 1963.

The survival of this fine old church has been something of a miracle. Surrounded by decay and neglect for many years, the church, through want of a congregation, was dissolved in 1892 by Andrew Wheelright, who held the building as a public service until the Boston Public Library took it over as its West End branch. Sold by the city in 1962 to the Methodists, it is once again being used for religious purposes.

Paul HOGARTH – Old Well Chu

Bulfinch Pavilion

Portico of the Bulfinch Building
Massachusetts General Hospital

Massachusetts General Hospital (Bulfinch Pavilion)

Check at Warren Lobby, 243 Charles Street for free guided tour of Bulfinch Pavilion and slide-show of hospital history. T stop: Charles on Red line. Five minute walk. Open to the public, Tuesday and Thursday. Call 726-2000 for schedule. Time: 40 minutes.

This optional last stop on the Beacon Hill trail won't take longer than an hour. Those of you who have walked both North and South loops and have seen enough should now walk up Bowdoin Street back to the State House, then walk down Park to Tremont, back to our starting point, Park Street subway station.

If you don't wish to take the tour of the **Bulfinch Pavilion (21),** but just want to look at the outside, look out for the black and green cupola of the Ether Dome sitting astride a gray pediment, at the junction of Parkman and Anderson Streets. Enter the gateway and follow the path by the tennis courts.

Designed by Bulfinch in 1818 and erected under the supervision of Parris between 1818 and 1823, the Bulfinch buildings comprise a superb example of an early nineteenth-century hospital. The great dome houses the old amphitheater, or Ether Dome; graceful, massive Ionic columns, wreathed with Virginia creeper, make it look more like a mansion of the colonial South. But many momentous events in medical history have taken place here, notably the first demonstration by Dr. Morten of the use of ether for major surgery.

Walk Four

OLD CAMBRIDGE

Distance: 3 miles. Time: one leisurely day of 5 to 6 hours is recommended, including, lunch in or around Harvard Square. But if time is short, 2 to 3 hours, depending on how many sites are visited. Start your tour at Harvard T stop on the Red line.

Farther to the west of Beacon Hill, on the far side of the Charles River, lies Cambridge, established in 1630 as Newtowne by the Massachusetts Bay Colony. The original settlement was a fortified village located on a small, defensible hill between the Charles River and the path from Charlestown to Watertown, far enough up the River to be accessible, but difficult to approach by surprise. Later, the town spread eastward and westward, and by 1786 the Charles Street Bridge enabled farmers to cross and sell their produce where Faneuil Hall now stands.

Newtowne became Cambridge in 1638 when the Massachusetts Great and General Court decided to build their newly established "colledg" there, and renamed the town Cambridge, in honor of the English University where so many Puritan clergymen had been educated. The college was named Harvard in 1636 for John Harvard (1607–1638), a graduate of Emmanuel College, Cambridge, a Puritan stronghold, who immigrated to New England in 1637 but died soon after, leaving half of his estate and his library to the infant college. Harvard is the oldest, the most prestigious and probably, still the wealthiest, university in the United States; and with MIT (founded 1861) and other important institutions, it is the academic heart of America.

Although Cambridge can hardly be considered a separate entity today, the city retains much of its own personality. Old Cambridge remains a residential, commercial, and academic center, refining and invigorating the character of its bigger, brasher brother.

First impressions may be disappointing. Much of Harvard Square is a bustling chaos of stoplights which only briefly regulate ceaseless traffic. But a closer look reveals historic sites and landmarks of old-world elegance, rivaling the Downtown and Beacon Hill Walks in interest and importance. Old Harvard Yard, for example, is a tranquil, shaded expanse of green, lined with stately, mellowed red-brick college buildings erected between 1718 and 1813. Christ Church, built in 1761, is one of the most exquisite wooden colonial churches in New England. At 105 Brattle Street is the Longfellow National Historic Site, the home of Henry Wadsworth Longfellow from 1837 to 1882, furnished as the poet left it. On your way

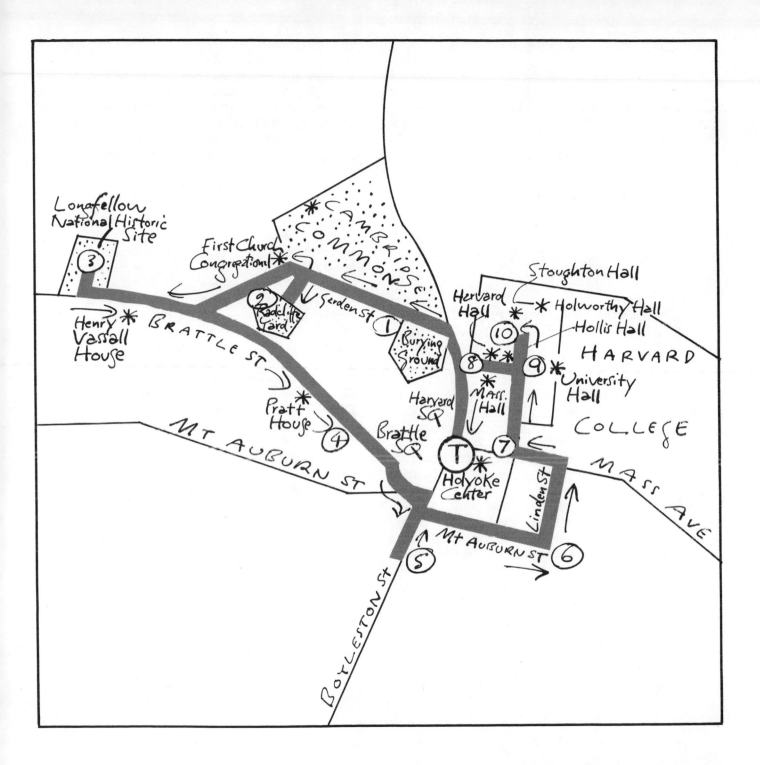

Longfellow National Historic Site

③

First Church Congregational *

CAMBRIDGE COMMONS

*

Stoughton Hall

Harvard Hall * * Holworthy Hall

Hollis Hall

Garden St

⑩ Hollis Hall

Henry Vassall House *

BRATTLE ST

② Radcliffe Yard *

①

Burying Ground

⑧ * * ⑨ * University Hall

H A R V A R D

Pratt House * ④

Harvard SQ

Brattle SQ

Mass. Hall *

⑦

C O L L E G E

MT AUBURN ST

Ⓣ Holyoke Center *

M A S S   A V E

Linden St

⑤ Mt AUBURN ST ⑥

BOYLESTON St

to it you will pass two more sites, both colonial mansions, the William Brattle House and the John Vassall, Sr., House. There are many more. We begin at the Old Burying Ground at the northwest corner of Massachusetts Avenue, walking west on Garden Street to our first stop, Christ Church.

Christ Church

Garden Street. Telephone 876-0200. Open daily. September–June 7:30–6:00; July–August 7:30–5:00. Visitors welcome when services are not in progress. Time: 15 minutes.

Before turning into Garden Street, view the **Old Burying Ground*,** also known as "God's Acre," set aside from Cambridge Common in 1635. Here lie the first eight Harvard presidents, as well as many early settlers, such as Stephen Daye (1594–1668), pioneer of printing in the colonies. Several veterans of the Revolution, including two black patriots, Cato Stedman and Neptune Frost, also lie here.

Follow the iron fence past the old milestone dating from 1794. On your left, set back from the street, is gray and white wood **Christ Church (1),** the oldest church building in Cambridge. It was designed in 1759 by Peter Harrison, the architect of Kings' Chapel, Boston (see page 52). The church was consecrated in 1761.

Christ Church went through difficult times with the coming of the Revolution. Its first rector, East Apthorp, was a typical high-living eighteenth-century Anglican priest who invited both ridicule and disaster. Cambridge, like Boston and other parts of New England, had been settled by Puritans and nonconformists who had emigrated to escape religious oppression. Antagonism against Christ Church exploded in 1774; Apthorp and the Tory members of his congregation fled for their lives.

The church was turned into a barracks in April, 1775, shortly after the Battles of Lexington and Concord. The metal organ pipes and lead window sash-weights were made into bullets by a rollicking company of volunteers from Wethersfield, Connecticut.

After Washington assumed command of the Revolutionary Army on July 2, 1775, the church was temporarily reopened for a New Year's Eve (1775) service, attended by the General and his wife (pew 93 is sited as the spot where they worshipped), accompanied by General and Mrs. Gates and other officers and their wives. Both Washington and his wife, Martha, were Anglicans. A contemporary witness described the occasion as "something grand and yet incongruous." The doors were shattered and the windows broken, the organ destroyed and the elegant interior totally marred.

Christ Church was again damaged in 1778 when townspeople, in a wave of resentment, ransacked the interior. But by 1825 the church had been restored by Isaiah Rogers, who maintained the quality of Harrison's original design. Entered by an arched portal, the church itself is engagingly beautiful. The tower originally housed a single great bell cast in England. This was recast to become part of the thirteen bell Harvard chime, donated by Harvard students to celebrate the centenary of Christ Church in

Christc Church

CLASS OF 1912

Radcliffe Yard

100

1861. One of the students was Richard Henry Dana, who contributed the royalties of *Two Years Before the Mast* to the project.

The original communion silver (now in the Museum of Fine Arts), bearing the name of William III and Mary, is still used on special occasions.

Radcliffe Yard

Buildings not open to the public. Visitors welcome to view the yard itself. Time: 10 minutes.

Continue down Garden Street, past Appian Way. Across the street to your right is **Cambridge Common***, the focal point of political, religious, and social activity in Cambridge for over three centuries. The land was set aside as early as 1631 for grazing cattle, militia training, and public ceremonies. Elections were held under the "Election Oak" and under another tree, the "Whitefield Elm," British revivalist George Whitefield (1714–1770), a founder of Methodism, moved townspeople to tears with his eloquent sermons.

The Common was long the training ground of the Cambridge militia and the hub of patriot activities; it immediately became the nerve center of the Revolution when Washington arrived in July, 1775. A bronze plaque and a scion of the "Washington Elm" commemorate the spot where the newly appointed generalissimo took formal command of 9,000 men who had gathered here to form the new Continental Army. Nearby stand three cannon captured from the British in that year.

A little farther along Garden is the gateway to **Radcliffe Yard (2),** the administrative center of the world-famous college. Buildings on the yard, or campus, include Fay House, built in 1806 and attributed to Bulfinch; the Gymnasium, built in 1898, and Agassiz House, named for Elizabeth Perkins Agassiz, the wife of Professor Louis Agassiz, Radcliffe's first president. Mostly these are Georgian in style or derivation, and enclose the yard in a protective embrace, exuding the ambience of peaceful academe. But the memorial apple tree seemed more essentially Radcliffe. What had happened, I wondered, to the "Class of 1912," the donors of the tree so dear to the heart of every graduate since?

Founded in 1879 as the Society for the Collegiate Instruction of Women, Radcliffe was created, unofficially, as an association of Harvard instructors, who agreed they would give women "some opportunity for systematic study in courses parallel to those of the University." There was no official connection with Harvard until 1894. In that year, the college was judged a complete success and named for Ann Radcliffe of England, donor of the first Harvard scholarship fund. Today, Radcliffe students sit with Harvard students in many of the latters' classes.

Continue down Garden. Turn left on Mason Street. **First Church Congregational*** on the corner, a Victorian building, has a Shem Drowne weathercock on the spire. Made in 1722 for the New Brick Church in Boston, it is an unbelievable five-foot tall, hollow-bodied rooster weighing over 170 pounds.

Walk down Mason. On your right is the

Longfellow's House

fine modern library of the Episcopal Theological Seminary. Turn right on Brattle to view the library which mixes agreeably with the rest of the seminary buildings, all ivy-covered Gothic, except the beige and white Greek Revival Hastings House.

Brattle Street itself, during the eighteenth century, was dubbed "Tory Row." In its large, detached, handsome mansions lived the stalwarts of the Old Christ Church congregation: colonial officials with estates stretching down to the Charles River. When they fled, their homes were confiscated and used as barracks, hospitals, and headquarter accommodation for the Continental Army.

The John Vassall House, now the **Longfellow National Historic Site (3),** our next stop, is perhaps the most famous example.

Longfellow National Historic Site

105 Brattle Street. Telephone 876-4491 or 4492. A National Historic Landmark administered by the National Park Service. T stop: Harvard Square on Red line. A fifteen minute walk. Open year-round. May–October: Monday through Friday 10:00–5:00; Saturday 12:00–5:00; Sunday 1:00–5:00. November–April: Monday through Friday 10:00–4:00; Saturday and Sunday 9:00–4:30. Closed New Year's Day, Easter, Thanksgiving, and Christmas. Admission: 50 cents; under 16, free if accompanied by adult. Guided tours every 20 minutes. Advance notice required of group visits. Time: 25 minutes.

The Longfellow National Historic Site is a mansion of exceptional interest, rich in historical and literary associations. The handsome colonial residence was given to the National Park Service by Longfellow's grandson, Henry Wadsworth Longfellow Dana, in 1973.

Built in 1759 by Major John Vassall, a wealthy Loyalist who fled from Cambridge on the eve of the Revolution, the house became Washington's headquarters in 1775. After the British left Boston in 1776, the house was empty until 1781, when it was occupied by Nathaniel Tracy, a wealthy shipowner. Admiral d'Estaing was entertained by him, and given the celebrated "frog soup" which caused some amazement, as each French officer found a full-size frog on his plate!

Dr. Andrew Craigie, who had served as apothecary-general during the Revolutionary War, bought the property. He had made a large fortune from land speculation, and in 1793 added the banqueting room and piazzas. The house, at this time, was known locally as Craigie House, or "Castle Craigie." Craigie died in 1819, after losing much of his money. To pay his debts, his widow took in lodgers. One of them, in 1837, was young Henry Wadsworth

William Brattle House

Longfellow (1807–1882), who had just been appointed Smith professor of modern languages at Harvard. The house became his home for life.

After Mrs. Craigie's death in 1841, Joseph Worcester, the lexicographer, and his wife rented the house. Longfellow was allowed to retain his rooms. Here, Charles Dickens joined the poet and other Harvard professors for breakfast in February, 1842, prior to the novelist's tour of the college. Longfellow married Fanny Appleton in 1843, and her father, the wealthy Nathan Appleton, bought the old house as a wedding gift. Well-educated and well-traveled, Fanny qualified to share her husband's life. Soon the house became a mecca for visitors from Europe. Here, Longfellow and Fanny created much of the warmth that made so many feel that Boston with Cambridge was, in the words of the Marquis of Lorne, "the abode of all that are first in literature, culture, and civilization in America."

Dickens again visited Longfellow on his second trip in 1867 when the great novelist came out for a family Thanksgiving dinner. It was on this occasion that Longfellow told him the story of the Craigie love-letters. The poet had accidentally discovered several old letters, written by a young girl to Craigie, that he had hidden away from his wife under the stairs. Longfellow told Dickens how, going down to the cellar one day, he had found the letters one after another, on the stairs, where they had dropped through a crack. A fitting subject for a story by Dickens, but used instead by Saxe Holm (Helen Hunt Jackson) in her story, "Esther Wynn's Love-Letters."

The old house, graced with its original furniture, books, and pictures, is much the same as Longfellow left it in 1882; including the famous chair, made from the wood of the "spreading chestnut tree," presented by the schoolchildren of Cambridge on the poet's seventy-second birthday.

William Brattle House

42 Brattle Street. Headquarters of the Cambridge Center for Adult Education. Not open to the public.

Return to Harvard Square on the south side of Brattle. On your way note the **Henry Vassall House*** at the corner of Hawthorn Street. The eight-foot-square chimney in the house dates from 1630. Later in the eighteenth century, it was rebuilt by the wealthy Vassall family, who lived there until 1775. During the Revolution the house was used as the medical headquarters of the Continental Army under Dr. Benjamin Church, who was confined here in his room after Deacon Davis discovered that he was a British spy. Replicas of eighteenth-century patriot flags are displayed here.

Continue along Brattle, past the Loeb Drama Center built in 1959. At 56 is the **Pratt House***, built *circa* 1808, and once the house of Dexter Pratt, Longfellow's village blacksmith. The forge is now a coffee and pastry shop and the original chestnut tree, long gone, is commemorated by a granite marker. A few more steps bring us to the red frame **William Brattle House (4).**

Built in 1727, the house originally stood in grounds extending from Brattle Street to the Charles River. Today, shorn of such a splendid setting, it stands as a modest three-story clapboard, gambrel-roofed dwelling unnoticed in the hustle and bustle of modern Cambridge.

Its original owner, William Brattle (1706–1776), was a man of restless ambition, who found it difficult to back one side or the other on the issue of independence. He was at various times a physician, lawyer, and in his spare time, general of the local militia. But in those troubled days, allegiances changed and re-changed. At first, the proud and portly Brattle was a Whig and friendly to the Sons of Liberty. But by 1774 he was a Tory and like his neighbors on Tory Row was compelled to quit Cambridge for good. He left Boston with the British and died homesick shortly afterwards in Halifax, Nova Scotia. The house was confiscated by the Committee of Public Safety, and after Washington's arrival in July, 1775, became the quarters of Major Thomas Mifflin, aide-de-camp and Commissary General.

Brattle House was also the residence of the great feminist, Margaret Fuller (1810–1850), between 1840 and 1842. Through her father, Timothy Fuller, a Harvard lawyer and politician, she came into contact with Emerson, Thoreau, and Channing, the circle that came to be known as the Transcendalists. She lived here while she was managing editor of their journal, *The Dial*.

Continue down Brattle, cross to the traffic island, and walk over to Mt. Auburn Street. After one block, you will reach Winthrop Square. During the seventeenth and eighteenth centuries this was the original market square of Old Cambridge. Now a city park, it is a pleasant place to rest your feet and watch the Cambridge characters pass. A short detour down Winthrop Square leads to an old stone wall of the eighteenth century which reveals the original grade of the hill that once rose from Eliot Square to Winthrop Square.

Return to Boyleston Street. Farther down, on the corner of Boyleston and South Street, is the **John Hicks House (5),** our next stop.

John Hicks House

64 Boyleston Street. Not open to the public. Old houses have a way of reaching out to you as if to say, "Oh, I may be plain but there's much more to me than what you see." The Hicks House is one such place.

Master carpenter John Hicks built a six-roomed, gambrel-roofed colonial homestead, laid out on the usual plan of one room each side of a front hall, with a staircase winding up in front of a large central chimney with closets taking up the space behind. John and Elizabeth Hicks, with a growing family of sons and daughters, came to live here in 1762, when the house was completed.

Hicks led a double life. He was a member of the Sons of Liberty, while his eldest son, John, had grown up to be violently Tory. Political arguments were a daily occurrence. But John Hicks, Sr., did more than argue. One cold December night in 1773 according to family tradition quoted by Esther Stevens Fraser, John Sr. rose from his bed and while the rest of the fam-

John Hicks House

Harvard Lampoon Building

ily were sound asleep, let himself out of the second-story north bedroom window by a sheet rope. Then he hastily made his way to Boston to join that merry band of "Mohawks" to empty chests of tea into Boston Harbor.

He returned to Cambridge in the small hours, and tried to enter his second-story bedroom window by the same means he had left it. But, having imbibed freely that night in celebration, he could not make it, and entered by the front door, leaving his muddy boots at the foot of the stairs.

He had intended to rise early to conceal all traces of his nocturnal adventure, but slept longer than planned. Morning came all too soon and the boots were discovered by his wife when she came down to make breakfast. Angrily, she waited for him to appear. When he did, the following conversation is said to have taken place:

"John, you were out last night, weren't you?"

"No," lied John, as he was bound to do if the secret of the Tea Party operation was to be properly kept.

"John Hicks! How can you say such a thing! You *were* out last night."

"No . . ."

"Well, look at your boots standing there. . . . Of course you were out last night!"

So Elizabeth Hicks picked up the telltale muddy boots, out of which tea leaves fell. Then she guessed what had happened and softened her tone. *That* kind of night prowling was quite all right!

John's next nocturnal foray did not end so happily. On the night of April 18, 1775, British troops marched out of Boston to Lexington and Concord. The next morning, when news of the fighting came back to Cambridge, John went out to his barn behind the house, lifted up the loose floorboards under which a musket lay hidden, and saddled his horse. He rode out toward North Cambridge where he joined in an attack on the Redcoats returning to Boston. Shortly afterwards, he was one of three Cambridge patriots killed during a skirmish.

Hicks House is now the library of Kirkland House, part of Harvard University.

Harvard Lampoon Building

Mt. Auburn Street. Not open to the public. Continue walking down Mt. Auburn past the back of the **Holyoke Information Center***. Open Monday through Saturday 9:00–5:00; Sunday 1:00–4:00. The center forms part of a precinct of shops and offices built 1961–1965 and designed by Jose Luis Sert, former Dean of the Harvard Graduate School of Design.

A little farther along Mt. Auburn is the **Harvard Lampoon Building (6),** a Dutch-*cum*-English flatiron edifice built between 1909 and 1910 on a triangular site donated by the young and then radical William Randolph. Hearst, the *Lampoon's* successful business manager at the time. One of Harvard's more flamboyant hellraisers, Hearst was later expelled for sending his professor a chamber pot. The architect was Edward Martin Wheelright, who delighted in the bizarre. One can readily imagine the building to be some monstrous beast kept alive only by a perennial diet of exams, slobbish roommates, and unpopular professors.

This is the editorial office of the famous bimonthly satirical paper, founded in 1876, where, between weekly Rabelaisian feasts in the odoriferous mock-medieval dining hall, generations of student editors have poked fun at the establishment and mounted their parodies of national magazines. *Lampoon's* editors usually distinguish themselves, and some have achieved fame, notably humorist Robert Benchley, actor Fred "Munster" Gwynne, and novelist John Updike.

Turn left up Linden Street, left again on Massachusetts Avenue. At the edge of Harvard Yard opposite the Holyoke Center is our next stop, historic **Wadsworth House (7).**

Wadsworth House

1341 Massachusetts Avenue. Office of the Harvard Alumni Association. Not open to the public.

Built in 1726 as the official residence of the Harvard president, the Reverend Benjamin

Wadsworth House

Harvard Hall and Massachusetts Hall with the Johnson Gate (8)

Old Harvard Yard

Old Harvard Yard: Fall

Wadsworth, Wadsworth House is a yellow clapboard, two-and-a-half story building of great charm and dignity. The front entrance door is its main feature. Two plain wooden columns support a pediment with triglyphs. It is simply ornamented. In those days it looked even more impressive. The house then had large gardens, a coach house, and a stable. Unhappily, all these gradually disappeared with successive widenings of Massachusetts Avenue.

The fine old house, the home of Harvard presidents until 1849, has seen many auspicious occasions "of ladies in the drawing-room," as Samuel Eliot Morison wrote, "band in the back parlor; Governor and aides and other distinguished foreigners, arriving and departing . . . ice creams and coffee circulating all the time."

Be that as it may, but to most people, Wadsworth House is where Washington made plans for driving the British army from Boston.

115

Holden Chapel

Harvard: The Holden Chapel

In 1775, the house was occupied by the Reverend Samuel Langdon, president of Harvard. Apparently a man of no great learning or administrative skill, nonetheless he was, Christopher Reed tells us, an ardent patriot who served the cause as chaplain of the new Continental Army. When Washington rode into Cambridge, exhausted after the long trek from Philadelphia, Langdon moved into a single room, and turned the rest of the house over to the new commander-in-chief and his entourage. Wadsworth House, from July 3 to the middle of that month, became Washington's first headquarters.

With Washington, as his second-in-command, was the eccentric Major-General Charles Lee (1731–1782), an able soldier of fortune who joined the British Army in 1747, and served in America in the Seven Years' War. On returning to England, Lee became a radical, and in 1773 settled in America. Boastful and ill-dressed, Lee was nonetheless a brilliant strategist. Had he not been so old, many would have preferred him as generalissimo. He was often critical of Washington, who regarded him with suspicion. At this time, however, the two men worked together to build their large unwieldy volunteer force into something resembling an effective fighting army.

While resident at Wadsworth House, Lee thought he might try to persuade his former comrade-in-arms, the British General Burgoyne, to see the futility of fighting the colonists. Burgoyne, on the other hand, thought he might bribe his old chum, in a gentlemanly manner of course. But although Burgoyne's trumpeter arrived with a letter for Lee, and was led to Wadsworth House blindfolded, the meeting between them never took place.

Walk now between Wadsworth House and Lehman Hall to enter Harvard Yard.

Old Harvard Yard

Between Cambridge Street and Massachusetts Avenue. Yard open to public, but not buildings. Year-round free guided tour from Information Center, Holyoke Center, Massachusetts Avenue, includes other Harvard buildings. Monday–Saturday 10:00, 11:15, 2:00, and 3:15. Sundays 1:30 and 3:00. Time: 45 minutes.

Perhaps the most beautiful of college campuses in America, **Old Harvard Yard (9)** was originally called College Yard, to distinguish it from the cowyards on each side. The yard was enclosed in 1636. It quickly became the focal point of undergraduate life.

Here are the most historic college buildings in America. Stand with your back to the Johnson Gate (the main entrance to the Yard). On your right is **Massachusetts Hall*** (1718) (see page 113). Designed by Harvard president John Leverett, the hall's handsome ivy-clad and ark-like bulk seems the essence of Harvard.

On your left, parallel to Massachusetts Hall, is majestic **Harvard Hall*** (1764) (see page 112) with its elegant bell tower and azure cupola. It was designed by Sir Francis Bernard, the royal governor whose misfortune it was to occupy that office from 1761 to 1769; a stormy period in which the Writs of Assistance, the Stamp Act, and the introduction of troops brought criticism and abuse of his administration. He had great affection for Harvard and gave the college much of his library. It was built by Thomas Dawes, later his enemy and a Revolutionary hero. The Hall has been the scene of many historic receptions and commencement banquets.

Walk forward a few steps. Farther to your left is **Hollis Hall*** (1762), a stiff, box-like, dormitory block designed and built by Dawes. It was named for the Hollis family whose generosity over many years helped the college with endowments, professorships, and scholarships. Opposite the middle of the Hall (on the left of my illustration) once stood the famous Liberty or Rebellion Tree, predictably the rallying point for student confrontations in 1818 and 1823 ("The Great Rebellion"), when resolutions were passed to organize resistance against injustice, real and imaginary. Later, the Rebellion Tree became the terminus of the annual parade of seniors who, headed by a band, cheered the buildings and danced around the old tree in dress suits and top hats. Immediately behind Hollis is **Stoughton Hall*** (1804), a Bulfinch design of great dignity, which had such famous freshman residents as Emerson, Thoreau, Holmes, and Edward Everett Hale.

Walk past Hollis Hall and turn left on the path between Hollis and Stoughton. This leads you to the baroque-looking **Holden Chapel (10),** immediately identified by its large Tuscan-style entablature and pediment embellished with a wooden armorial carving picked out in white against a background of ultramarine blue. The motto *Teneo et Teneor* means "I hold and I am Holden."

Such an unsual design was so different from anything Harvard had seen before that it is thought to be English. The chapel was built with a gift of £400 from the widow of Samuel Holden, a prominent Dissenter and director of the Bank of England. Thomas Hutchinson, a Harvard graduate himself and a future governor, acted as the go-between. Since that time it has been almost everything but a chapel, being used successively as lecture room, barracks, lumber room, fire engine house, medical hall, carpentry shop, and museum. It now houses the Harvard Glee Club *and* the Radcliffe Choral Society.

We now return to the Yard. The dormitory block on the left is **Holworthy Hall*** (1812), built with the proceeds of a state lottery and named in honor of another English Puritan, the merchant Sir Mathew Holworthy, who in 1681 gave £1,000, the largest gift received by Harvard during the seventeenth century.

Before we turn right and walk back to our starting point, the Johnson Gate, glance across to **University Hall***. Designed by Bulfinch and built in 1813, it is the most imposing building in the Yard. Its gray granite façade with white wood pilasters and white chimney stacks stand out against the Georgian red-brick which surrounds it on every side. In front of the Hall is the idealized bronze of John Harvard, an early work executed in 1883 by Daniel Chester French. Unable to find a print or portrait of

Harvard, French based his figure on a typical Harvard student of the time; his friend, Sherman Hoar of Concord (Harvard College, 1882), obliged. The statue itself was given to the University in 1884 by Samuel James Bridge.

Walk Five

CHARLESTOWN

Distance: 4 miles. Time: a day of 5 to 6 hours including the climb up to the top of the Bunker Hill monument, tour of the U.S.S. *Constitution* (*"Old Ironsides"*) and visit to Bunker Hill Pavilion to see *Whites of Their Eyes*, an 18-minute multimedia presentation sponsored by the Raytheon Historical Foundation, a non-profit institution. If not possible, limit your tour to 2 or 3 hours, concentrating on the Bunker Hill pavilion, *"Old Ironsides"* (next door) and the Bunker Hill monument.

Charlestown, just across the Charles River, is older than Boston. The first village was founded in 1629 by English settlers sent in by the Massachuesetts Bay Company, later reinforced in 1630 by John Winthrop and a fleetload of Puritan colonists. The rest of the story has already been told (see page 20). Charlestown's bad water led to the founding of Boston.

Nonetheless, Charlestown grew to become a busy seaport, and as resentment of British taxes spread, its sentiments became those of radical Boston. When the Revolution finally came, the townspeople found themselves in the frontline, the site of the first major conflict on June 17, 1775—the historic Battle of Bunker Hill. But they paid a heavy price when the British burned their town to the ground.

Reconstruction began after the end of the war, leading to a large influx of Irish immigrants in the 1850s, and making the town a major shipbuilding center (The Boston Naval Shipyard). Much of its Late Colonial and early Federal character remains but the setting and intimate scale of the town is overshadowed by surrounding urban blight and encroaching expressways.

Although this is quickly left behind once the walker enters the town, I found Charlestown a walk strictly for the dedicated: those who prefer to see their history actually in the process of being saved and preserved. Except for the Bunker Hill monument (a State Park), the Navy Yard (a National Historic Park), and a nucleus of restored eighteenth-century houses (the Thompson Square Triangle) much of the town is undergoing the agonies of renewal. Many old houses (clapboard or brick), mainly in the Federal style, are being revitalized by the Historic Preservation Program of the Boston Redevelopment Authority, particularly in the neighborhood of Town Hill.

First impressions, therefore, may not be favorable, but depending on how you look at historic buildings, these may be soon replaced by an appreciation of what has been, and what will be, done to restore much of Charlestown's former ambience.

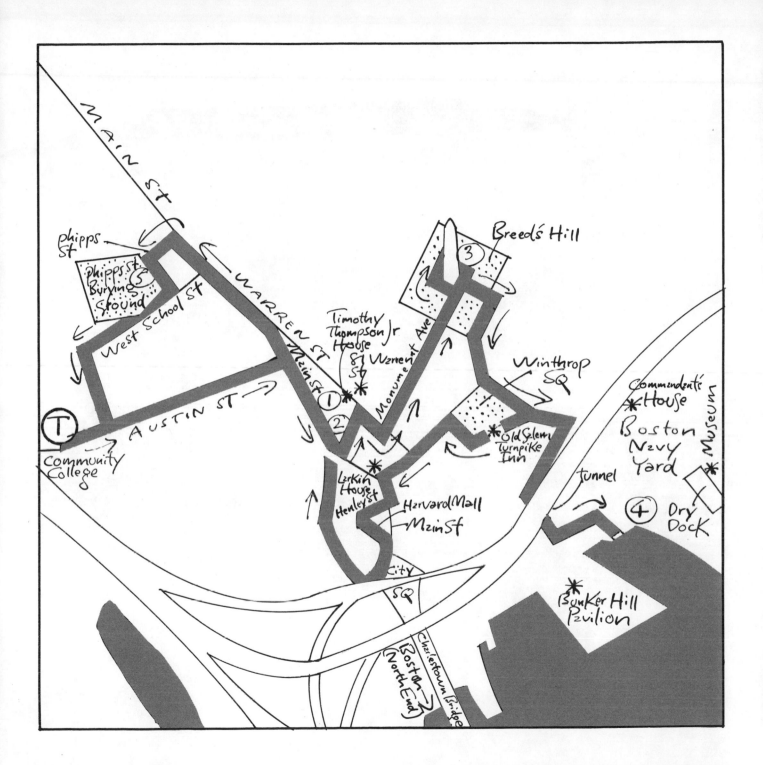

Timothy Thompson House

We begin at the new T stop, Community College on the Orange line, and follow the map up Washington and Union Streets to Thompson Square where the walk begins.

The Timothy Thompson House

119 Main Street. Not open to the public.

We begin our tour with a look at the Thompson Square Triangle, a three-sided lot between Warren and Main Streets once known as Craft's Corner. Here, one Elias Craft kept an apothecary shop which faced the public square. In 1869, the shop was demolished and the square enlarged and named Thompson Square in honor of Dr. Abraham Rand Thompson, a prominent local citizen. Thompsons have lived for generations in Charlestown. A James Thompson arrived with Winthrop in 1630 and refused to budge when that great colonist decided to move on to Shawmut and fresh water.

The Triangle contains three buildings of historic interest saved for posterity by the timely intervention of the Charlestown Preservation Society and restored between 1971 and 1975.

The first of these lies just ahead of us, the handsome **Timothy Thompson, Sr., House (1)**, built about 1794. It is a splendid example of a Federal woodframe mansion, three storys high and pleasantly enriched by quoins at each corner and an ornate doorframe graced by an open pediment and carved cornice. Incredibly, some of the original features have survived, including wood paneling around one of the fireplaces. My illustration shows the front entrance, which looks out onto a pleasant enclosed garden.

Timothy himself fought at Bunker Hill and not only lived to tell the tale but to head an illustrious family. His son, Senator Benjamin Thompson, a man once well-known in Massachusetts politics, was born here. Dr. Abraham Rand Thompson also lived here.

Old Warren Tavern

2 Pleasant Street. Telephone 241-8500. Open 11:30–2:30 and 6:00–9:00. Summer: Monday–Saturday. Winter: daily. Reservations recommended Friday and Saturday. Jackets after 6:00.

Next door to the Timothy Thompson, Sr., House, on the corner of Main and Pleasant, is the **Old Warren Tavern (2).** Built shortly after the burning of Charlestown, it is thought to be the town's oldest standing structure. Records reveal that in 1780 the building belonged to a baker, Eliphalet Newell. Shortly afterwards it became the General Warren Tavern, in honor of the much beloved patriot and revolutionary leader, Joseph Warren (1741–1775) who died at the Battle of Bunker Hill at the age of thirty-four.

Warren's short life was so devoted to the cause of independence that this seems as good a place as any to pause and reflect about him as a soldier-citizen; a man who perhaps all too eagerly sacrificed himself for what he believed. He was, it is said, handsome, articulate, and good-tempered, but cautious and uncompromising. He had practiced medicine in Boston and joined Samuel Adams during the agitation over the Stamp Act in 1765. He was president of the Provincial Congress and a member of the Boston Committee for Public Safety, and in 1774 had presented the Suffolk Resolves, advocating armed resistance to British demands. It was Warren who observed the unusual deployment of British troops on Boston Common, April 18, 1775, and dispatched Revere and Dawes on their famous errand to warn patriots that the Redcoats were marching on Concord to seize and destroy their arms and supplies.

Congress elected Warren a major-general of the Continental Army but he had no command; he wished only to be of service. When Colonels Prestcott and Putnam were sent to occupy Bunker Hill (and chose Breed's Hill instead), Warren left Cambridge to join them on June 17. Declining to assume command, he placed himself at the disposal of the more experienced Prestcott and Putnam and fought as a private, arming himself with a musket dropped by a retreating minuteman. He was killed on the day of the third and final British assault. One of the last to retreat, he was shot in the head and died instantly. "When he fell," wrote Abigail Adams

to her husband, John, "liberty wept." Howe said Warren's death was worth five hundred men to him. His body was buried by the British, but lay undiscovered for ten months until it was identified by Paul Revere, who had carried out dental work for Warren and recognized two artificial teeth he had fastened in for his friend.

For many years the Tavern was the headquarters of the first Masonic Lodge in Charlestown. Revere spoke here at its consecration in 1784 (both he and Warren were Masons). He spoke here again in 1794 when members of the Lodge marched to Breed's Hill to dedicate the Warren monument. This statue by Henry Dexter can be seen in the museum of the Bunker Hill Monument.

Only the square shape, the hipped roof, and the upper-story windows are original. Yet great care has been taken to restore the building to its original appearance. Wide floorboards and massive beams and posts give it a congenial ambience. It is a good place to have lunch or dinner, serving hearty Boston fare of seafood, beef, and poultry at moderate prices.

Before leaving Main Street, take a look at the quaint old free-standing stone building at 92, on the corner of Deverson and Prestcott. Built by Nathaniel Austin, who had the stone transported from Outer Brewster Island in Boston Harbor, it is one of two surviving splitstone buildings in Charlestown, but like many historic houses in the town, it awaits restoration.

Walk up Pleasant to Warren. On the way you will pass the third historic house on the Triangle, the **Timothy Thompson, Jr., House*** immediately on the left. Built in 1805, the beige woodframe clapboard house was at one time

Old Warren Tavern

125

the residence of another prominent member of that indefatigable family, Timothy Thompson Sawyer, grandson of Timothy Sr. and local historian.

As you turn right on Warren, look at the picturesque cluster of one late Georgian and two Federal houses at the corner of Warren and Pleasant. One of the Federal houses, **81 Warren Street*** is especially striking, with much of its original features still intact, including a fine doorframe and entablature with blocks and sidelights flanking the paneled door. Set behind is 81b Warren Street, a free-standing Georgian woodframe house with a gambrel roof.

Now turn left up Monument Avenue, and climb the historic hill, the scene of the first major battle of the war for independence, and our next stop, the **Bunker Hill Monument (3).**

Bunker Hill Monument

Monument Square (Breed's Hill). A National Historic Landmark owned by the National Park Service. Telephone 241-7205. T stop: from Sullivan Square on Orange line take Bunker Hill bus #93. Fifteen minute walk. Open daily and holidays 9:00–5:00. Adults: 75 cents; children under 12: 50 cents; school groups: 25 cents. Admission includes audio tour and museum. Time: 25–30 minutes.

The Battle of Bunker Hill, which began in the early morning of June 17, 1775, is an event so well-documented that it seems hardly necessary to add my nickle's worth. At the base of the mall you can follow the course of the battle in sequence with a headset by going to the marked locations and listening to the appropriate tape at each one. Note: if you and the family are especially interested, then I do recommend a visit to the **Bunker Hill Pavilion*** on Water Street, where a dramatic multimedia presentation, *Whites of Their Eyes* is shown daily from 10:00 to 6:00. Adults: $1.50; children under 12: 75 cents. Bus #111 from Haymarket Square stops at gate to Navy Yard and U.S.S. *Constitution*, 100 yards from Pavilion.

The Bunker Hill Monument itself is on the actual site of the redoubt on Breed's Hill where the main fighting took place. Here, Colonel William Prestcott walked back and forth, ignoring the cannon fire from HMS *Lively*, to give his untried men confidence to meet the assaults of the British infantry with those immortal words, "Don't fire till you see the whites of their eyes!"

It was up the eastern slopes that the King's grenadiers and marines strode forward in disciplined ranks, to recoil, reform, and charge three times before shortage of powder ended resistance. Burgoyne later wrote that "Howe's corps ascending the hill in the face of entrenchments" while Charlestown burned was "one of the greatest scenes of the war." The

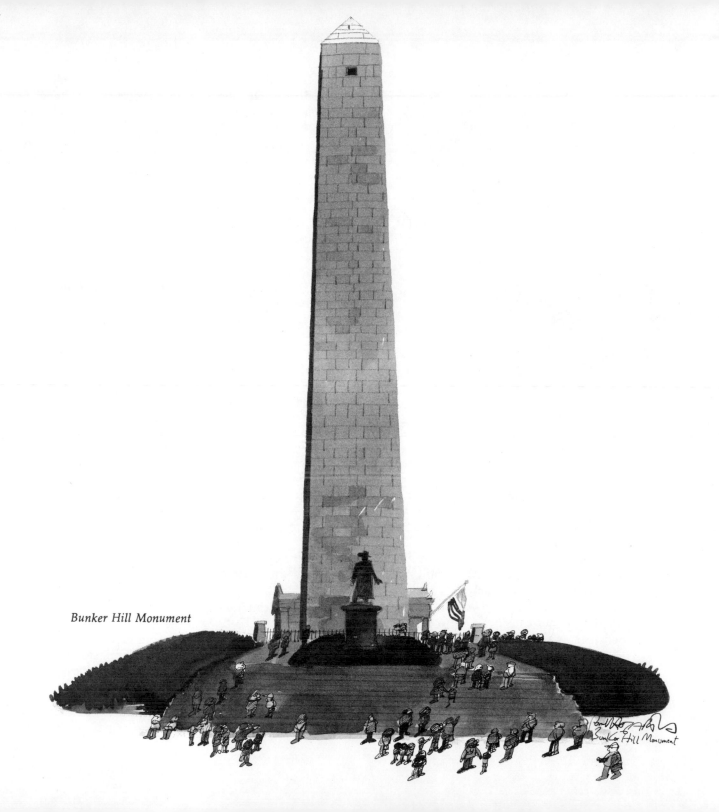

Bunker Hill Monument

It was the first edifice to commemorate an event during the Revolution. The cornerstone was laid by Lafayette on June 17, 1825, and Daniel Webster spoke at the ceremony. Webster also delivered the address of dedication eighteen years later on June 17, 1843, when the 13 survivors present inspired the moving words, "Venerable men, you have come down to us from a former generation!" Completion was delayed by chronic lack of funds. That is, until the ladies came to the rescue. A great bazaar organized by Sarah Josepha Hale raised the $30,000 required.

The ascent to the top (not to be attempted by anyone with a heart condition) offers a spectacular panorama of Greater Boston, including the Charles and Mystic Rivers.

As you leave the monument take a look at Monument Square with its range of splendid houses built through successive decades of the Victorian era. Go down Winthrop Street to Winthrop Square (also known as the Old Training Field). Here men trained for combat and left for active service in 1775, 1812, and 1860. Two large memorials name men killed at Bunker Hill and in the Civil War. As you walk around the square, note the low-slung woodframe clapboard **Old Salem Turnpike Inn*** at 16 Common Street. Once a well-known hostelry in the days of coaches and horses, it is now a private residence.

From Winthrop Square you can continue along the trail to the Boston Navy Yard and **Old Ironsides (4)** to complete the Charlestown walk (see page 120). But if you would rather devote another day to that, this will give you a chance to round off your tour of Old Charlestown. Continue down Winthrop Street. Cross Warren and continue to Main Street. Before crossing Main

British swept the redoubt, and pressed on to take Bunker Hill, the second of the two hills above the town, and won the day. It was a costly triumph; British losses numbered over 1,054 killed and wounded, whereas the Americans suffered only 450 casualties.

In the Tower of London, there is a cannon which was captured at Bunker Hill. Some years ago, author Robert Shackleton relates, the old cannon was proudly shown to a visiting American. The American looked it over calmly; and then just as calmly said, "Oh, I see, *you* have the cannon, and *we* have the Hill!"

The monument itself, an obelisk of Quincy granite 221 feet high, was designed by Willard.

glance right to view the white frame **Larkin House*** at 55–61 Main Street, built around 1795 on the site of the house where Paul Revere got his horse to begin his historic ride.

Cross Main and proceed up Henley Street opposite, one of the oldest streets in the town. This brings us to Harvard Square with its tiny splitstone house at 27, once the town's free dispensary (established in 1814). Turn left into **Harvard Mall*,** the gift of a Harvard alumnus to commemorate John Harvard, who lived here on Tower Hill in 1637; and the site of the first permanent Charlestown settlement. Here Governor Winthrop and his sturdy men built a fort anticipating Indian attacks, then after deciding it wasn't necessary after all, built a house for Winthrop.

Walk down the Mall and turn right on Main Street. This brings us to City Square, once the bustling market square of the town, but now little more than a traffic circle. Turn right and walk up **Harvard Street*,** a pleasantly winding street of Federal and Victorian houses, some of which are being restored to their former glory. Continue past the Warren Tavern on Main to Phipps Street. Turn left on Phipps. At the end of the short street is the **Phipps Street Burying Ground (5).**

PH Charlestown Navy Yard

Boston Navy Yard & U.S.S. Constitution (*Old Ironsides*)

Water Street, Charlestown. Telephone 242-3734. A National Historic Park. By bus from Haymarket Square, take bus Woodlawn via Mystic #111. By car: from North, Tobin Memorial Bridge, or Mystic Bridge, I-95 South, first exit after toll. (Exit sign: Charlestown, U.S.S. Constitution, Bunker Hill) or I-93 South to I-95 North, first exit. (Exit sign: Constitution Road, City Square, Charlestown) From South: Southeast Expressway to I-95 North. (Exit sign: Constitution Road, City Square, Charlestown) From West: Massachusetts Turnpike to Expressway North to I-95 North. (Exit sign: Constitution Road, City Square, Charlestown) Parking available. Open daily year-round 9:30–4:00. Free guided tours of *"Old Ironsides."* Time: 45 minutes.

If you decide, after visiting the Bunker Hill Monument, to go ahead and take in the Boston Navy Yard as well, continue down the Trail from Winthrop Square down Adams Street. Turn left on Chelsea and proceed to the underpass at the expressway on your left, which takes you to Water Street. Turn left on Water. On your right is the **Bunker Hill Pavilion***. Turn right to enter the Navy Yard. At this point you may want to see *Whites of Their Eyes* and relax for a half hour or so to round off your impressions of Bunker Hill. If not, proceed to view the historic **Boston Navy Yard & U.S.S. *Constitution* (4).**

Boston Navy Yard, the birthplace of so many innovations which transformed shipbuilding from a craft to a sophisticated industrial enterprise, is located on Moulton's Point, the very spot where the British began their assault at the Battle of Bunker Hill. Founded in 1800, the Yard covers some 43 acres, 30 of which form a segment of the Boston National Historical Park established in 1974 after the Yard was officially closed.

The Park contains the oldest and more interesting buildings, such as the **Commandant's House*** (1805) (not open to the public) said to have been designed by Bulfinch; and the **Dry Dock*** (1830) and **Engine House*** (1832) (now the U.S.S. *Constitution* Museum), both designed by Alexander Parris. Parris, who had worked with the great Bulfinch, and whose work I previously discussed on Walks two and three, became the architect of the Navy Yard in 1848. He designed over fourteen buildings, three of which, including the famous **Ropewalk,** are open to the public.

By far the most interesting sight is the U.S.S. *Constitution*, or *"Old Ironsides."* This ship, perhaps the most famous in the history of the United States Navy, was designed by Joshua Humphreys, Chief of Naval Construction, and launched in 1797. She put to sea in 1798 during the undeclared war with the French; and from that time on, hardly missed a war. Here are just a few of her triumphs.

Boston Navy Yard: Commandant's House

In 1803, under the command of Commodore Edward Preble when he blockaded Tripoli, she helped free American merchant ships held for ransom by Algerian corsairs. In the War of 1812, she served as a flagship for Captain Isaac Hull and won a famous victory over the British frigate, *Guerriere*, on August 19, 1812, off the coast of Nova Scotia. Battle began when British gunners fired salvo after salvo of hot shot, but the *Constitution* remained silent and worked in close. Then, suddenly, she let loose a succession of raking broadsides which ripped off the masts of the *Guerriere*, killing 79 of her crew, and tearing huge holes below her waterline.

There seems to be a difference of opinion as to whether this was the battle which won her the illustrious nickname of *"Old Ironsides,"* or a subsequent battle with another British frigate, *Java* which took place some months later on December 29, 1812, off the coast of Brazil.

Like everyone else, I enjoyed clambering about, looking at old cannon, the Captain's quarters, the hammocks that were beds for the crew; not to forget the brass and copper-fixtured galley where soups and stews were prepared for 500 men.

After many further adventures, *"Old Ironsides"* was condemned as unseaworthy in 1830, but popular sentiment, aroused by Oliver Wendell Holmes's poem, *"Old Ironsides,"* saved the ship from being broken up, and she was rebuilt in 1833. She was laid up again at the Portsmouth Navy Yard in 1855 and used as a training ship. In 1877 she was rebuilt again, and sailed across the Atlantic. Her long and active career finally ended in 1881, and in 1897 she was stored at the Boston Navy Yard, where she has lived in retirement ever since.

Phipps Street Burying Ground

Between Main and Rutherford Streets. Entrance via Phipps Street. T stop: Community College on Orange line. Five minute walk. Open daily 8:00–4:00. (Check with Visitor Information Center). Time: 15 minutes or longer according to your interest.

This quaint old cemetery is one of the three oldest in Boston, and probably in New England. It was first mentioned in 1640 although it was laid out in 1631. At that time, the little graveyard looked much more impressive as it stood on the mound flanked on two sides by the Charles River.

The oldest marker dates from 1642 but at least a hundred more predate 1700. Most of Charlestown's first families lie buried here: Frothingham, Hunnewell, Hurd, Larkin, Phipps, Tufts, plus a sprinkling of illustrious sons and distinguished residents including Nathaniel Gorham, president of the Constitutional Congress and Constitution signer, and

Phipps St Burying Ground

Oliver Holden (1765–1844) a popular composer of religious music who made his home in Charlestown, which he helped rebuild after the holocaust of 1775.

The obelisk at the top commemorates John Harvard (1607–1638). Born in Southwark, London, John was baptised in the Cathedral where his father was a churchwarden. His mother owned a popular local tavern, the Queen's Head. After her death, John sold the inn and immigrated to New England shortly after his marriage. It was the money from the sale of the inn that helped establish America's oldest university. In 1637 he and his young wife settled at Charlestown, where he became a teaching elder of the First Church. Tragically, within a year the former Cambridge graduate died of tuberculosis. He left half of his estate of £780 and library of 320 volumes toward the foundation of the new college at Cambridge.

Originally, Harvard was buried on Town Hill, close to his home which stood at the south end of Main Street, but the grave vanished after the burning of Charlestown. The monument was erected in 1828 by graduates of the college.

As at Copp's Hill, Granary, and Old Puritan, the earliest stones show the transition from the simple life and death symbols of the Puritans to the willow branches, urns, and broken columns of the Federal era. Many of these are ideal for those of you interested in graverubbing. But don't forget to take along the equipment you need. Charlestown's art supply stores are few and far between!

Phipps Street Burying Ground is the last stop on the walk. From here it is a five minute walk along West School Street to our starting point, Community College Station.

Walk Six

VICTORIAN BACK BAY

Distance: 4 miles. The trail includes a sampling of the more interesting mansions and public buildings. It begins at Copley Square T stop on the Green line and ends there. Nearby Newbury Street is a good halfway point for lunch if you start midmorning. Time: 2 to 3 hours.

Back Bay, which lies southwest of Beacon Hill and Downtown Boston, is a large residential district of great style, and is rich in historical associations. Flamboyant Victorian townhouses and mansions of every decade make it an immense museum of nineteenth-century architecture, enabling the walker to follow the constant changes in style and decoration during the last half of the century. Nowhere else in America is this possible.

In the eighteenth century, the site was a vast salt-water mudbasin of the Charles River. As Boston changed from a bustling town to a booming metropolis, more and more land was needed to accommodate the mounting pressures of expansion. Draining and filling Back Bay from 1857 on solved the problem, if only temporarily.

The gracious provincial lifestyle of Old Federal Boston now gave way to another created by the Industrial Revolution with a new, tougher set of material values, and, need one add, even greater wealth. And with greater wealth came a taste for the Fine Arts. Again, European influences (especially Victorian England and Second Empire France) made themselves felt. Modeled on the boulevards of Paris, Back Bay was transformed into an elegant district of flamboyant mansions, handsome churches, elaborate public buildings, ornate clubhouses, and luxurious hotels.

Here lived a new generation of Boston Brahmins who came to symbolize Boston ("The Athens of America") at the very peak of its achievement: authors, Oliver Wendell Holmes and William Dean Howells; artist, John Singer Sargent; architects, Henry Hobson Richardson and William Morris Hunt; plus a host of great financial and industrial dynasties—the Adamses and the Ameses, the Forbeses and the Gardners, the Lawrences and the Lowells, and many others.

Today, many of Boston's First Families live elsewhere. Some may still live in Back Bay or even Beacon Hill, but they are more likely to be found living more modestly in the suburbs. Lacking the servants to run them, many of Back Bay's mansions (and public buildings) have fallen into disuse or partial use and face a doubtful future. Many have been recycled as

STORROW DRIVE

BEACON ST

MARLBOROUGH ST

Cushing Endicott House ④

First Corps Cadets Museum

Higginson House ✳

Ames Webster House

✳ Gibson House

COMMONWEALTH

Side Trip to Symphony Hall via Mass' Ave ⑤ ✳

AVE

⑥

Hotel Vendome ✳

③

Trinity Church ✳ Rectory

Church of Holy Covenant ✳

Ritz Carlton Hotel ✳

NEWBURY ST

⑦

New Old South Church ✳

Old Museum of Natural History ✳

Arlington St Church ✳

BOYLESTON ST

Lennox Hotel

Boston Public Library ✳

Ⓣ

Copley SQ ①

→

⟶

⟶

Ⓣ

Arlington

Prudential Tower

FAIRFIELD ST

HUNTINGTON AVE

EXETER AVE

DARTMOUTH ST

Copley Plaza Hotel

John Hancock Tower

CLARENDON ST

ST JAMES AVE

BERKELEY ST

STUART PLY

Statler Hilton Hotel

Ⓣ Prudential

②

PUBLIC GARDENS

ARLINGTON ST

apartment houses, residence halls, offices, theaters, and art centers. One hopes that as building costs continue to escalate, recycling will continue to provide the intelligent alternative to demolition and reconstruction.

Trinity Church

Copley Square. Telephone 536-0944. T stop: Copley Square on Green line. Open daily 7:30–5:00. Sunday services 8:00 and 11:00. Visitors welcome. Free guided tours last 30 minutes (on Sundays after 11:00 service).

As you emerge from the Dartmouth Street exit of the subway you will enter Copley Square. Although framed by more ornate edifices than it is now, the square is a showplace of High Victorian architecture. The majority of these great buildings were built of stone in Gothic or Renaissance styles, which gave Back Bay its strongly European flavor, still exemplified by the Edwardian Copley Plaza Hotel, Trinity Church, the Public Library, and New Old South Church.

Cross the street and walk across the modern plaza to Boston's tallest building, the 790-foot, 60-story Hancock Tower. Designed by I. M. Pei, 1968–1969, it gained worldwide fame in 1973 when its windows kept popping out. To your left is **Trinity Church (1),** its glories enhanced by its glittering neighbor. The splendor of its massed towers, pinnacles, and turrets are the embodiment of a High Victorian style which not only revived the glories of the great Romanesque churches of France and Spain but rivaled them!

The construction and decoration of Trinity was an impressive achievement. It was, moreover, a cultural event of great importance, bringing together on a medieval scale architects, painters, and craftsmen to create one of the most sumptuously satisfying religious buildings of the nineteenth century.

Designed by the celebrated architect, Henry Hobson Richardson (1838–1886) and built between 1872 and 1877, Trinity is Richardson's masterwork of church architecture. Over the next twenty years or so, architectural historians tell us, many churches in the United States, particularly in the Midwest, followed in some degree what became known as Richardsonian Romanesque. A large striking man, Richardson brought worldwide recognition to American architecture during the two decades following the Civil War. He was a native of Louisiana, and was graduated from Harvard and the Ecole des Beaux Arts, Paris. Unfortunately, he was the victim of diabetes, which gave him as one biographer put it, "the waistline of a hippopotamus." He ate and imbibed with the courage of one who thought he would live forever. Friends marveled at the champagne, burgundy, and schooners of iced beer he downed on special occasions while sampling enormous helpings of oysters and roast beef rare. He declared on more than one occasion, that he would "never take the time to die." But he died at his prime at the tragically early age of forty-eight. We shall be looking at more of his work.

Trinity Church

Different in temperment but no less remarkable was dynamic Phillips Brooks (1835–1893), Rector of Trinity and later Bishop of Massachusetts. Brooks was invited by Trinity, the stronghold of Boston Episcopalianism, to become its rector in 1869. He lost no time, and, under his genial driving leadership, the present location on Copley Square was purchased in 1872 and fellow Harvard student Richardson chosen as architect. Here, Brooks distinguished himself as a man of broad and generous sympathies, who did much to add a new dimension to Boston life. His statue, by St. Gaudens, stands outside the North Transept. There's also a bronze bust of him by Daniel Chester French in the Baptistry.

The construction and decoration of Trinity also reflects the technological as well as the spiritual optimism of the time. The church stands on a manmade landfill. No less than 4,500 wooden piles support the foundations. Of these, over 2,000 are in the area, supporting the foundations of the great blocky Lantern Tower which, incidentally, weighs 9,500 tons. Water levels under the foundations are checked regularly, since the piles must be kept saturated at all times.

The interior is unusually intimate and relaxing for a Victorian church of this size, perhaps because of the rich but harmonious scheme of reds, browns, and greens with gold accents devised by painter John La Farge (1835–1910). Note especially the polychrome paintings and decorations on the walls of the Tower, above the arches (and above the windows of the Nave). These were planned and executed by La Farge in cooperation with Richardson and St. Gaudens, and represent the first major fresco scheme to be successfully carried out by an American artist. La Farge also designed the magnificent stained-glass window, *Christ in Majesty*, above the West portal or gallery. Those in the Baptistry, *David's Charge to Solomon*, and in the North Transept (South wall, above the gallery) were designed in 1878 by the English artist-designer William Morris (1834–1896) with the figures by Sir Edward Burne-Jones (1836–1898).

Before leaving Copley Square, turn to view the interesting buildings situated on the west side. Directly opposite you is the richly ornate frontage of the **Public Library***, one of the world's greatest, completed in 1895 and designed by Charles Follen McKim (1847–1909) of the famous partnership, McKim, Mead and White. Faced with the problem of harmonizing his design with the adjacent Romanesque Trinity and Italian Gothic New Old South Church, not to mention other buildings long since demolished, McKim concluded that, to hold its own, his library must be horizontal, simple in outline and above all, classical in style. In doing so he created a masterpiece of American public architecture, "a Florentine place," as Henry James wrote, "magnificently superseding all others."

Set on a low, stepped terrace, the Rennaissance-style building is built around a central courtyard. It has a low-slung granite façade, with a series of arched windows and portals that overlook the Square. Flanking the triple entrance doors are clusters of huge Florentine-style cast-iron lanterns with spikes. Note also the carved panels by St. Gaudens emblemizing the arms of the library, the city, and the commonwealth, and the great bronze doors designed by French. The two bronze figures representing Science and Art are by Bela Pratt (1867–1917).

The interior of the library is enormous and, even without the equally impressive modern annex designed by Phillips Johnson, covers a whole city block to house its many famous collections. If you do have the time, take a look at the grand marble staircase, with murals, *The Allegory of Wisdom*, by the French painter, Puvis de Chavannes, which lead to the huge reading room known as Bates Hall. On the Huntingdon Avenue side, another reading room forms the setting for a frieze of Arthurian mural decorations, *The Quest for the Holy Grail*, by the American artist, Edwin Austin Abbey (1852–1911) a Philadelphian then living in England. Press on to the third floor stair hall, to view the murals, *The Triumph of Religion* by John Singer Sargent (1856–1925). This was the commission which took the famous portrait painter to the Middle East and produced some of his most vivid and memorable watercolors. Both the Abbey and Sargent decorations are embellished by gold-leaf sculpture executed by St. Gaudens.

Immediately to the right of the Public Library, on the southeastern corner of Newbury and Dartmouth Streets, is **New Old South**

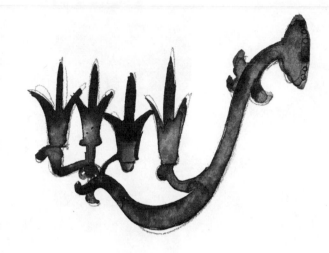

Boston Public Library

Church* designed in North Italian Gothic style by Cummings and Sears and completed in 1877, when the Third Church of Boston abandoned the Old South Meeting House.

Leave Copley Square by way of Newbury Street. Walk up Newbury to Arlington Street.

139

Armory of the First Corps of Cadets

Armory of the First Corps of Cadets

97–105 Arlington Street and Columbus Avenue. T stop: Arlington on Green line. Three minute walk. Call Visitors Information Center to check if open to public.

Originally lined with fine mansions and institutions, Newbury Street is now famous for its elegant shops, art galleries, and cafes. On your left, at the end of the first block is Richardson's **Trinity Rectory***, built in 1879. At the corner of Berkeley and Newbury is the **Church of the Covenant***. Designed by Howard and Richard Upjohn, and built in 1867, the Presbyterian-Congregational church is noted for its stained-glass windows, designed by J. A. Holzer of the Tiffany Studio in 1893. The building opposite, designed by William Gibbons Preston (1842–1910) is the former **Museum of Natural History***, built in 1862. The museum moved to the Museum of Science on the Charles River, and this graceful building began a new life in 1947 as Bonwit Teller's Boston Shop.

Turn right on Arlington to Stuart Street. Continue past Arlington Street Church, which also has Tiffany windows. On the southwest corner of Arlington and Columbus Avenue is our next stop, the fabulous **Armory of the First Corps of Cadets (2).**

Richardsonian in style, this massive, granite-faced, Romanesque fortress is one of the more unsual buildings I have drawn. It consists of a four-story Head House, a six-story hexagonal tower, and a vast single-story Drill Hall. Both house and tower have huge, high-ceilinged, elaborately-fitted rooms big enough to house as well as train a brigade of cadets. Bostonians call the Armory "The Castle," and certainly, as I drew it against the setting sun one spring day, it did look like some Kafka-esque pile transplanted from central Europe.

Built between 1891 and 1897 after designs by Preston, the Cadet Armory is one of the last surviving examples of the American Victorian armory built to house and provide training facilities for the local militia units required by the 1878 Act of Congress. Boston, however, was unable or reluctant to allocate funds. Undaunted, the Cadets decided to raise the necessary funds themselves and established one of the finest armories in America.

The history of the Corps suggests a characteristically pugnacious independence, and goes back to 1741 when they functioned as a bodyguard to the Governor of the Province of Massachusetts Bay. Reorganized in 1777, the Corps became the Boston Independent Company and served with distinction in the Revolutionary War. Subsequently, the Corps became part of the State Militia and during the Civil War supplied officers to the Union Army. Military buffs note: Memorabilia and weapons from these wars and others can be viewed at the **First Corps of Cadets Museum,** 227 Commonwealth Avenue. Telephone 267-1726. Open Friday through Monday, May 16–September 1. Admission: $1.00 for adults, 50 cents for children under 12.

Today, the Cadet Armory faces an uncertain future and possible demolition. It became the Library of the University of Massachusetts at Boston from 1966 to 1974; and then in 1975 was adapted as the venue of the city's bicentennial exhibit on Victorian Boston. But this closed at the end of 1976 with no definite plans for adaptive reuse.

The historic Armory may not, therefore, be open at the time of your visit, but I hope you can at least view its impressive exterior. The best side to do so is from narrow Columbus Avenue. Note the top story of the Head House and tower. Carved detailing includes a spectacular winged dragon and pairs of grotesque heads which complete the moldings above the window arches.

Note also the "drawbridge" to the Drill Hall with its steeply pitched roof and pyramid-shaped dormer windows. The "moat" is suggested by the space between the sidewalk and the building and allows for light to enter the basement storage rooms, furnished, as are all the windows of the Drill Hall, with retractable bullet-proof steel shutters!

Retrace your steps along Arlington Street. Continue past Newbury Street. Pause to view the **Ritz-Carlton Hotel*** on your left at the corner of Newbury and Arlington. Built in 1912, it is the last stronghold of elegance from a bygone era. The opulent dining room overlooking the Public Gardens ranks among the finest of America's restaurants. The menu is á la carte and expensive, too. If you wish to savor the ambience of this famous Back Bay hotel with the minimum strain on your budget, do as I did. Try the café downstairs—more moderately priced, but still of very high quality. Open

daily 12:00–2:30 and 6:00–9:00. Jackets and ties required.

Before turning left on Commonwealth Avenue, glance at Boston's first equestrian statue; the striking George Washington mounted on his horse by Thomas Ball (1819–1911). The model for the horse was Black Prince, which the Prince of Wales rode when he reviewed the troops on the Common during his visit to Boston in 1860.

Now, walk down Commonwealth as far as Berkeley Street. One of the finest residential streets in America, the Avenue is even more imposing than it appears in early photographs of Back Bay. At that time, the trees had yet to reach their full maturity. Now they cast their genial shade on the stroller, enhancing the gracious perspective of handsome mansions.

Turn right on Berkeley and continue to Beacon Street. At 137 is the **Gibson House***, a museum devoted to Back Bay's Victorian Era. Open to the public daily 2:00–5:00 except Mondays and holidays. Admission: $1.00 includes a guided tour.

If you took the Beacon Hill tour, you will have had an opportunity to see what a Beacon Street home looked like at the Appleton-Parker House (Women's City Club). Here at the Gibson House, you have the opportunity to see its Back Bay counterpart. Built in 1860 and designed by Edward Cabot as one of a pair of brownstones (135-137 Beacon Street) for the related families of Russell and Gibson, the six-story houses have a central entrance fitted with double doors, and are approached by a massive flight of stone steps. Despite the somewhat forbidding exterior, the overstuffed interior fascinates with its high-ceilinged rooms crowded with fine objects and furnishings, set off by heavy, dark woodwork and red-carpeted floors and stairs.

Leaving the Gibson House, resume your walk down Beacon to Clarendon Street. Note the abundance of fine Victorian mansions of every style from 1860 to 1900. Many of these are now colleges or residence halls for students, although a less fortunate fate awaits such houses when they become the prey of the rooming-house proprietor, or worse still, the speculator concerned only with the sale of the site.

One such house on the north side, 150 Beacon Street (now Emerson College) was the former home of the late Governor Alvan T. Fuller. In the elegant ballroom, now a cafeteria, the Fullers gave musical evenings and debut dances. One of their guests was the celebrated British painter, and *bon vivant* Augustus John (1879–1861), who lived here with the family for several months in 1927 while he painted their portraits. The Fullers, however, didn't like the portraits or his unconventional behavior. "John," wrote Michael Holroyd, "was almost as bad for them as the Sacco-Vanzetti Trial." (Governor Fuller, with Abbott Lawrence Lowell, upheld the verdict of Sacco's and Vanzetti's guilt, a decision which caused him and his family much anxiety.)

Turn left on Clarendon. A few more steps brings you to our next stop, the ivy-clad, Romanesque **First Baptist Church (3)**.

The First Baptist Church

Commonwealth Avenue at Clarendon Street. Telephone 267-3148. T stop: Copley Square on Green line. Five minute walk. Open daily. Visitors welcome. Services: Sunday, 11:00. Time: 15 minutes. Free guided tour.

This former Unitarian Church, begun in 1870 and completed in 1872, was Richardson's first church, and gained him the commission to design Trinity, which stands but two blocks away. Like Trinity, the exterior has an extraordinary richness of detail. The 176-foot tall tower, built between the nave and the transept, is a striking feature. Above the belfry arches is the famous frieze, modeled by Frederic Auguste Bartholdi (1834–1904) and carved on location by Italian stonemasons. This was the young French sculptor's first major project in America. His colossal figures of Charles Sumner, Longfellow, Emerson, Hawthorne, Lincoln, and Garibaldi, included in groupings representing Baptism, Communion, Marriage, and Death, established his reputation even before his celebrated Statue of Liberty was completed. Enough was never sufficient for the Victorians: Standing at the four corners of the frieze are giant angels with gilded trumpets. This gave the church the affectionate nickname, "The

First Baptist Church

Church of the Holy Beanblowers."

Incorporated into the tower are quoins and cornerstones from the old Brattle Street Meeting House of 1772, which the Brattle Square Unitarian Society sold to move here. One cornerstone bears the magic names of "John Hancock, Esq., July 27, 1772" and "Jno. Greenleaf. 1772." Both were members and benefactors of the Society. The bell from the colonial Meeting House, cast in 1809, hangs in the tower.

No less remarkable are the three immense rose windows in each of the ends of the cross-gable roof. Later in the nineteenth century, the Baptists, not to be outshone by its various rivals, added stained glass by Louis Tiffany (1848–1933). Tiffany's windows, of which there are many in Back Bay churches (art historian Susan Fondiler Berkon tells us), brought revolutionary effects in varicolored glass. Field of color was enlarged as well as the adaptability of stained glass to contemporary architecture.

The interior of the church, with its high, unadorned walls and galleries, provides a striking contrast to the outside. Some historians think there may have been plans to embellish and decorate the walls, plans which were abandoned when the Unitarians lost the church through mortgage foreclosure.

Proceed along the mall of Commonwealth Avenue. The spacious tree-lined park, which runs its entire length, sets off the houses and provides a pleasant walk. The houses of Commonwealth Avenue, while similar in date and style to those we have seen on Beacon Street, are larger and more flamboyant. The north, or sunny side, was considered the "right" side, so the houses there are generally more grandiose or more elegant than those on the "wrong" side.

Just ahead, on the other side of Dartmouth Street, is the seated bronze statue of William Lloyd Garrison, the abolitionist and reformer who was dragged through the streets of Boston with a rope around his neck—a rope that might have led to a lynching had it not been for the courageous intervention of Mayor Theodore Lyman. In 1886, half a century later, when the statue by Olin Levi Warner was unveiled on the Mall, Garrison had become a respectable figure. Almost but not quite; there were some nearby residents who talked of moving.

Across the Avenue, on the southeast corner of Dartmouth, is the once celebrated **Hotel Vendome***, now an apartment house-*cum*-shopping precinct, but a good example of an historical building recycled for modern use. Decidedly French in style with its mansard roof and châteauesque trimmings, the white-marble-faced hotel was, in the 1880s, a Boston showpiece and one of the world's most elaborately furnished accommodations. The great dining hall, which seated almost four hundred, was of carved mahogany and cherry with huge plate-glass mirrors and mural decorations. The wood-paneled elevator had a built-in seat for passengers. Rooms were stuffed with great pieces of ornate furniture and luxurious drapes trimmed with fringes and tassels. Here, in October, 1879, Thomas Edison demonstrated the incandescent lamp for the first time in Boston. This led to the installation of fifty colossal chandeliers fitted with his lamps in the great dining hall in 1882.

Although built in 1871 from the designs of W. G. Preston, the essentially Back Bay extras such as octagonal and round bays, the mansard roof, and other flamboyant touches were added in 1881 by J. F. Ober.

The Vendome had hardly time to enjoy this new look when Oscar Wilde descended from his carriage on the snowy night of January 28, 1882, for his memorable three-week visit to Boston. A visit which apparently had few dull moments, culminating as it did with the celebrated lecture at the Music Hall which stood opposite Part Street Church on Hamilton Place. Back at the Vendome, the bellboys were kept busy delivering notes and cards including the dinner invitation from the oft-quoted Oliver ("Autocrat of the Breakfast Table") Wendell Holmes, which caused the poet to remember Boston as a great civilized city and the abode of that "lovely old man, who is himself a poem."

The list of the famous who stayed at the Vendome is long: President Grant, Mark Twain, John Singer Sargent, Sarah Bernhardt, P. T. Barnum, and Sir Arthur Sullivan are just a few of the celebrities who graced its threshold.

Leaving the Vendome and its ambience of departed grandeur, turn left to walk north on Dartmouth. At 306 Dartmouth and Commonwealth Avenue is the **Ames-Webster House***, now the headquarters of Neil St. John Raymond's Cattle Company. Designed by Peabody and Stearns in 1872 and remodeled by John Sturgis a decade later, the Frederick L. Ames House is perhaps the grandest Back Bay mansion of them all. Its enormous. reception rooms, richly decorated in styles ranging from Jacobean Revival to Frankenstein Baronial, have been preserved and imaginatively recycled into office space. The grand staircase rises through three storys to a domed ceiling covered with murals by the French painter, Benjamin Constant, and stained-glass windows by La Farge. Ames, its last great owner, was once

connected with seventy-five of America's railroads, notably the Union Pacific.

Continue now to Marlborough Street. At the northeast corner of Dartmouth and Marlborough is the **Cushing-Endicott House (4),** another large and impressive townhouse, now a residence for working girls and college students, and known as Endicott Manor. Designed by Snell and Gregerson for Thomas Cushing and built in 1871, the house was occupied until 1958 by Mrs. William (Louise) Endicott, Jr. It is described by Bainbridge Bunting as being the handsomest house in Back Bay. The house isn't open to the public, but its history and associations are so well-documented that it would be a pity not to look upon its walls and think of what used to happen there.

Its builder, Thomas Forbes Cushing, was the son of John Perkins Cushing, a wealthy and benevolent Yankee merchant prince. As a youth of sixteen, John had announced that he wanted to become a writer, but his father's answer was to hustle him off to China on a company clipper. All was forgiven when he returned at the age of twenty-three with a fortune of seven million dollars! Most was inherited by Thomas, who was to marry Fanny Leslie Grinnell of New York. The house was completed in 1873, while the young couple were in Europe.

Elegance even to the smallest detail was characteristic of the mansion. Red-velvet carpeting set off black and gold balustrades, and, for the weary climber on his way up to the second, or third, or even fourth floor, there were velvet hand ropes. Opening off the second floor were the main rooms: dining room, drawing room, and library. The dining room, with a huge bay window facing south and another to

146

Cushing-Endicott House

147

Symphony Hall

the west, was the most beautiful of these, hinting of the family's links with the Orient, with a great oval table and green-covered chairs, twin china cabinets and mirrored sideboard, all imported from China, as was also the gray-green wallpaper, with orange, green, and gold figures. On each side of the sideboard were black and gold doors; one to the pantry; the other a dummy to preserve balance.

The drawing room, only a trifle less elegant, featured a white marble fireplace and a great crystal chandelier. From the drawing room double doors led to the dining room, hall, and library. The library overlooking Dartmouth Street was a world in itself, stuffed with tables, chairs, lamps, books, and pictures. On the third floor were the main bedrooms with two adjoining dressing rooms and bath, together with a nursery with its own bathroom. Two more spare rooms and a dressing room with bath completed the family quarters on the fourth floor, which also contained, under the mansard roof, rooms for eight servants, who shared a common bathroom.

The house was bought by William Crowninshield Endicott in 1898 to house his wife and two children. A lawyer who had served as Secretary of War in President Cleveland's first administration, William traced his ancestry to Governor John Endicott. Mary, his only daughter, became the wife of Joseph Chamberlain, British statesman and father of Neville Chamberlain, the British Prime Minister and coauthor of the controversial Munich Pact.

As the Victorian age gave way to the Edwardian decade, there were changes in the decor and furnishings of the great house. The Oriental style was now unfashionable. Instead, large, elaborately ornamented furniture mixed with pieces from earlier periods in luxurious confusion. Among the more valuable pictures were four large portraits by Sargent, of Mrs. Ellen Peabody Endicott, Mary Endicott Chamberlain, Louise Thoron Endicott and her husband, William Crowninshield Endicott, Jr. All are among the more impressive of Sargent's portraits of Boston families.

The most striking of these was his uncompromising view of the matriarchal Mrs. William Crowninshield Endicott, exquisitely severe and beautifully painted. Mary Chamberlain sat for hers in London. Both portraits are in the National Gallery, Washington D.C. Louise's portrait was painted in her bedroom in the house. Sargent was then at the climax of his distinguished career. He had completed the mural decorations for the Boston Public Library, and, after a trip to Washington to paint President Roosevelt's portrait, returned to Boston to carry out the many commissions that had accumulated in his absence. He arrived at 163 Marlborough Street on March 4, 1903, to begin the portrait of Louise, and selected a black and white lace dress with pink roses as her costume. William, her husband, stood on the sidelines, hoping that Sargent wouldn't paint his wife with her mouth open! William himself was painted in London at Sargent's Chelsea studio.

Although he lived for most of his life in Europe, Sargent himself came from a great merchant family of Gloucester, Massachusetts, established by shipowner Epes Sargent during the eighteenth century. Tall, vigorous, with touches of Puritan reserve, John studied painting in Paris at eighteen with the master portraitist Carolus Duran. In 1885, Sargent settled permanently in England to become, in Edward VII's words, "the most distinguished portrait painter in England."

Yet when Sargent had arrived in London, he was so poor that he almost gave up and thought of returning to America and becoming a businessman. His brilliant and sophisticated style, thought to be "avante-garde," was then unacceptable, but friends like Henry James and Robert Louis Stevenson opened the doors. For a while the commissions were slow in coming, until the offer of one in Newport, Rhode Island, brought him back to America in 1887–1888 and almost immediate success. From 1890 to the end of his life in 1925, he shuttled back and forth to become the painter of Boston Society.

Sargent never owned a house in America but he did live for months at a time in Boston, usually in Back Bay. He liked painting his sitters in their habitat, usually in their own houses. As I drew the house I couldn't help wishing it could be the same as in his time. But, unlike the Gibson House which miraculously survives like a time-capsule, the Cushing-Endicott House has assumed another personality and is beyond recall.

Symphony Hall

251 Huntington Avenue and Massachusetts Avenue. Telephone 266-1492 or 267-0656. T stop: Symphony on Green line.

Performances are given Tuesday, Thursday, and Saturday evenings and Friday afternoons from late September to late April. There are also Wednesday evening open rehearsals and the Boston Pops series Monday through Saturday in May and June. Evening concerts begin at 8:30, afternoon concerts at 2:00. Tickets: $1.50–$8.00. Advance booking required.

Continue down Marlborough and turn left on Exeter Street, then left again on Commonwealth Avenue. The enormous mansion on the corner, **191 Commonwealth Avenue***, was the home of Major Henry Lee Higginson (1834–1919) financier and philanthropist extraordinary, and the most powerful of Boston First Family patriarchs between 1880 and World War I. When Theodore Roosevelt, then president, attacked the monoplies of the day, it was the Major who brusquely told him to stop his nonsense "about corporations and capitalists."

The Puritan ideal of plain living and high thinking was strongly embodied in Henry Lee Higginson. He didn't like automobiles and wisely preferred to save cab fare by walking each day to his office on State Street. Yet, to Harvard, he gave Soldiers Field and the Harvard Union and presented the first great Flemish painting to cross the Atlantic, Roger Van der Weyden's *St. Luke Painting the Virgin*, to the Museum of Fine Arts.

His biggest gift, however, was a symphony orchestra, the world-famous Boston Symphony, which he founded in 1881 and supported until 1918, when old age compelled him to share what had become a prestigious burden. His idea was new in its day, to hire an orchestra by the year to give concerts of classical music and also to give, at other times, concerts of a lighter

Exeter Street Theater

kind of music; and most important, to always keep prices low.

The Major was immensely wealthy. He had served in the army during the Civil War, and after his marriage to Ida Agassiz, daughter of the famous zoologist, joined the family brokerage firm in 1868. Well-informed connections and the post–Civil War boom did the rest. Yet money to him was often the means of giving people what they needed to boost the quality of their lives. "My money," he wrote, "may fly away; my knowledge cannot. One belongs to the world, the other to me."

At this stage you may succumb to curiosity and see this unique institution. I would recommend that you take a cab and save time. This is a long, fifteen minute walk and will take you west on Commonwealth Avenue to Hereford Street. Turn left on Hereford and cross Boyleston. Turn right on Boyleston, then left again on Massachusetts Avenue. Symphony Hall is on the corner of Massachusetts Avenue and Huntington Avenue.

Completed in 1900, **Symphony Hall (5)** was designed by McKim, Mead and White. It is a massive, red-brick Renaissance Revival structure, two storys high with the central portion rising to a fourth story. The auditorium itself, richly embellished with classical figures and gilded ornamenation has excellent acoustics and is considered one of the three best concerts halls in the world.

After viewing Symphony Hall, take the subway at nearby Symphony station, back to our starting point, Copley Square.

Back at Commonwealth Avenue, walk south on Exeter Street to our next stop, the Exeter Street Theater.

152

The Exeter Street Theater

26 Exeter Street at Newbury. Telephone: 536-7067. T Stop: Copley Square on Green line.

This fortresslike brownstone and granite building is not another armory but a famous Back Bay institution which received a special award from the National Trust for Historic Preservation in 1973. It is, in fact, the oldest continuously operating movie theater in Boston. Built in 1885 as the First Spiritualist Temple for Marcellus S. Ayer, founder of the Working Union of Progressive Spiritualists, the **Exeter Street Theater (6)** became a cinema in 1914.

The architects were Henry Walker Hartwell (1833–1919) and William Cummings Richardson (1854–1935) who, as you will have noted, were much influenced by Henry Hobson Richardson's Trinity Church. They even used the same construction company, Norcross Brothers.

Yet the building has its own peculiar character, well-suited to its original purpose. The most interesting part of the outside is the huge, richly carved Romanesque arch leading to the stylish interior, set off by bands of brownstone masonry and rows of irregularly-placed windows. Above the enormous basement, which contains a lecture room or lower auditorium and library, the main floor rises three storys, occupied by a large auditorium, today the Exeter Street Theater.

Until 1974, the theater was managed by the charismatic Viola Berlin, an Englishwoman with a B.A. from the University of London and

Old Boston Art Club

an accent to match. Under her enlightened guidance it became a showcase for first-quality films. The new owner, Neil St. John Raymond, carries on the tradition but stories are still told of Miss Berlin's legendary reign. It seems that her patrons were mostly Proper Bostonian ladies who, suspicious of Hollywood and its products, nonetheless were attracted to the theater simply because of Miss Berlin's faultless good taste. If she didn't call them, they would call her to ask if they should come and she, in turn, would tell them quite frankly whether or not she thought they would enjoy themselves. Those days have gone, and new life has been brought to the old building with improved facilities—a live theater in the lower auditorium and even a restaurant. Yet the strangely refined atmosphere lingers on, or was it all in the mind?

Old Boston Art Club

152 Newbury and Dartmouth Streets. Not open to the public. Now Copley Square High School.

From the Exeter Street Theater walk a few steps south and turn left into Newbury Street. Although much spoiled by commercial alteration, the houses of Newbury Street still proclaim their distinguished past when the street was residential in character. Note again the abundance of various Victorian styles, culminating in the Queen Anne Revival **Old Boston Art Club (7)** on the corner of Newbury and Dartmouth.

Completed in 1881 and designed by William Ralph Emerson (1833–1937), a well-known Boston architect who specialized in country houses, the Club House of the Boston Art Club is said to be his finest urban building. Distinguished by its bulbous four-story tower, elaborate terra cotta ornamental panels, and Dutch gables, it is a striking example of a fashionable style first introduced in England by Norman Shaw and Phillip Webb during the 1870s.

Inside, club facilities were lavish, and included a gallery, library, and restaurant, all embellished with finely carved mantelpieces and paneling. But although the majority of New England's more well known artists were members and participated in its annual exhibitions, the Club, nonetheless, shared the fate of so many of Back Bay's fine old buildings and closed its doors shortly after World War II. Between 1950 and 1970 it was occupied by the Bryant and Stratton Business School before conversion in 1970 to an alternative high school by the Boston Public Facilities Department—a useful but depressing function for such a distinguished building.

Cross Newbury at Dartmouth Street and continue walking south. This will bring you back to your starting point, Copley Square.

Footscrapers

In the thriving, bustling towns of colonial America, streets were generally unpaved. Deep ruts and mud-holes during bad weather made walking any distance a difficult and messy exercise. Shoes and boots quickly got covered with mud or snow while crossing a busy street or even descending from a coach or carriage to enter a house, store, or inn. The humble footscraper, perhaps the earliest labor-saving device in the New World, performed the vital function of removing the mud.

Before iron became generally available, the earliest scrapers were made of thick pieces of seasoned oak with a wood or iron blade. But soon they were made entirely of wrought-iron by blacksmiths and craftsmen. Simple and practical in form, the earliest types were adapted from common English models which were little more than a plain or curved scraper blade in-serted in the house wall or on the riser of the doorstep. Such types, known as Boston Side Wall, were still being made well into the nineteenth century, and can still be seen outside the more modest townhouses of Beacon Hill, that is, in Pinckney and West Cedar Street.

Later, as streets were paved with cobbles and stone sidewalks began to appear, footscrapers began to be made with side supports and became more ornate. The most popular design was the scroll, which first made its appearance in colonial times. This is found in many varieties throughout the original Thirteen Colonies. Later still, in the Federal period, the scroll form was used to support the standards or vertical posts and was topped by balls, ovoid, or hexagonal-shaped ends. Sometimes, when railings adorned entrance steps on a much wider scale, a scraper was included at the lower end of the newel post. Perhaps the most unusual are the Greek Revival designs which were cast in molds. Boston, however, unlike Philadelphia, doesn't have many examples.

Colonial. Boston side wall type. 98 Pinckney Street, Beacon Hill. Wrought iron. 1750–1820.

Colonial. Boston side wall type. 58 Mt. Vernon Street, Beacon Hill. Wrought iron. 1750–1790.

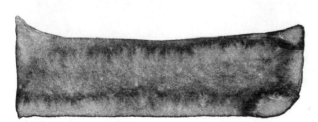

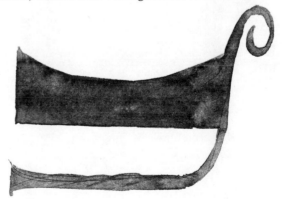

155

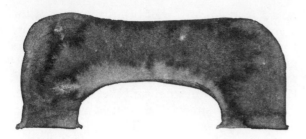

Colonial. Boston step type. 50 Chestnut Street, Beacon Hill. Wrought iron. 1790–1800.

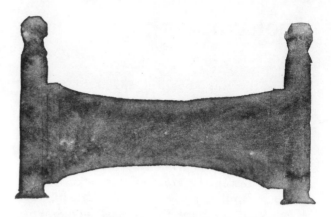

Colonial. Charleston type. 90 Mt. Vernon Street, Beacon Hill. Wrought iron. 1770–1790.

Federal. 54 Beacon Street. Wrought iron. 1790–1800.

Federal (Greek Revival). 95 Pinckney Street, Beacon Hill. Cast iron. *Circa* 1830–1840.

Perhaps the casualty rate of such accessories, now valuable relics, may account for this.

Nonetheless Boston, especially Beacon Hill, can boast of a wider range of designs than any other city in America. Not only are its streets full of several uniquely Boston and New England variants of the side wall type but it also has many types made by craftsmen and foundries in Connecticut, Massachusetts, Maryland, New Jersey, Pennsylvania, and South Carolina. Obviously, Boston's weather made its citizens good customers.

See how many different designs you can spot.

Colonial. Connecticut type. 32 West Cedar Street, Beacon Hill. Wrought iron. 1780–1790.

Colonial Style. Side wall type. 20 Mt. Vernon Street, Beacon Hill. Wrought iron. *Circa* 1790–1820.

Federal. Boston type. 6 Mt. Vernon Street, Beacon Hill. Wrought iron. *Circa* 1800–1820.

Rubbing Graves the Right Way

Before you reject the whole idea as an exercise in morbidity, stop at an art supply store for rice paper, masking tape, oil crayons, and chalk fixative. Take along a dishtowel, a measuring tape, and old newspapers to kneel or sit on, and try some grave-rubbing. Besides resting your feet for the day and getting away from the hustle and bustle of the everyday world, there is no better way of savoring the historic past of old Boston.

Basically, the idea is like rubbing a penny, but in reverse. Only the surface of the stone, which you cover with the finely textured rice paper, is reproduced in the rubbing. The inscription remains untouched by the crayon and appears in negative. Symbols like willow trees, hourglasses, skulls, and angels appear like magic, as do the ancient, often very moving epitaphs.

The earliest stones or markers were usually carved by blacksmiths or stonemasons whose sense of layout and spacing seldom allowed for the exact placing of an inscription; words are separated without regard for syllables. They simply continue on the next line, or a letter or two sits above the rest, or even vertically along the side of the stone.

Begin by making a sample rubbing to get used to the technique. A graphite stick or wax lumber marker (available in six colors) will do. Some art stores offer rubbing blocks made for the job but the common wax lumber marker is just as good and much cheaper. In addition you will need a 3-inch mailing tube to store your completed rubbings. Finally, you should have a shoulder or utility bag to carry your supplies.

There are at least five cemeteries, or burying grounds, in Boston which offer superb examples of this unique folk art. In fact, they offer the best examples of early funeral art to be found in North America. **Copp's Hill Burying Ground** (see North End to Waterfront Park Walk, page 16), colonial Boston's second largest, was established in 1660. The Old Puritan Burying Ground, now the **King's Chapel Burying Ground** (see Downtown Walk, page 52) also has many colonial markers. **Old Granary Burying Ground** (Downtown Walk, page 38), has a remarkable collection not only of colonial gravestones but also of the Federal era, including many famous patriots and statesmen. On the other side of the Common is the **Central Burying Ground,** laid out in 1756 and containing the graves of the celebrated portrait painter, Gilbert Stuart (1754–1828) and Julien, the restaurateur for which a soup was named.

Cambridge, with its **Old Burying Ground** (see Old Cambridge Walk, page 98), opposite the main (Johnson Gate) entrance to Old Harvard Yard, has many historic stones, as does **Mt. Auburn Cemetery,** which contains the graves of Longfellow, Lowell, Sumner, Channing, Phillips Brooks, and many others. Being essentially Victorian, however, many of these are more suitable for drawing or photography than rubbing.

Finally, Charlestown has the **Phipps Street Burying Ground** (see Charlestown Walk, page 130) one of the oldest in Boston, and laid as early as 1631.

One last reminder. Do check opening times. Usually, the hours are 8:00–4:00 daily.

Note: In some places no permission for rubbing is necessary, in others, one must secure permission from the church or the Boston Parks Department.

Glossary of Architectural Terms

ACANTHUS. Stylized ornament based on the leaf of a thistle. Used on Composite and Corinthian Capitals and sometimes on a frieze. Greek Revival.

ADAMESQUE. A decorative style based on Roman classicism, introduced by Robert Adam (1728–1792), Scottish architect who influenced the architecture of London and Edinburgh.

ANTEFIX. Upright ornamented motif placed above the eaves or gutter to decorate ends of a roof ridge. Greek Revival.

APSE. End of a church, usually semicircular or polygonal.

ARCADE. Group of arches on columns or pillars.

ARCHITRAVE. Lowest of the main divisions of an entablature. Molded frame over door or window.

ART NOUVEAU. Style of architecture and interior decoration using flat or three-dimensional writhing plant and animal forms.

BALUSTER. Small, usually bottle-shaped column that supports a parapet. Georgian Colonial.

BALUSTRADE. A series of upright forms supporting a railing.

BANDING. Continuous course of masonry.

BAROQUE. Period roughly 1600–1700; also applied to painting, sculpture, music, literature, and lifestyle of the period.

BASILICA. In medieval architecture, a church with a nave higher than its aisles. In early Christian architecture, with apse at one end. Name and form, Roman.

BATTLEMENT. Indented parapet. Openings are called embrasures or creneles (crenellated) and raised parts are called merlons.

BAY. An architectural unit. In this context, it is used as a width measurement, corresponding to one section between two vertical supports, usually marked by a window. Each building is described in height by stories and in width by bays.

BAY. Bay window. An octagonal, elliptical or rectangular form that projects from the exterior wall. It is a structural projection which means that the foundation wall itself projects, in contrast to the oriel, which is just applied to the façade without any structural change.

160

BELFRY. Part of a tower or turret in which bells are hung. Georgian Colonial.

BOND. Brick laid to effect maximum rigidity, comprising headers and stretchers. A stretcher brick is laid so that the side only shows on the wall side. *English Bond* consists of alternating courses of stretchers and headers. *Flemish Bond* consists of headers and stretchers laid alternately in the same course.

BRACKET. Supporting member projecting from wall, sometimes used ornamentally in the form of a scroll or volute to carry cornice.

BROWNSTONE. A reddish-brown sandstone, a popular building material in the Back Bay.

BULL'S EYE WINDOW. A round or oval window, usually with glazing bars radiating from a circular center.

CAMPANILE. Italian word for a free-standing bell tower.

CAPITAL. The head of a column, pillar, or pilaster.

CARTOUCHE. Shaped tablet enclosed in an ornamental frame or scroll, usually bearing inscription or heraldic device.

CHÂTEAUESQUE MANNER. This revival derives from the sixteenth century châteaux of the Loire Valley, France. Recognized by the use of lavish sculptural decoration, picturesque massing of gables and towers.

CHINOISERIE. Style incorporating Chinese elements. In America found in architecture of Federal period.

CLASSICAL REVIVAL. A revival of the use of classical ornament, concentrated on doorways, windows, and cornices. Buildings usually of light stone. No attempt, however, to recreate an ancient building. In the Back Bay the Classical Revival begins in the 1890s and continues through the early twentieth century.

CLASSICISM. Style or tendency originally derived from ancient Greece or Rome.

COLONIAL. Style developed in eastern United States by European colonists using classical elements.

COLONNADE. A columned walk without arches; a feature of neoclassical architecture. Greek Revival.

COLUMN. Vertical supporting member; in classical architecture it consists of a base, shaft, and capital.

COMPOSITE CAPITAL. Most elaborate of five orders, having many variations. Combines volutes, or spiral scrolls, of the Ionic with the foliate bell of Corinthian.

CONSOLE. A bracket of classical form, usually scrolled at the top and bottom.

CORINTHIAN CAPITAL. Bell-shaped capital ornamented with acanthus, olive, or laurel leaves from which eight small, spiral scrolls emerge. Shaft usually fluted.

CORNICE. Upper member of entablature, also molded projection of stone or wood which tops or finishes part to which it is fixed, e.g., a wall, door, or window (see Entablature).

CRYPT. Underground burial place.

CUPOLA. A small domed roof, or small domed turret built on a roof. Georgian Colonial.

DORIC CAPITAL. Plainest and most massive of five orders. Squat in proportion, the relationship between thickness and height usually being 1:4. Greek Revival.

DORMER. A window form that projects out from a sloping roof. Its own roof may be flat, pedimental, or hooded. (See also *Shed Dormer*.)

DRUM. Circular or polygonal wall on which a dome rests. Georgian Colonial.

ECLECTIC. Style which doesn't belong to any period of the past but borrows freely from various sources.

EGG AND DART. Classical ornamental molding.

EGYPTIAN REVIVAL. Adoption of Egyptian forms and motifs as a result of archaeological discoveries around 1800. See also *Obelisk*.

EMPIRE. See *French Second Empire*.

ENTABLATURE. In classical architecture, the superstructure that rests upon the capital of a column—architrave, frieze, and cornice.

EPITAPH. Memorial tablet for the dead.

FAÇADE. Face or front of a building.

FANLIGHT. A semicircular or fan-shaped window above a Georgian door.

FEDERAL. American version of Georgian architecture.

FLUTING. Vertical grooving on the shaft of a column.

FRENCH REVIVAL. A revival of Boston's architecture, as seen in its original form on Beacon Hill, recognizable by the use of graduated story levels, red brick, fanlight doorway, and flared window lintels. From 1890 a popular revival style in the Back Bay.

FRENCH SECOND EMPIRE. A Neo-Roman or Renaissance Revival style, fashionable in France (1852–1870). Common in the Back Bay.

FRET. Ornamental band of repetitive, interlocking forms.

FRIEZE. Decorative band, usually horizontal, along a wall or entablature. May be painted, carved, ornamented, or figured.

GAMBREL. A form of curved mansard roof with a short upper slope and a ridged gable.

GARGOYLE. Carved waterspout in the form of a grotesque human or animal head, usually projecting from top of a wall.

GEORGIAN. English adaptation of Renaissance style during reign of the four Georges (1714–1830).

GEORGIAN REVIVAL. Revival of English architecture of the eighteenth century, both the early Georgian, which is recognizable by heavy stone ornament—pediments, consoles, quoins—and the delicate decoration of swans, garlands, etc., applied to flat or bowed brick façade. This revival began in the Back Bay in the last decade of the nineteenth century.

GOTHIC REVIVAL. Use of architectural features, characteristic of Gothic architecture in Europe during the Middle Ages. It appears in the Back Bay as early as 1869.

GREEK REVIVAL. Adaptation of Greek style to the architecture of mid-nineteenth-century America.

HIGH BASEMENT. The extension of the basement above ground, sometimes over half a story, requiring an entrance stairway to the raised first floor. A common architectural motif in the Back Bay.

IONIC ORDER. Greek style originating in the Ionian Islands; characterized by voluted capitals and canalized columns.

ITALIANATE. Style derived from Italian motifs.

ITALIAN RENAISSANCE REVIVAL. Revival of Italian elements in the Renaissance architecture as opposed to the French Renaissance. Starts in the Back Bay in the 1890s under leadership of McKim, Mead and White. Use of light stone, Palladian window, string courses at sill levels, etc., are characteristic.

JACOBEAN. Style of architecture predominant during the reign of James I of England (1603–1625). A development of the Elizabethan style using purer classical forms.

LANTERN. Small open or glazed structure crowning a dome; usually cylindrical or polygonal.

LINTEL. The horizontal member spanning an opening above a door or window.

LUNETTE. A semicircular window or panel.

MANSARD. A roof with two slopes: the lower is steeper than the upper.

MULLION. Vertical shaft of stone, iron, or lead, dividing lights or panes in a window. Greek Revival.

NARTHEX. A vestibule stretching across the main entrance to a church.

NEOCLASSICAL. A style which dominated Europe from 1760 to 1790 and was the product of a new interest in antiquity which resulted from archaeological discoveries in Rome, in newly excavated Herculaneum, Pompeii, and other places. Unlike their predecessors, who accepted a textbook view of antiquity, architects of a practicing style generally made first hand investigation of the monuments themselves. In England, the leading exponents were Robert Adam, James "Athenian" Stuart, and Sir William Chambers. In the United States: Benjamin Latrobe, Charles Bulfinch, and William Strickland.

OBELISK. An Egyptian cult symbol for the sun-god. A tall, tapering stone pillar having four sides and a pyramidal top. Used in small sizes as a decoration on neoclassical buildings.

ORATORY. A small chapel or room for private prayer.

ORDER. Essential components of a complete order are a column base, a shaft and, a capital, and an entablature with architrave, frieze, and cornice. Size and proportion vary with each order. Three Greek orders are Doric, Ionic, and Corinthian. The Romans added two more: Tuscan and Composite. (See also entries under these headings.)

ORIEL WINDOW. A projecting bay window supported by corbels or brackets.

OVOLO. A convex molding usually a quarter of a circle and sometimes ornamented with egg and dart or similar motifs.

PALLADIAN. Style named for Andrea Palladio (1508–1580). Introduced to England by Inigo Jones in 1615, and from England it later spread to America. Georgian Colonial.

PALMETTE. Stylized ornament resembling fan-shaped palm (or palmetto) leaf. Alternating with lotus, it forms the classical anthemion pattern.

PARAPET. Low wall at the edge of a bridge, gallery, balcony, or above the cornice of a building. Georgian Colonial.

PEDIMENT. A low-pitched triangular gable usually above an entablature. Also used as ornamental feature above doors and windows.

PILASTER. Rectangular column projecting slightly from a wall. Georgian Colonial and Greek Revival.

PINNACLE. Pyramidal or conical ornament used to terminate a gable, buttress, etc.

PORTAL. An imposing entrance.

PORTE-COCHÈRE. A porch, often a portico, large enough to admit a carriage.

PORTICO. Covered colonnade forming an entrance to a building.

QUEEN ANNE. Phase of late Victorian or Edwardian architecture based on English architecture of Queen Anne's reign (1702–1714).

QUOINS. Cornerstones at the angle of a building.

RECONSTRUCTION. To rebuild according to original plans or drawings.

REGENCY. Georgian style characterized by elegant details fashionable during the regency of Prince of Wales (1811–1820). Also exotic, e.g., Nash's Pavilion is typical as are his Regent's Park Terraces in London.

RESTORATION. To repair and make a good building in its original form.

RICHARDSONIAN. Victorian style introduced by H. H. Richardson. (See Romanesque Revival.)

ROMANESQUE REVIVAL. Style derived from early Christian architecture of Southern France, characterized by use of round arches, contrasting rough masonry. Begins in Back Bay 1879, under leadership of H. H. Richardson and continues to 1892, in row housing.

ROTUNDA. A round building or internal space, circular, or oval in plan and usually domed. Greek Revival.

RUSTICATION. Mode of building masonry. Individual blocks of courses of stone have deeply recessed joints, and often a roughened surface. *Banded:* horizontal joints emphasized. *Chamfered:* stones are smooth but have V-joints. *Rock Faced:* stones have irregular surface to appear unhewn. *Vermiculated:* stone given appearance of being worm-eaten.

SHED DORMER. A dormer window with horizontal eave line. (See also *Dormer Window*.)

SPIRE. Tall tapering structure in the form of a pyramid or cone, erected on the top of a tower, turret, roof, etc.

STEEPLE. Complete tower of a church, with spire or lantern.

STRETCHER. A brick or stone laid with its length parallel to the face of the wall.

TURRET. Small decorative tower usually set on the ridge of a gable roof.

TYMPANUM. Triangular or segmental space between enclosing moldings of a pediment. Greek Revival.

TRANSEPT. Either arm or side of cruciform or cross-shaped plan of a church.

For Further Reading

The following books, catalogues, and articles were invaluable to the author and are recommended to anyone interested in learning more about Boston.

Amory, Cleveland. *The Proper Bostonians*. New York: Dutton, 1947.

Bacon, Edwin M. *The Book of Boston*. Boston: 1916.

Bearse, Ray (Ed.). *Massachusetts: A Guide to the Pilgrim State*. Boston: Houghton Mifflin, 1971.

British Library, The. *The American War of Independence 1775–1783*. London: British Library, 1975.

Bruce, James L. *The Old State House*. Boston: The Bostonian Society, 1965.

Bunting, Bainbridge. *Houses of Boston's Back Bay*. Cambridge: The Belknap Press, Harvard University, 1975.

Chamberlain, Allen. *Beacon Hill*. Boston: 1925.

Childs, Charles D. & Hitchings, Sinclair H. *The Metropolis of New England: Colonial Boston, 1630–1776*. Boston: Massachusetts Historical Society, 1976.

Conn, Stephen R. "America's Most Contemporary City: Boston," *Town & Country*, April, 1976.

Crowe, Eyre. *With Thackerary in America*. London: 1893.

Dickens, Charles. *American Notes*. Philadelphia: 1843 and subsequent editions.

Drake, Samuel Adams. *Old Landmarks and Historic Personages of Boston*. Vermont: Tuttle, 1971.

Fields, Mrs. James T. *Biographical Notes and Personal Sketches*. Boston: 1881.

Foote, Henry Wilder. *John Smibert, Painter*. Cambridge: Harvard University Press, 1950.

Fraser, Esther Stevens. "The John Hicks House," *Journal of the Cambridge Historical Society*. January, 1932.

Freeman, John (Ed.). *Boston Architecture*. Cambridge: MIT Press, 1970.

Frost, Jack. *Fancy This: A New England Sketchbook*. Boston: Waverly House, 1938.

——. *Harvard and Cambridge: A Sketch Book*. New York: Coward-McCann, 1940.

Hamlin, Talbot. *Greek Revival in America*. London & New York: Oxford University Press, 1944.

Hitchings, Sinclair & Farlow, Catherine H. *The Massachusetts State House*. Boston: Commonwealth of Massachusetts and John Hancock Mutual Life Insurance Company, 1964.

Howe, M. A. De Wolfe. *The Boston Symphony Orchestra*. Boston: Houghton Mifflin, 1931.

————. *Memoirs of a Hostess* (Mrs. James T. Field). Boston: Houghton Mifflin, 1922.

James, Henry. *The American Scene*. New York: Harper Bros., 1907.

Kirker, James & Harold. *Bulfinch's Boston*. New York: Oxford University Press, 1964.

Mann, Dorothea Lawrence. *The Story of the Old Corner Bookstore*. Boston: *The Transcript*, 1928.

McCord, David. *About Boston*. Boston: Little Brown, 1973.

McIntyre, A. McVoy. *Beacon Hill*. Boston: Little Brown, 1975.

McKibbin, David. *Sargent's Boston*. Boston: Museum of Fine Arts, 1956.

Morison, Samuel Eliot. *Three Centuries of Harvard*. Cambridge: Harvard University Press, 1936.

————. *William Hickling Prescott: 1706–1859*. Boston: Massachusetts Historical Society, 1958.

————. *Francis Parkman: 1823–1893*. Boston: Massachusetts Historical Society, 1973.

Norton, Bettina A. *The Boston Naval Shipyard, 1800–1974*. Boston: The Bostonian Society, 1975.

Okie, Susan & Yee, Donna. *Boston: The Official Guidebook*. New York: E. P. Dutton Co., 1975.

Parrington, Vernon Louis. *Main Currents in American Thought*. New York: Harcourt, Brace & Company, 1930.

Pearson, Kenneth (Ed.). *1776: The British Story of the American Revolution*. London: National Maritime Museum, 1976.

Place, Rev. Charles A. *Charles Bulfinch: Architect and Citizen*. Boston: Houghton Miflin, 1925.

Rapson, Richard L. *Britons in America: Travel Commentary 1860–1935*. Seattle: University of Washington, 1971.

Reed, Christopher. "George Washington Slept *Here*" (Wadsworth House), *Harvard Magazine*. Vol. 77: No. 10, June 1975.

Ross, Marjorie Drake. *The Book of Boston* (published as three volumes: Colonial Period, Federal Period, and Victorian Period). New York: Hastings House, 1961.

Shackleton, Robert. *The Book of Boston*. Philadelphia: Penn Publishing Co., 1917.

Soun, Albert H. *Early American Wrought Iron*. Vol. III. New York: Scribners, 1928.

Swift, Lindsay. *Literary Landmarks of Boston*. Boston: 1922.

Vogel, Susan Maycock. "Hartwell and Richardson," *Journal of the Society of Architectural Historians*. May, 1973.

Wadsworth, Ann. *A Reader's Guide to the Boston Athenaeum*. Boston: Boston Athenaeum, 1975.

Weinberg, Helena Barbara. "John La Farge and the Decoration of Trinity Church, Boston," *Journal of the Society of Architectural Historians*. Dec., 1974.

Weinhardt, Jr., Carl J. *The Domestic Architecture of Beacon Hill, 1800–1850*. Boston: The Proceedings of the Bostonian Society Annual Meeting, 1958.

Whipple, Sherman L. *The Locke-Ober Café*. Boston: Locke-Ober, undated.

White, Margaret E. (Ed.). *A Sketch of Chester Harding, Artist*. Cambridge: Houghton Mifflin, 1929.

Whitehill, Walter Muir. (Ed.). *A Seidel for Jake Wirth*. Boston: Jacob Wirth & Co., 1964.

———. *A Boston Athenaeum Anthology*. Boston: Boston Athenaeum, 1973.

———. *The Metamorphoses of Scollay and Bowdoin Squares*. Boston: The Bostonian Society, 1973.

———. *Boston: A Topographical History*. Cambridge: Harvard University Press, 1975.

Williams, Alexander W. *A Social History of the Greater Boston Clubs*. Boston: Barre Publishers, 1970.

Williamson, Jefferson. *The American Hotel*. New York: Knopf, 1930

Zaitzevsky, Cynthia. *The Architecture of William Ralph Emerson, 1883–1917*. Cambridge: Fogg Art Museum, 1969.

Index

Warren Lobby, 94
Warren Street, 123, 124, 128
Warren Tavern, 123–126, 129
Washington, George (points of interest), 18, 29, 98, 101, 103,
    115, 117, 142
Washington Street, 20, 29, 30, 37, 123
Waterfront Park, 17, 18
Waterfront Urban Renewal Project, 18
Water Street, 126, 131

West Cedar Street, 65, 86, 155
West School Street, 131
Willard (works of interest), 40, 42, 81, 128
William Brattle House, 98, 105–106
William Hickling Prescott House, 76–78
Willow Street, 62
Winter Place, 34
Winter Street, 34
Winthrop Square, 106, 128, 131
Winthrop Street, 128
Wirth's Restaurant, 33–34
Women's City Club, 81, 142

Zapotec city, 23

Dedication

To the true pioneers in integrative health care: Linus Pauling, PhD; Abram Hoffer, MD, PhD; Adelle Davis; Weston Price, DDS; the Shute brothers, MDs; Max Gerson, MD; Virginia Livingston-Wheeler, MD; and many others. Your courage, independent thinking and brilliance have built a road for the rest of us.

Acknowledgements

A special salute to the many scientists who labor to unravel the mysteries of healing foods, like cayenne, which are found in Nature and have no drug company to champion their cause. Where would we be without your persistence and brilliance?

CHAPTER ONE

OVERVIEW AND HIGHLIGHTS

IS CAYENNE
A WONDER DRUG?

Epithets, like pepper, Give zest to what you write;
And if you strew them sparely, They whet the appetite
But if you lay them on too thick, You spoil the matter
quite!   *Lewis Carroll*

I t is a gift to humanity and a puzzle to
scientists. A "gift" because, next to garlic, it
has more health benefits than any other
food/herb on earth
with over 3000 scientific
studies to support its use in
preventing and reversing
many common health
ailments. A "puzzle" because
it simultaneously heats and
cools, rewards and torments.
"It" is cayenne pepper, the
most widely studied and easily

available of the many hot chili peppers on earth.
      Some people love it and some people hate it,
but everyone has to respect the impact that this

humble little fruit, cayenne, has had on the history of mankind. It has been used as a weapon, a food, a spice, and an herbal medicine for over 9000 years.[1] Chili peppers, including cayenne, are consumed regularly by over 1.5 billion people each day, or 25% of the world's population, which makes it one of the most popular foods in the world. Chili peppers, also spelled as "chile" or "chilli", may well be the first cultivated food when our "hunter gatherer" ancestors decided to settle down to farming.

The list of ailments that can be improved with the use of cayenne boggles the imagination. From asthma to pain reduction to melting away pounds to preventing heart disease; there are only a handful of "superherbs" on the planet earth that can match cayenne for its versatility, taste, therapeutic value and safety.

The list of enigmas regarding cayenne is impressive:

* How can it cool you and warm you at the same time?

* How can it feel like its burning, but actually reduces the pain from burns?

* How can it hurt so bad when the amateur eats it, yet it helps the body to generate an internal form of morphine-like pleasure?

* How can it be so selectively good for your body cells while it is viciously lethal to intestinal bacteria and parasite cells?

This book is a complete compilation of valuable facts about cayenne. It just may be the most important book that you ever read.

SOME HISTORY AND DETAILS

NAME CONFUSION

It's not from the country Chile and it's not really a pepper, and, much to the dismay of East Indians, hot peppers were first cultivated in the Americas. So who started all of this name confusion? You have to admire the courage, persistance and creative thinking of Christopher Columbus. When he set sail in 1492 in pursuit of peppercorns found along the

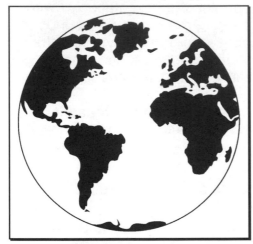

coast of India, most everyone watching him disappear over the horizon thought that he would fall off the edge of the earth. Instead of sailing over some cataclysmic waterfall or landing in India, Columbus landed in the Caribbean, some 11,000 miles short of his destination. Undaunted, he called the locals "Indians", a name distortion that Native Americans have grappled with ever since; and he called the local "aji" food spices "peppers" to try to please his patrons back home.

Columbus was not looking for gold or real estate, but rather for spices to liven up the otherwise boring menu items consumed by royalty throughout Europe. Remember, in those days, without refrigeration, food began rotting as soon as it was slaughtered or picked, thus spices were more than a hedonistic pleasure, they were necessary to overcome the stench of food that was beginning to decay. Pepper, or Piper nigrum, from the Malabar coast of India was the spice of choice in those days; it was first brought overland to Europe by Chinese and Arab traders. Due to the extraordinary effort of moving pepper, ginger, cinnamon and other spices across 6,000 miles of treacherous land, the cost for these spices in Europe was quite high and only available to royalty.

Columbus found no black peppercorns in his "India", but on his second voyage to the New World, his accompanying physician, Dr. Diego Alvarez Chanca, picked up some of the local spices, then called "aji", which were regularly served by the native Arawak people. In an attempt to please his "venture capitalists" in England, Columbus called the aji "peppers", but the food was initially deemed unfit for consumption by the royal physicians and scientists throughout Europe. Columbus died as an unheralded pauper.

From Europe, the chili plants and seeds were brought around the world by ocean explorers and thrived in many parts of South America, Africa and Asia. It took 50 years before the tomato from America and the potato from the Andes highlands of South America were accepted as a food in Europe. In that same time frame of 50 years, chilis circumnavigated the globe and were grown on every continent but Antarctica. Such was the appeal of this humble little fruit. While we know that the "cradle" of chili cultivation was somewhere in Central or South America, the best guess for its exact location is

Bolivia. The hottest pepper in the world is the habanero, grown only in the Yucatan area of Mexico. The Mayan natives there consider the regular consumption of the habanero to be a "rite of passage", which few outsiders can pass.

Later, this aji, or chili pepper was more accurately classified as a fruit belonging to the genus Capsicum annuum, which includes red pepper, anaheim, ancho, cayenne, cherry, chili, green bell pepper, hot pepper, jalapeno, paprika, pimento, piquin and red bell pepper.[2] Tabasco pepper belongs to the Capsicum frutescens genus and the hottest pepper in the world, Habanero, belongs to Capsicum chinense. This Capsicum genus belongs to the family Solanaceae, which includes tomatoes and potatoes. So realize, that as we charge ahead with discussion of "cayenne", that this is only one of many chili peppers, more accurately called Capsicum, that is found throughout the world. What we are really talking about in this book is the incredible healing and pleasurable value of hot chilis from around the world, with the most commonly available and best studied one being cayenne.

It was the Greek spice merchants in the 16th century who decided to end the confusion between black peppers and these "quasi" peppers by calling the red, green and yellow chilis: chili pepper. Hungarians decided to call their prize chilis "paprika". Italians called it "peperone". The English called theirs "red pepper", Germans "Indianifcher pfeffer, the French "poivre de l'Inde", and "mircha" in India. "A rose by any other name is still a rose" and all of these delightful varieties of hot chilis have pleased and healed billions of people for the past 90 centuries.

WHO GROWS IT?

Capsicum plants grow around the world in many climates on many continents. But there are some basic ground rules:

1) the hotter the climate, the hotter the chili

2) the smaller the chili, the hotter the taste.

New Mexico along with parts of Louisiana are the epicenters of chili farming in the United States. Most chilis require an optimal growing temperature of 24 degrees C. (93 F.) with a tolerable temperature range of 32 C. (103 F.) and 15 C. (59 F.). Humidity is a must. Three to five months is the average growing time for most chilis before harvest. There are over 1,700 different varieties of both wild and cultivated

peppers known.[3]

Hungary uses twice as much acreage to grow paprika chilis as tomato plants, producing over 62,000 tons per year. India produces over 800,000 tons of chilis annually and consumes 95% of it right there at home. The chili growing nations of India, Hungary, China, Pakistan, Mexico, Sri Lanka, Nigeria, Ethiopia, Thailand, and Japan produce over 4 million tons per year.[4] Mexico cultivates the widest assortment of chilis in its 53,000 tons per year, with only a small percentage being the bland bell pepper and nearly all of that going to the United States. The hottest pepper commonly found in American markets is the Jalapeno, grown in Jalapa, Veracruz in Mexico. New Mexico grows around 47,000 tons of chilis annually, leading all American states. American farmers wishing to diversify their crops may consider the humble chili as a "cash crop", which nets a profit of $1600 per acre, compared to $300 per acre for hay. Meanwhile, the infamous black pepper that Columbus sought, amounts to only 200,000 tons of production per year around the world.

HELPED WIN A NOBEL PRIZE

Dr. Albert Szent-Gyorgyi was a Hungarian scientist doing research in the United States during the 1930s. He was trying to isolate hexuronic acid from the adrenals of cattle. After laboring for years and tediously extracting hexuronic acid from vast quantities of cow adrenal glands, he managed to gather a mere 20 grams (less than an ounce) of pure hexuronic acid from the hundreds of kilograms of adrenals that he had processed.

Then, once back home in Hungary, his wife fed him a paprika chili pepper for dinner. Lacking an appetite, he decided to take the paprika down to his laboratory and see if it had any hexuronic acid. As we now know, chili peppers have more hexuronic acid, or vitamin C, than almost any other food on earth, as much as 500% more vitamin C per gram than an orange. Dr. Szent-Gyorgyi was elated, able to extract enough vitamin C to identify the chemical structure and was awarded the Nobel prize in 1937 for what Time Magazine then called "the Paprika Prize". Vitamin C has since become one of the more valuable nutrients in human nutrition, since it bolsters the immune system and slows down the aging process.

AS A WEAPON?

When the Spanish Conquistadors were attacking the Mayan and Incan people in Central and South America during the 16th century, one of the few weapons those people had was to burn large mounds of dried chili peppers in the path of the oncoming invaders, which temporarily blinded the advancing soldiers. More recently, 13 shoppers at a mall in San Fernando, California were hospitalized when a fire broke out in a restaurant and then began burning hot chilis. The fumes from these burning chilis acted like spray Mace on the eyes and lungs of the shoppers.

The bite of chili peppers has been used for brutal purposes. The British rubbed hot Bahamian peppers in the eyes of mutinous slaves in the Caribbean region. In 1640, Sir John Parkinson wrote that dogs detested hot peppers, which eventually produced the aerosol pepper sprays carried by postmen and many women today. It is still custom in some regions of Africa to spray water containing hot pepper juice in the eyes of misbehaving children. The U.S. Army considered using chili powder as a non-lethal form of tear gas. The Grebo tribe in Liberia still conduct a sadistic ritual of smearing mashed hot peppers in every orifice of an infant's body as a means of "initiating" the child.

WHAT'S IN IT?

When we arrive at the HEALTH BENEFITS section of this book, you are going to be amazed at the healing properties of cayenne. Therefore, we need to peer inside of this humble little fruit in order to better understand how it may help an alphabet soup of health problems. Bear with me for a minute. There is a purpose to this section.

The "bite" in cayenne is from a compound called "capsaicin", with the family of related compounds called "capsaicinoids" found in hot peppers throughout the world. Chemists call capsaicin "8 methyl N vanillyl 6 nonenamide". Capsaicin has a chemical structure very similar to the active ingredient in ginger, both of which have a pungent "bite" and many therapeutic values.

In addition to capsaicin, which we will spend considerable time discussing in the next section, a fresh cayenne chili pepper contains[5]:

Water: 9%
Carbohydrate: 54%
Starch: 1%
Protein: 13%
Fiber: 31%
Ash (minerals): 6%
Fat soluble "others": 22%
Vitamin C: 29 mg per 100 grams
Capsaicinoids: 177 micrograms per gram
Beta carotene: 1733 micrograms per gram
Iron: 10 mg per 100 grams
Phosphorus: 356 mg per 100 grams
Calcium: 210 mg per 100 grams

The health of Americans is suffering from too much fat and the wrong kind of fat. Chili peppers are both low in fat and contain the right kind of fat: 66% of the fat as linoleic and 5% as linolenic acid, the two essential fats in the diet of humans. Phospholipids are valuable fats that are bound to the mineral phosphorus and make up much of our cell membranes and escort molecules in the blood. In chili peppers, 76% of the phospholipids are lecithin (phosphatidylcholine), which is an extremely valuable nutrient for the heart and brain.

The fabulous rainbow of colors that are found in chili peppers contain thousands of bioflavonoids and carotenoids, which may be partly responsible for the healing properties of cayenne. These natural pigments help chlorophyll in capturing the sun's energy in the process called photosynthesis. Some of these colorful and healthful substances are: beta-carotene, zeaxanthin, cryptoxanthin, violaxanthin, neoxanthin, antheraxanthin, cryptoxanthin, and lutein. Free range chickens eat a wide assortment of these natural pigments and produce eggs with deep reddish orange yolk, which reflects the healthful nutrients in the chicken's diet. Cayenne powder is added to commercial chicken feed to give their egg yolk the healthy color that we look for.

The real "business end" of cayenne is the "bite", which comes from capsaicin. There are varying levels of capsaicin in the multitude of hot peppers found around the world. Capsaicin content ranges from a high of 1.8% in the newly bred Jwala from India to a low of 0.02% found in Hungarian paprika. Topical ointments with capsaicin contain anywhere from 0.025% to 0.075%. Keep this in mind as we later talk about toxicity of cayenne and other chili peppers. Nature never puts much more than 1% of capsaicin in its chili fruits.

MECCA FOR "CHILIHEADS"

Those people who develop a passion for the bite of chili peppers are affectionately called "chiliheads". They will go to any length to get their high from their favorite chili. Zubin Mehta, the famous philharmonic conductor, brings his own hot peppers with him, even to the finest restaurants in the world, where the chef's eagerly greet him and take his peppers into the kitchen to be added gracefully to his meal. The King of Spain plucked a few peppers from Mehta's garden and brought them home for his garden. It was "chiliheads" like these celebrities who spread the hot pepper around the world in only 50 years.

Mrs. Frank Sinatra is an equal fan of hot peppers and carried them with her everywhere as well as grew her own in her California home. Gregory Peck was so enamored of Mrs. Sinatra's flavorful habit, that he too became a chilihead and started his own garden. All U.S. astronauts are provided a "kit" for space travel that includes hot peppers, which wasn't quite good enough for astronaut and chilihead extraordinaire William Lenoir who took a jalapeno with him on a space voyage in 1982.

For chiliheads looking for pilgrimages to the "promised land", there are many regions and countries willing to fight for the title of chili capital. In the U.S., the Rio Grande area of New Mexico and Texas grow the most chilis. Meanwhile, Edmund McIlhenny, developer of the infamous Tabasco sauce, founded a chili pepper empire on Avery

Island, Louisiana in 1862. If you are looking for the world's hottest chili pepper, then buy a ticket to the Yucatan Peninsula of Mexico and dine with the native Mayans. If it is serious hot chilis that you are after, then people in Thailand consume 5 grams daily, twice the amount of Indian chiliheads. If its chili commerce that you are after, then head to Guntur in southeast India, where the planting, harvesting, processing and eating of chilis occupies most of the locals most of the time. Koreans and their kimchi and Chinese Szechwan residents might protest these verdicts, due to their own chili obsessions.

WHAT DOES CAYENNE DO TO THE BODY?

Here's where it starts looking "too good to be true"; but it is true. The whole concept of a simple fruit, like cayenne, generating healing benefits for such a wide assortment of ailments seems a bit preposterous. Until you realize that bread mold was used for centuries in Ayurvedic medicine as an antibiotic before Alexander Fleming isolated the mold extract, penicillin, that specifically kills bacteria. White willow bark was used for centuries by Native American medicine men for treating aches, pains and the flu before a scientist in this century was awarded the Nobel prize for explaining how aspirin (the active ingredient in white willow bark) works.

Curare is an herbal extract that has been used for centuries as a muscle relaxant in the Amazon jungle. The local people apply curare to the tip of a dart, shoot a monkey, and the curare weakens the monkey until it drops out of the tree and becomes dinner. In the past few decades, curare has become a favorite medication for anesthesiologists in the operating room to keep the patient's muscles relaxed.

Ephedra, used as a pure drug to treat asthma, was originally derived from the Chinese herb, Ma Huang. Robitussin is one of the more common over-the-counter drugs used to loosen mucus, called an expectorant. The active ingredient in Robitussin is guaifenesin, which is derived from guaiacol, which has the same chemical structure as capsaicin. In fact, one third of all prescription drugs in the United States were derived from a plant compound--just like cayenne.

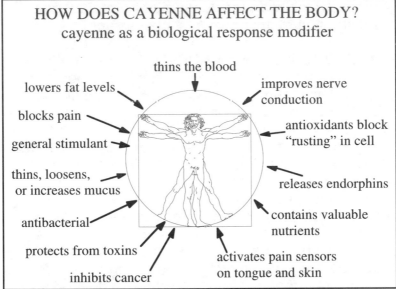

HOW DOES CAYENNE AFFECT THE BODY?
cayenne as a biological response modifier

thins the blood

lowers fat levels

improves nerve conduction

blocks pain

antioxidants block "rusting" in cell

general stimulant

thins, loosens, or increases mucus

releases endorphins

antibacterial

contains valuable nutrients

protects from toxins

activates pain sensors on tongue and skin

inhibits cancer

What is even more amazing is the 3000 plus scientific studies listed in the National Library of Medicine on the health benefits of capsaicin and cayenne. Nearly all research money in America comes from major drug firms, or the National Institutes of Health, which uses 95% of its money to fund drug studies. Drugs are patentable substances, which can be protected against competition, thus improving the chances of making a substantial profit during the 17 year life of the patent. Natural substances, like cayenne, cannot be patented, and hence are of little interest to drug companies, except to create drug analogs (molecules that are similar to the natural molecule but different enough to be patented). The fact that 3000 studies exist on the merits of capsaicin, with no serious drug patron to fund the studies shows how valuable this humble little fruit may be to our future health care system. Imagine how many studies would be done on capsaicin if we invested research dollars based upon a simple formula of risk to benefit to cost of that item.

The lengthy alphabetical listing in the next section regarding the health benefits from cayenne all stem from the basic mechanisms on how it influences the human body:

Thins the blood. My wife and I took a tour of a southern plantation in Louisiana near the Mississippi River. The tour guide told us that the river would sometimes get "too thick to drink and too thin to plow." The same might be said for the blood of the typical American. With too much fat, saturated fat, cholesterol, and sugar in the diet; and not enough fish oil, flax oil, fiber, vitamin E and cayenne--we end up with blood that is sludgy. Imagine how much harder a swimming pool pump would have to work if the pool was filled with yogurt instead of water. That's how much harder your heart has to work to move the sludgy blood that is a product of our lifestyle.

Our bodies are a miraculous network of 60,000 miles of blood vessels with a heart muscle that pumps 55 million gallons of blood over the course of a lifetime to feed all 60 trillion cells in your body. Some blood vessels are so narrow that the blood cells must squeeze down the passageway like a water balloon being forced down a pipe in order to feed the peripheral cells in the outlying regions.

When the blood gets too thick, it cannot fit into tiny capillaries and many cells that rely on this precarious flow of supplies begin to starve for oxygen and nutrients; then start to accumulate waste products and die in their own toxic mess. When the blood gets too thick, the heart must pump harder to get blood to all areas, thus stressing the heart muscle. When the blood gets too thick, the pressure in the vessels goes up, with hypertension being the result. High blood pressure pounds away at delicate capillaries in the brain and kidney and can cause stroke or organ failure. Cayenne can change all of that.

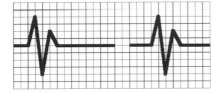

An extremely important research project was conducted by Sukon Visudhiphan, MD, PhD and colleagues in 1981 in which they tested the viscosity of the blood in Americans living in Thailand versus native Thais, who eat copious quantities of hot chilis.[6] Fibrin is the substance in the blood that forms clots when we are cut--something we don't want to happen before we are cut. Fibrinolytic (breaking of fibrin) activity was much higher in the native Thais eating all those spicey chilis. More on this therapeutic activity of cayenne later.

Blocks pain. Certain types of nerves in the human body seem to have receptor sites for capsaicin, kind of like having a keyhole that fits a certain lock. Capsaicin topically applied is able to block the production of substance P (stands for "pain") in nerves without affecting the ability to sense hot, cold or touch.[7] No other substance even comes close to the low risk analgesic benefits of cayenne in certain conditions.

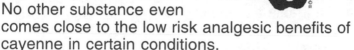

Enhances nerve conduction. Capsaicin is able to stimulate the conduction of nerve impulses, with the net effect of energizing the nerves, muscles and brain. Given the fact that one of the most common complaints among Americans is fatigue, this should come as welcome news.

Increases mucus flow. Since capsaicin is a mild irritant to mucus membranes, the capsaicin heightens the flow of mucus which flushes out bacteria, virus and debris from the sinuses and lungs. This mildly irritating quality of cayenne seems to put it on the "no-no" list for people with ulcers. Actually researchers find that cayenne, taken in reasonable quantitites, may accelerate the healing of ulcers by creating a flow of protective mucus while also directly killing the bacteria Helicobacter pylori that can cause ulcers.

Changes fat metabolism. Capsaicin is able to block the reabsorption of cholesterol in the gut and to slow down the manufacturing of cholesterol in the liver. It also helps to mobilize fats as serum triglycerides to keep them from permanently parking in the liver, which helps to prevent fatty liver. More on this feature of cayenne in later sections.

Antioxidant slows oxidation and aging. After nearly 40 years of research, scientists have generally agreed on the importance of free radicals (a.k.a. reactive oxygen species, prooxidants) and antioxidants. Free radicals are like little fires that crop up around your body all day every day. Free radicals come from the toxins we inhale, eat and drink (like tobacco and alcohol) and the free radicals that we generate as part of living. These fires can burn up valuable tissue, like the DNA to start cancer, or the cornea of the eye to begin cataracts, or the brain to begin Alzheimers, or the lining of the blood vessels to begin heart disease. Antioxidants are the "fire extinguishers" that put out these free radical fires. In the process of putting out the fire, antioxidants get used up. Hence, there must be a continuous flow of antioxidants into the body to slow down the incessant onslaught of degenerative disease and aging.

Antioxidants include:

⇒ vitamins, like C, E and betacarotene
⇒ minerals, like selenium
⇒ amino acids, like glutathione
⇒ bioflavonoids, like quercetin from orange peelings
⇒ mixed carotenoids, like lycopenes from tomatoes
⇒ other substances, like chlorophyll from spinach or Coenzyme Q from liver.

There are several known antioxidants in cayenne, including betacarotene, bioflavonoids and vitamin C; but these do not quite account for the ability of cayenne to slow the aging process and retard the effects of free radicals. Scientists are giving up on trying to find that one "magic bullet" antioxidant, and have realized that a mixture of antioxidants give much better protection against free radical damage.[8] We are only beginning to understand the complexities and importance of antioxidants. Since paprika peppers have already played such an important role in the understanding of antioxidants through the discovery of vitamin C, no doubt there are more antioxidant mystery substances waiting to be uncovered in hot chilis.

Releases endorphins. The reason that a morphine addict can get "high" off of his drug is that the human brain has receptor sites for heroine and morphine, more accurately known as endorphins ("endo" for inside us and "orphin" for morphine). The body uses these "rivers of pleasure" to reduce pain during childbirth and major cuts and burns, while also letting endorphins flow when we are doing something that we enjoy. When we eat cayenne, we feel an initial burning sensation, though it doesn't really burn anything. The body thinks that a burn has occurred and lets a little endorphin flow to soothe the wound. People who eat hot chilis on a regular basis actually become addicted to the endorphin flow, not unlike long distance runners who get high from their endorphin flow.

Valuable nutrients. High in protein, fiber, vitamin C, bioflavonoids, mixed carotenoids and some essential fatty acids; cayenne is a "nutrient dense" food, not unlike Uranium is an energy-dense radioactive element. No doubt, there are as-yet undetermined nutrients lurking within the shadows of cayenne that add to its healing value.

Inhibits cancer. Eating too much hot peppers was once considered a mild risk for getting cancer.

We now find that capsaicin can inhibit the transformation of cells that gear up toward full blown cancer. Capsaicin was able to block the generation of cancer from one of the more cancer-causing substances on earth, aflatoxins.

Protects stomach from alcohol and aspirin. While many people labor under the misconception that cayenne irritates the stomach, and it can in higher doses, actually aspirin is one of the more lethal compounds on the stomach. Aspirin causes microscopic bleeding in the lining of the stomach, which kills 3,300 older Americans each year from hemorrhaging. Alcohol is a milder irritant on the stomach lining. Cayenne has been shown in scientific studies to protect the lining of the stomach from potential damage caused by aspirin and alcohol.

Kills microorganisms. Cayenne has been shown to be one of the more potent and selectively toxic substance known in killing bacteria, viruses, worms, and parasites.

Based upon the above list of actions on the human body, in the next section you will read a very impressive list of health benefits from cayenne.

SUPERFOODS & SUPERHERBS

There are many nourishing foods among the 20,000 edible plants and thousands of edible animals and insects on earth. Yet, there are only a handful of "superfoods" which are so nutrient-dense that they merit inclusion in your diet on a regular basis. "Nutrient density" refers to the amount of vitamins, minerals, protein, fiber and conditionally essential nutrients (like lipoic acid, carnitine and EPA) found per 100 calories of that food. So, for instance, the nutrient density of broccoli is much better than for chocolate cake;  liver is better than prime rib, spinach is better than iceberg lettuce, and so on. Based upon these guidelines there are several foods that should be eaten often by nearly everyone (unless you have an allergy to that food) to achieve optimum health:

SUPERFOODS

-hot chili peppers, including cayenne
-garlic
-dark green leafy vegetables, including spinach, collards, beet greens
-tomatoes
-whole grains, like oats, wheat and rice
-legumes, like soy and garbanzo beans
-fruits rich in enzymes, including kiwi, papaya, and pineapple

-cold water ocean fish, including salmon, tuna, halibut, anchovies

-cruciferous vegetables, including cauliflower, brussel sprouts, broccoli

There is another set of "superherbs" that are so potent and so non-toxic that they need to be included on a regular basis to ensure optimal health. These herbs stimulate "host defense mechanisms" for a stronger immune system, more balanced blood glucose levels, healthier prostaglandins and more.

SUPERHERBS

-hot chili peppers, including cayenne
-garlic
-echinacea
-ginger
-tumeric
-ginseng
-goldenseal
-astragalus
-green tea (Camellia sinensis)
-licorice

Note that only two items on the planet earth qualify in both "superfood" and "superherb" category: hot chilis and garlic. For more on garlic, see my book HONEY, GARLIC AND VINEGAR (Available by calling toll-free 1-800-899-6117).

HOW MUCH IS ENOUGH?
CAN YOU EAT TOO MUCH?

Nothing in life is perfectly safe. Last year in America, 17 people died from electrocution while using a hair dryer and standing in a bathtub full of water. That doesn't mean that we should ban hair dryers, which are relatively safe. Over 3,300 Americans died last year from the hemorrhaging effects caused by aspirin, one of the most widely used and most valuable over-the-counter medications. No one has died from the use of cayenne, although some novices accidentally  biting into the infamous habanero firecracker might briefly wish for a peaceful death. On a risk to benefit to cost ratio, cayenne is extremely safe and useful at improving the health for most people.

As with anything in life, you want the right amount. Too much cayenne will not only send your mouth into a 4 alarm fire drill and burn you at the other end, but may end up doing more harm than good. Cayenne is a mildly irritating substance on the gastro-intestinal tract. Cayenne should be avoided by people with hemorrhoids, since the "burn at both end" slogan at many chili festivals will antagonize hemorrhoids.[9] Small amounts of cayenne increase the flow of gastric secretions, which improves digestion, appetite and elimination. Too much cayenne and you have stomach irritation, nausea, maldigestion of nutrients and possibly diarrhea. The novice is going to find that cayenne requires an adaptation period. Build up to eating a reasonable level. See the section at the end of this chapter on "getting started". Do not eat cayennes to demonstrate your macho ability to withstand pain. Too much or too little exercise, sunshine and cayenne are all bad for you. Good judgment needs to be used in finding the right amount of cayenne for you.

Cayenne should never be rubbed on an open wound. Do not inhale cayenne powder or serious spasms of coughing and sneezing will follow. Do not get any hot peppers in your eyes. If applied to the skin in high concentrations (greater than 1% solution) it can create serious irritation spots. Originally, there was some concern that hot chilis taken in excess could increase the risk of stomach cancer; however more research points to moderate use of cayenne as a potent protector against cancer. See the section following on "cancer prevention". All of the above precautions regarding the use of cayenne should be heeded, yet realize that you don't need to go to the emergency room if you get some cayenne in your eyes. Just flush it out and wait for the "burn" to subside. Cayenne may be occasionally painful, but it is not poisonous. Cayenne is found on the Generally Recognized As Safe (GRAS) list by the Food and Drug Administration.[10]

AMERICA'S HEALTH CARE MELTDOWN
WHY WE NEED CAYENNE

America spends over $1 trillion each year on what we euphemistically call "health care", which is more "disease maintenance" than anything else. We spend twice the money per capita as any other nation on earth for health care. And our "health state of the union" is less than spectacular:

-58 million Americans have high blood pressure
-half of us die from heart disease and one fourth from cancer, both diseases were relatively unknown prior to the 20th century
-24 million have insomnia
-50 million have regular headaches
-55 billion aspirin are consumed yearly
-9 million Americans are alcoholics
-40% are overweight
-40 million have mental illness
-9.6 million older adults each year suffer drug-induced side effects, including 659,000 hospitalizations and 163,000 with memory loss

When the doctor sets a broken bone, he or she does not heal the patient, but rather sets in place the tissue so that Nature can heal us from within. Same thing happens in stitching up a cut, or when you recovered from your last bought with the flu. The only way you stay well or heal from a health challenge is by nourishing that "God-given life force" within us. When we stop trying to change natural biochemical laws, then we will find a quantum leap in our health and improved results at the doctor's office.

America has among the highest incidences in the world for heart disease, cancer, diabetes, mental illness, osteoporosis, and other diseases. We have a worse infant survival record than such undeveloped countries as Venezuela and the Phillipines.

MALNUTRITION IN AMERICA
THE GREAT NUTRITION ROBBERY

America is the most agriculturally productive nation in the history of the world. We grow enough food in this country to feed ourselves, to make half of us overweight, to throw away enough food to feed 50 million people daily, to ship food overseas as a major export, and to store enough food in government surplus bins to feed Americans for a year if all farmers quit today. With so much food available, how can Americans be malnourished? The simple answer is: poor food choices.

People in Western Society chose their food based upon taste, cost, convenience and psychological gratification--thus ignoring the main reason that we eat, which is to provide our body with the raw materials to grow, repair and fuel our cells. We take Nature's elegantly designed nutritious foods and:

⇒ use drugs, hormones, and antibiotics to raise animals faster, while spraying 1.2 billion pounds of pesticides over our food crops

⇒ fail to properly fertilize the soil with organic matter and trace minerals, which creates mineral-poor crops

⇒ remove vitamins, minerals, and fiber during extensive food processing

⇒ add over 2800 Food and Drug Administration approved additives, including salt, fat, sugar, and unsafe food additives, like saccharin and MSG

⇒ dramatically increase the cost of the food, which compounds the problems for the poor.

The fact is: the nutrients were in that food for a very good reason. When we tamper with the food supply, we usually wreak havoc on the food's nutritional content. The most commonly eaten foods in America are white bread, coffee and hot dogs, which have little to offer the body. Based upon our food abundance and affluence, Americans could be the best nourished nation on record. But we are far from it.

In the late 1930s, Dr. Weston Price, a dentist, and his wife, Monica, who was a nurse, were intrigued by the possible link between diet and health. In true "Indiana Jones" adventuresome fashion, they travelled the world logging over 100,000 miles on primitive aircraft to investigate 17 different cultures.[11] What they found was startling to scientists then. The more refined (read: adulterated) the food supply, the worse the health of the people. Those people who ate their ancestral diet had excellent health, teeth structure, energy, and appearance. Those who deviated from their ancestral diet suffered everything from mild symptoms, such as acne, skin and hair problems, and poor dental formation to the severest forms of mental retardation and even paralysis.

Another group of researchers from Emory University in Atlanta followed up on Dr. Price's work in 1988 and found similar results. They stated that the "paleolithic" diet was very different from our current refined diet, and that difference may contribute to many of our ailments.[12] Our ancestors, the hunter and gatherers, ate a superior diet and enjoyed superior health. See the chart below which compares our modern diet to that of our hunter gatherer ancestral era.

MOST POPULAR GROCERY ITEMS IN AMERICA

1. Marlboro cigarettes
2. Coke Classic
3. Pepsi Cola
4. Kraft processed cheese
5. Diet Coke
6. Campbell's soup
7. Budweiser beer
8. Tide detergent
9. Folger's coffee
10. Winston cigarettes

from "1992 Top Ten Almanac"
by Michael Robbins

Overwhelming evidence from government surveys of 200,000 Americans and numerous respected universities shows that many Americans are low in their intake of:

-VITAMINS: A, D, E, C, B-6, riboflavin, folacin, pantothenic acid

-MINERALS: calcium, potassium, magnesium, zinc, iron, chromium, selenium; and possibly molybdenum and vanadium.

-MACRONUTRIENTS: fiber, complex carbohydrates, plant protein, special fatty acids (EPA, GLA, ALA), clean water

Meanwhile, we also eat alarmingly high amounts of: fat, salt, sugar, cholesterol, alcohol, caffeine, food additives and toxins.

This combination of too much of the wrong things along with not enough of the right things has created epidemic proportions of degenerative diseases in this country. The Surgeon General, Department of Health and Human Services, Centers for Disease Control and Prevention, National Academy of Sciences, American Medical Association, American Dietetic Assocation, and most other major public health agencies agree that diet is a major contributor to our most common health problems, including cancer and heart disease.

The typical American diet is high in fat while being low in fiber and vegetables. "Meat, potatoes, and gravy" is what many of my cancer patients lived on for decades. Data collected by the United States Department of Agriculture from over 11,000 Americans showed that on any given day:

-41 percent did not eat any fruit

-82 percent did not eat cruciferous vegetables

-72 percent did not eat vitamin C-rich fruits or vegetables

-80 percent did not eat vitamin A-rich fruits or vegetables

-84 percent did not eat high fiber grain food, like bread or cereal

The human body is incredibly resilient, which sometimes works to our disadvantage. No one dies on the first cigarette inhaled, or the first drunken evening, or the first decade of unhealthy eating. We misconstrue the fact that we survived this ordeal to mean we can do it forever. Not so. Malnutrition can be blatant, as the starving babies in third world countries. Malnutrition can also be much more slow and subtle; first bringing the vague symptoms of chronic fatigue, constipation, mood swings, poor wound recovery, and frequent colds; followed by a decade of struggling with incontinence, poor memory, pain in the chest, poor digestion, and visual problems. Malnutrition in America is a progressive and silent saboteur from within the body, not an instant knockout punch.

It was the Framingham study done by Harvard University that proclaimed: "Our way of life is related to our way of death." While many Americans are overfed, the majority are also poorly nourished. The typical American, statistically speaking, is overweight, has six colds per year, is regularly plagued with lethargy, mild depression, and constipation, gets dentures by age 45, begins a marked decline in function and vitality by age 50, and dies in their 60s or 70s from heart disease or cancer. Another scientist has stated the problem more bluntly: "We are digging our graves with our teeth." A return to healthier foods, including cayenne, would make a marked difference in the health of Americans. But remember, it is always best to adopt a healthier lifestyle rather than relying on one "magic bullet" drug or food (even cayenne) to rescue you from a health challenge. A healthier lifestyle includes moderate exercise, a good diet, rest and avoidance of toxins.

USE AND ABUSE OF MODERN MEDICINE

"Let food be your medicine and let medicine be your food." Hippocrates, father of modern medicine 400 BC

America has the most expensive and technologically advanced health care system in the world. For acute critical care, no medical system in the world can match ours. Yet, oftentimes we fight the symptoms of degenerative diseases with drugs and surgery in a futile losing battle, when the real answer to the patient's health problems might have been something as simple as diet improvement, or gentle herbal healers like cayenne, or a sympathetic ear. Think of a sink overflowing with a mess of water all over the floor. Our medical system spends an incredible amount of time and money trying to wipe up the mess on the floor when the easiest solution is to turn off the faucet that produces the diseases.

Dr. Christiaan Barnard, the pioneering heart transplant surgeon, claims that the greatest advancement in health care in the last 500 years came from, not a drug or surgical procedure, but the invention of the indoor flushing toilet, thus eliminating the many plagues caused by contaminated water supplies. The World Health Organization has reported that 70-80% of the world's population uses herbs and foods as their primary healing instruments, many of which are in jeopardy of being lost as the tropical rain forests disappear. Hippocrates, the Greek father of modern medicine told us 2400 years ago "Let food be your medicine and medicine be your food" and "...in nature there is strength."

Throughout the world and recorded history, natural healing agents were the main tools of the physician, with herbs serving as the favored medicines. Avicenna was an Arab herbalist who lived in the 11th century and travelled extensively throughout the known world to catalog the medical uses of herbs. He eventually wrote 100 books on this subject, culminating in his 1 million word tome: CANON OF MEDICINE. This book was considered a standard for medical education throughout Europe and Asia until the 17th century. Hippocrates, the father of modern medicine, used cayenne in several of his healing herbal remedies.

The big shift in medical outlook began with a Swiss physician, Theophrastus von Hohenheim, who became discontent in the early 16th century with his training and began wandering Europe. While in the mines in Italy, Hohenheim was intrigued by the refining of minerals. He took this knowledge and began using mercury, a known poisonous metal, to treat his patients. He further dabbled in the use of strong minerals for medicines. His methods were widely criticized and he died after being tossed from a window by his adversaries while only 50 years old.

By 1928, Alexander Fleming had taken penicillin from bread mold and injected it into a patient with an infection. The recovery process was astoundingly quick and the era of anti-biotics was born. By the end of World War II, the development of chemicals was coming faster than they could be cataloged or tested for safety. The chemical age was born, and with it came the mixed blessings of miracle chemicals and the immoral contamination of our planet. In the 1950s, Jonas Salk brought us the polio vacccine, and helped to end one of the worst scourges of mankind.

There is a difference between using our knowledge to improve our lot and abusing our knowledge through ego to worsen our lot. Drugs and surgery have their places in the healing arts, especially as short term fixes to get an acutely ill patient through a crisis phase. There are times when no other form of healing will work. But when we rely on these invasive therapies to heal a problem which can only be healed by following natural biochemical laws, we end up worse off. We need to be more restrained with medical therapies and more liberal with natural healing therapies, like cayenne. The intelligent combination would leave us with astoundingly good health. First, try the "cell restoration" therapies which include cayenne, and only as a last resort should we use the symptom-treating therapies of drugs and surgery.

I have worked with many patients who were defying all of Nature's laws: poor food, smoking, no exercise, stress, and a body loaded with toxins. Without a thought for changing this semi-suicidal lifestyle, the doctor will put the patient on an endless array of prescription drugs, which all have dastardly side effects, until the patient eventually develops a really serious disease, like cancer. We arrogantly assume that drugs can reverse the abuse caused by decades of poor nutrition and toxic burden. We are not respecting the laws of nature.

Cayenne is one of Nature's truly remarkable healing forces. But cayenne alone cannot negate the influence of living off junk food, cigarettes, TV and stress. Start incorporating an overall healthy lifestyle if you want to derive maximum benefits from the use of cayenne.

ANTIDOTES FOR THE "SINS" OF AMERICAN EATING

There was a report published in the Journal of the National Cancer Institute which found that the more pizza men ate, the lower was their risk for prostate cancer.[13] Not that pizza is good for you, with high fat cheese, white flour crust and lots of fat added. But, the tomato sauce is one of the richest sources of lycopenes, which are such a powerful healing factor that lycopenes, even with the rest of the unhealthy baggage from pizza, can reduce the risk for one of the more common killers among American men.

Scientists have found a similar "antidote" effect with red wine. Although the French eat as much fat as Americans, and have equally disastrous lifestyles, their regular use of red wine with its healing bioflavonoids has been shown in numerous studies to neutralize the otherwise damaging effects of a not-so-healthy lifestyle.

Garlic can do similar magic. You can commit many errors in your diet, yet include garlic and still have a lower risk for many disease. Cayenne is in this magical "antidote" category. Studies have shown that cayenne can reduce circulating levels of fat and cholesterol in the blood after a high fat meal. You can do many things wrong in your diet, but do a few very important things right and still come out ahead. I believe that Americans are dying more from what we are NOT eating rather than what we are eating. Add garlic, cayenne and tomatoes to an otherwise marginal nutrient intake, and you may help neutralize some of the "sins" of the typical American diet.

HOW "HOT" IS HOT?

Based upon the modern 0-10 "heat intensity" rating system, here's how some chilis from around the world rate for "fire power":[14]

HEAT-CHILIS	COUNTRY GROWN
1-Hungarian sweet chili	east Europe, California
1-Pimento	Hungary, Spain, Calif
3-Anaheim (green, red)	southwestern USA
3-Poblana (green & red)	central Mexico
4-Chawa	Yucatan, Mexico
4-Chilaca	Central Mexico
4-New Mexico	southwest US
5-Guero	southwest US, n. Mexico
5-Jalapeno	Mexico, southwest US
5-De Agua	central Mexico
6-Huachinango	central Mexico
6-Santa Fe grande	southwest US, n. Mexico
6-Dutch	Holland
6-Fresno	southwest US
7-Korean	Japan, Korea, California
7-Manzana	Central America
7-Peter Pepper	Texas, Louisiana
7-Rocotillo	South America
7-Serrano	southwest US, Mexico
7-Thai	southeast Asia
7-Aji	Peru
7-Amatista	South America
7-Fiesta	north Mexico, Louisiana
8-Peruvian	South America
8-Tepin	Central & South America
9-Jamaican Hot	Caribbean
9-Macho (green & red)	Mexico
9-Scotch Bonnet	Cent.America, Caribbean
9-Tabasco	Louisiana, Cent. America
10-Habanero	Yucatan

Methods of measuring the heat index of chilis
has become a complicated process. The Aztecs had
6 categories of heat value for their chili peppers: hot,
very hot, very very hot, brilliant hot, extremely hot,
and runaway hot. This method worked for the
Aztecs, yet for centuries, spice merchants around the
world grappled with some way of describing the heat
value of the chili peppers being sold to their
customers. Finally, in 1912, Wilbur L. Scoville, a
pharmacist at the Detroit pharmaceutical firm of
Parke-Davis (now part of Warner-Lambert) devised a
system using the human tongue to detect dilutions of
chili extracts. His rating scale went from zero for bell
peppers to 300,000 Scoville units for the revered
habanero. A more current method uses a zero (bell
pepper) to ten (habanero) system.

In your basic well-stocked American grocery
store, you should be able to find the following hot _Hottest_
chilis: Poblano, green and red Jalapeno, Habanero,
Serrano, Tomatillos, Anaheim, Yellow peppers, and
dry peppers.

HOW TO GET STARTED WITH CAYENNE

For the uninitiated, hot chilis may seem like a
daunting prospect, having tried a chili at a family
picnic, then chugging a glass of cold beverage to try
to put out the fire. There are many chilis that are
grown around the world. If you want to become a
connoiseur of chilis, then consult the appendix for
mail order companies who will sell you the most
exotic chili, either dried or as a seed to plant in your
garden.

For the rest of us who want a little of the
cayenne "bite" and all of the cayenne health benefits,

start slow. The easiest "entry level" cayenne product is:

1) Tablet form of cayenne. Heat units (HU, or Scoville units) of 40,000 is adequate to get some health benefits. Take 1 to 2 capsules with lunch and dinner. Unless you have an uncommonly strong stomach, do not take capsules of cayenne at breakfast. Mixing cayenne with ginger and guar gum (seaweed) seems to tame some of the fire in cayenne without neutralizing the health benefits. There are "cool" forms of cayenne capsules sold in your health food store. You may eventually venture your way up to the major leagues with the 100,000 heat unit cayenne capsules. Dollar for dollar, you cannot beat the health benefits of taking a few capsules of cayenne daily.

2) Powdered cayenne sprinkled on your food. Use it with or instead of salt for seasoning. Buy chili powder at your grocery store or Spike brand cayenne pepper (from Gayelord Hauser, Box 9398, Milwaukee, WI 53209) at your health food store. The Spike brand is not irradiated, which is an advantage. Since chilis grow best in hot humid Third World countries where regulations on pesticides and irradiation are virtually non-existent, I find comfort in buying cayenne and other herbs that are, hopefully, organically grown, or at the least have not been irradiated.

3) Salsa. There are many delicious salsas sold at your local grocery store. Try a few different brands. Most of them will rate the heat value with a thermometer on the side of the label, to give you some forewarning about the "bite" of their product. Mexicans, Indians, Thais, Koreans and other nationalities use their own form of hot sauce on nearly every food eaten.

4) Food. There are a few recipes later in this book that give you some ideas on how to incorporate cayenne and other hot peppers into your regular eating pattern. Start slow. Experts tell us that the best way to "put out the fire" from too much hot chilis is to eat dairy products, like yogurt, or bread, or some sugar or ginger, and of course, lots of cool water. You may wish to subscribe to Chili Pepper magazine (1-888-SPICY-HOT) for many more ideas on how to enjoy the flavor and health benefits of cayenne.

MY OWN "DANCE" WITH CAYENNE

The ancestral Irish diet does not use much spices. In college I was introduced to the tempestuous and tantalizing treats of hot Mexican food. I was hooked. Though my palate and stomach do not tolerate as much cayenne as many chiliheads, I enjoy the stuff.

   If you find no pleasure in a good hot salsa, but still wish to enjoy the health benefits from cayenne, then I suggest taking one or two 40,000 heat unit cayenne capsules with each meal.
   Cayenne has helped to clear up my sinuses, giving me more fresh air. Cayenne has improved my physical and mental energy levels and even helped to speed the healing of an occasionally sensitive stomach. From a personal and scientific standpoint, I heartily endorse the frequent use of cayenne for almost anyone.

ENDNOTES

[1]. Cordell, GA, et al., Annals of Pharmacotherapy, vol.27, p.330, Mar.1993

[2]. Palevitch, D., et al., Journal of Herbs & Spices, vol.3, no.2, p.55, 1995

[3]. Foster, S., HERBAL RENAISSANCE, p.63, Gibbs Smith, Salt Lake City, 1984

[4]. Naj, A., PEPPERS, p.17, Vintage Books, NY, 1993

[5]. Govindarajan, VS, et al., CRC Critical Reviews in Food Science and Nutrition, vol.22, no.2, p.108, 1991

[6]. Visudhiphan, S., et al., American Journal Clinical Nutrition, vol.35, p.1452, June 1982

[7]. Colpaert, FC, et al., Life Sciences, vol.32, p.1827, 1983

[8]. Chen, H, et al., Free Radical Biology Medicine, vol.16, p.437, 1994

[9]. Mindell, E., EARL MINDELLS HERB BIBLE, p.63, Simon & Schuster, NY, 1992

[10]. Murray, MT, HEALING POWER OF HERBS, p.76, Prima, Rocklin, CA 1995

[11]. Price, WA, NUTRITION AND PHYSICAL DEGENERATION, Keats, New Canaan, 1945

[12]. Eaton, SB, et al., PALEOLITHIC PRESCRIPTION, Harper, NY, 1988

[13]. Giovannucci, E., et al., Journal National Cancer Institute, vol.87, p.1767, 1995

[14]. Heinerman, J., HEALTH BENEFITS OF CAYENNE, p.43, Keats, New Canaan, CT 1997

CHAPTER TWO

★

HEALTH BENEFITS OF CAYENNE

Acne. See "skin problems" below.

Allergies. One of the most common symptoms in the world is upper respiratory allergic responses--sneezing, itchy eyes, runny or plugged up nose, wheezing and coughing. Cayenne may help. Capsaicin acts as an antagonist to the kinins and tachykinins that trigger allergic and asthmatic responses. Take 2 capsules of 40,000 heat unit cayenne powder with lunch and dinner. Results should begin within a week.

Angina. Angina is a severe pain in the chest region that basically is caused by the heart muscles being starved for oxygen and nutrients. In 1994, 945,000 Americans died of heart disease, including 487,000 from the later stages of angina (called ischemic heart disease).[1] People who have been through serious angina describe it as a "knife stabbing me right in the heart" followed by the "weight of an elephant sitting on my chest". These are serious signs of heart problems and must be treated with immediate medical attention. Patients who suffer from chronic angina get to experience the pinnacle of miracle drugs in nitroglycerin. Within seconds after placing the nitroglycerin under the tongue, the blood vessels in the heart region begin to dilate and allow some oxygen to reach the starved muscles on the other side of the blockage.

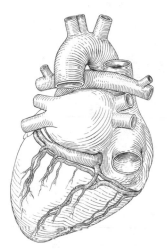

Cayenne can help. Capsaicin triggers the release of a substance called CGRP (calcitonin gene related peptide) which is a potent dilator of the blood vessels that surround the heart.[2] As you work with your doctor, add cayenne to your health regimen, preferably 1-2 capsules of cayenne powder with lunch and dinner. Cayenne will not reduce the effectiveness of any heart medications and may begin to change the underlying causes of the angina, which drugs never do.

Since the active ingredient in cayenne, capsaicin, is easily dissolved in an alcohol solution, you can prepare a special remedy for angina that has been used by a famous herbalist. In a glass jar with a tight fitting lid, mix one ounce of dried cayenne peppers in with a pint of vodka or gin. Shake several times daily for 2 weeks, then strain this mixture through cheesecloth. Twice daily in between meals, take 6 drops of this tincture either under the tongue or diluted in a glass of water.

Appetite/anorexia. For people with a poor appetite, cayenne may be able to help. Cayenne stimulates the gastro-intestinal tract, to help increase the flow of gastric juices (hydrochloric acid and digestive enzymes) along with stimulating the muscles in the GI region to move the food more speedily along--thus making the stomach empty sooner. For speed-eating Americans, you may find that this normally positive effect of cayenne can work against you. Many people report that if they eat too fast and include cayenne in the meal, then they overeat. Slow down your eating so that a meal lasts at least 25 minutes, otherwise the stomach does not have time to send signals to the brain that the stomach is full and the food intake should cease.

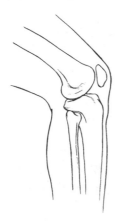

Arthritis. Over 2.5 million Americans suffer from rheumatoid arthritis so severe that it requires medical attention.[3] More than 40 million Americans have some degree of some form of arthritis. Rheumatoid arthritis usually involves an inflammation, thickening and eventually an erosion of the bone ending connective tissue. Osteoarthritis involves the dissolving of the spongy cartilage that cushions the pounding between bone endings. Cayenne to the rescue. Topical application of the more dilute 0.025% capsaicin ointment was able to provide substantial pain relief in patients with both osteo and rheumatoid arthritis within 4 weeks.[4] Another study found good results with capsaicin ointment in osteoarthritis, but no improvement in grip strength, swelling and morning stiffness.[5] In that same study, Drs. McCarthy and McCarty did not find improvements in rheumatoid arthritis from capsaicin. In another study, more than 80% of the patients using the capsaicin ointment felt improvement in morning stiffness and other arthritis-related symptoms, with only 55% of the placebo group feeling relief. There are numerous studies now showing the benefits in reducing pain for arthritis patients. One animal study even showed that capsaicin reduced the swelling from rheumatoid arthritis.[6] During pain response, Substance P is produced in the nerve endings near the joints. Substance P can cause a deterioration in the cartilage surrounding a joint, which means that people should not ignore the pain associated with arthritis, because of this self-perpetuating downward cycle instigated by Substance P. All of this can be helped by capsaicin ointment. See the section "pain" for more information.

Asthma. Asthma can be caused by poor diet (especially low intake of vitamin C and magnesium), stress, air pollution, overexertion in exercise, pollen, ragweed and food allergies. In some of these causes, cayenne can help. Capsaicin seems to be a potent antagonist to several compounds (kinins and tachykinins) which trigger bronchial constriction. The net effect is that regular consumption of cayenne or taking cayenne supplements may help to open the bronchial passageways for asthma sufferers. Take 1-2 capsules of cayenne powder with lunch and dinner. Dr. Jim Duke, a world-famous herbal specialist formerly with the United States Department of Agriculture, told a USA Today reporter that he cured an asthma attack while in the Costa Rican jungle by sipping a mixture of a pinch of dried cayenne pepper in a glass of hot chocolate.

Baldness. Remember, baldness is mostly a genetic condition. However, for those people who are going bald due to poor circulation in the scalp region, cayenne working as a potent vasodilator may help. Take 2 capsules of 40,000 heat unit cayenne powder with lunch and dinner. If you really want to accelerate the blood supply to the scalp, then mix the powdered contents from 2 cayenne capsules into a small container of pure aloe vera gel. Stir thoroughly. Apply this cayenne mixture to the scalp at bedtime, then wash off in the morning shower.

Bruises & sprains. Cayenne, when applied topically, is able to exhaust the nerve endings of their Substance P (for pain). Cayenne ointment will eventually reduce pain without the use of dangerous drugs, like Tylenol, or addictive drugs, like codeine. See the sections for "pain" and "osteoarthritis" for more information.

Cancer prevention. While there have been some conflicting reports in this area, it is clear that moderate use of cayenne is cancer protective, while excessive use of chilis may be counterproductive. In one study of Mexicans who ate lots of hot chilis, there was a noticeable increase in the incidence of stomach cancer.[7] To test the theory that capsaicin causes cancer, scientists painted capsaicin on the backs of shaved animals, then applied one of the most potent cancer-causing agents known (DMBA from tobacco smoke) to the skin, with a result of no tumors formed.[8] Other researchers found that cayenne used regularly lowers the incidence of cancer and seems to block the downhill spiral of initiation and promotion that begins cancer.[9] Now, there is an entire series of scientific articles showing that capsaicin prevents the cancer that would have formed from exposure to benzopyrenes (found in overcooked foods), aflatoxin (found in moldy grains and legumes), and tobacco nitrosamines. The conclusions from researchers who are very savvy on foods and cancer: "Although a minute amount of capsaicin displays few or no deleterious effects, heavy ingestion of the compound has been associated with necrosis (death of tissue), ulceration and even carcinogenesis." In other words, if a little hot chilis is good, then more is not better.

Cataracts. Cataracts involve the loss of transparency in the lens of the eye. Cataract surgery is one of the most common procedures done in American clinics and hospitals, costing Medicare billions of dollars annually. Cataract sufferers liken their problem to "trying to read after smearing Vaseline jelly on your glasses." Cayenne is rich in a collection of bioflavonoids that have been implicated in maintaining healthy vision. Fresh hot chilis (not the dried powder or capsules) are a rich source of vitamin C, which is a potent antioxidant that can slow down the free radical destruction that creates cataracts. Cayenne is also a potent vasodilator, which the lens of the eye can use, given the limited circulation available to that very unusual tissue. All in all, regular use of cayenne may reduce the risk of developing cataracts.

Clogged arteries. See "high cholesterol" and "heart disease" sections.

Colds and flu. If you add up all the amazing effects that cayenne has on the body, it becomes obvious why cayenne has been used for centuries to shorten the severity and duration of colds. Cayenne increases the flow of mucus, which washes away the invading viruses. Cayenne dilates blood vessels to speed the delivery of healing immune factors to the site of infection. As a "beginners" approach to using cayenne for your cold, take 2 capsules of at least 40,000 heat unit cayenne powder with lunch and dinner. For the more advanced followers of cayenne, make a hot tea to gargle with: into 1 cup of warm water mix 2 capsules of 40,000+ heat unit cayenne powder. Swish this fluid around your mouth and gargle. If it's too painful, then try half the cayenne powder. Do this 1-3 times daily to help shorten the severity and duration of your colds. Take cayenne supplements and eat cayenne daily to help prevent colds.

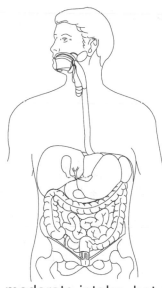

Constipation.
Constipation is one of the more common complaints among Americans. Given our low fiber, low fluid intake along with too much sugar, meat, cheese, and fat; it should not be surprising that the most commonly shoplifted item from American pharmacies is Preparation H, for hemorrhoids. Cayenne increases the flow of juices in the intestinal tract, which helps to speed the food through the GI tract. At moderate intake, hot chilis will encourage regularity. At a higher intake, chilis can cause diarrhea and irritation of the colo-rectal region, hence the slogan at many a chili fest: "Burns at both ends." Obviously, we are looking for healthy and daily bowel elimination, not diarrhea or irritation of hemorrhoids.

Cooling effects. Cayenne is a potent vasodilator. As it opens up the blood vessels near the surface and causes sweating, it creates an initial warming sensation, but is actually bringing the body's internal heat to the surface to be dissipated. Cayenne is regularly consumed by natives of hot humid climates to help them better tolerate the oppressive heat of the tropics. Animal research indicates that cayenne actually triggers the hypothalamus of the brain to cool the body.[10] Just when you think you are fully understanding the breadth of cayenne's healing abilities, then you notice it will also do the opposite. See the "warming effect" section below.

Cough. With its stimulating effect and mild irritation on the mucus membranes, cayenne helps the body to expell whatever is creating the cough. DO NOT breath cayenne powder. Using hot chilis or cayenne capsules will provide support (called an expectorant) in helping the lungs to expel dust, viruses and debris. Dr. Jane Guiltinan of Bastyr University in Seattle has found good success for relieving coughs by mixing: 1 teaspoon of salt, 1/4 teaspoon of cayenne powder and the juice of a half lemon in 4 ounces of warm water. Gargle with this solution as long as you can tolerate it, then spit it out. Do not swallow.

Diabetes. Diabetes mellitus is a common condition of abnormal blood glucose regulation. The name literally means "sweetness running through" since diabetics end up dumping substantial amounts of sugar in their urine, even though the cells of the body are being starved for sugar. Inadequate insulin production, or insulin resistance are common problems. Obesity often compounds diabetes. 55,000 Americans died last year from complications of diabetes, which usually includes heart disease, infection, gangrene and kidney failure.

There are several ways that cayenne can help diabetics:

1) as a vasodilator to increase circulation to the peripheral tissue which often gets starved in diabetics and results in poor circulation and gangrene

2) lowering blood glucose levels[11]

3) applied topically to reduce the common pain from diabetic neuropathy (see below).

Diabetic neuropathy. Among the many problems facing the diabetic is a painful neuropathy, which is caused by the nerve cells being starved of their favorite fuel: blood glucose. Diabetic neuropathy usually includes numbness, tingling and pain in the hands and feet. When diabetics were diligent about staying on their strict diet and following medication guidelines for blood glucose regulation, diabetic neuropathy was cut by 64%.[12] Other ways of controlling diabetic neuropathy include pain medication, of which the safest and most effective is cayenne ointment. Other analgesics (pain killers) that are widely used have numerous side effects. Kidney failure may accompany the excess use of Tylenol and other drugs containing acetaminophen.

Axsain is an ointment containing 0.075% capsaicin content. When applied topically, this ointment penetrates deeply into the skin to the surface nerves and depletes the nerves of substance P, which generates pain. Capsaicin ointments usually must be used for anywhere from 1-7 days before the pain killing effect is felt.

In one double blind study involving 227 men and women with painful diabetic neuropathy, 71% of capsaicin-treated patients reported improvement versus 51% in the placebo group.[13] Patients treated with the capsaicin ointment reported improvements in work, sleep, walking and participation in recreational activities. The capsaicin ointment was applied to the affected regions of the body 4 times daily and improvement was generally seen within a week. 63% of these patients reported the side effects of burning, stinging or warming sensation at the site of the ointment. But these side effects were minor and considered tolerable. Capsaicin depletes the substance P that causes pain, but still allows for normal pressure, heat and other sensations.[14] No medication can do what cayenne may be able to do for diabetics: knock out the pain yet still allow other sensations to the nerve endings without toxic side effects or addiction.

Fatigue & depression. As one of the most common symptoms reported to American physicians, fatigue and depression seem to be linked together. Cayenne, through some unknown mechanism, seems to excite and stimulate nerves.[15] The net effect is that many people feel energized by the regular use of capsaicin and hot chili peppers. The increased oxygen consumption of Thai people when eating hot chilis is similar to what is found with higher adrenaline output. Cayenne may be energizing people by stimulating the production of adrenaline, which definitely will relieve fatigue and possibly depression. A team of French scientists has found a definite energizing stimulating tonic effect from the consumption of hot chilis.[16]

One of the more intriguing aspect of cayenne is the "high" experienced by the seasoned user of hot peppers. The body carries its own pharmacy in the brain. When we are hurt, burned or in shock, the brain sends out morphine-like compounds, called endorphins, to sooth the pain. Cayenne feels like it is burning the skin, but it doesn't. The brain sends out the required "medication" of endorphins to reduce the expected pain from this burn. Scientists have actually found receptor sites on human nerve cells for capsaicin.[17] You may find it equally puzzling that there are receptor sites in the human brain for caffeine (from coffee, tea, and colas), theophylline (from tea), alcohol (benzodiazapine sites in the brain), morphine and heroine (endorphin sites in the brain), nicotine (from tobacco), and THC from marijuana.

What scientists, like Dr. Candace Pert from the National Institutes of Health, are discovering is that the human brain is a pharmacy, always generating chemicals based upon your thoughts and state of health. These chemicals can be pleasurable or stressful. No doubt, there is a chemical produced in the human brain that is similar in active receptor site to capsaicin. By eating cayenne, we generate more of these healthful and pleasurable effects. In a similar fashion, exercise can cause the brain to release endorphins for pleasure.

Fatty liver. The liver is one of the largest and, arguably, the most sophisticated organ in the human body. It converts, stores, processes and detoxifies millions of molecules a minute. When the liver develops fatty accumulation, all of the vital functions in the liver slow down. Due to its lipotropic action (means "breaking up fats), cayenne may be able to help prevent the collection of fats in the liver. Cayenne may also help reduce the toxic effects of alcohol, which can cause fatty liver, and possibly worse (fibrosis, necrosis).

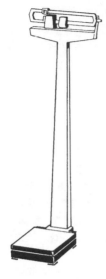

Fat reduction. Cayenne has the remarkable ability to favorably alter the levels of fats in the blood and the body. Country doctors have noticed for decades that people who eat lots of hot peppers rarely get overweight. In animals, giving capsaicin in the diet while feeding 30% of the calories as lard provided for a 29% reduction in serum triglycerides compared to animals fed the same diet but no capsaicin.[18] A human using cayenne pepper daily might expect to drop their triglycerides from 300 milligrams per deciliter, which puts them at risk for heart disease[19], to 213 mg per deciliter which is closer to the normal range.   In the animal study just mentioned, there was a 24% reduction in fat surrounding the kidneys (perirenal). Through some unknown mechanism, cayenne helps the body to mobilize and use up fats, which is a very healthy effect for fat-burdened Americans. For more information, see "obesity" below.

Food poisoning. See "worms" below.

Frostbite. See "warming effect" below.

Gas (flatulence). While everyone from the President to the Pope do it, sometimes gas can become a troubling issue. Intestinal gas is more likely to be produced when we eat foods that we do not digest well, but putrefactive intestinal bacteria thrive on; such as beans and nuts. Cashews, peanuts, soybeans, and other beans can generate an embarrassing round of gas. Obviously, one solution is to reduce the intake of foods that generate gas.

Another strategy is to encourage the aerobic bacteria in the intestines which compete with the nasty putrefactive bacteria. Yogurt and capsules of Lactobacillus acidophilus (available at your health food store), and soil based organisms (from Nature's Biotics 800-622-8986) can help to generate a healthier climate in the human gut. More vegetables, less sugar and fat in the diet helps. Exercise helps to stimulate peristalsis, or the muscular movement of the intestines that pushes the food to its end point. When food is properly digested within a reasonable period of time, there is very little gas. When high fat food is allowed to ferment in the gut, there can be considerable gas.

Cayenne can reduce gas (a.k.a. carminative) in a number of ways:

1) As a stimulant, cayenne encourages the flow of secretions from the intestines, including digestive enzymes, which helps to prevent fermentation of carbohydrates in the gut

2) Cayenne moves food through the intestines more rapidly to reduce the chance of fermentation.

3) Cayenne helps to kill the unfriendly bacteria in the gut that cause gas through putrefaction, or literally turning your intestines into an old moonshiner's still.

The bottom line is that hot peppers and salsa will likely reduce the gas from your Mexican meal which usually includes gas-making beans.

Headache. Cluster headaches are common and can last up to 3 days for some unfortunate people. Medication for this condition usually centers around heavy narcotics which can make the patient drowsy. Cayenne may be the drug of choice for these people. Cluster headaches were treated by applying a topical capsaicin ointment to the inside of the sinuses. This should only been done under medical supervision. After 30 days of this treatment, 70% of the patients reported improvement in their cluster headaches.[20] 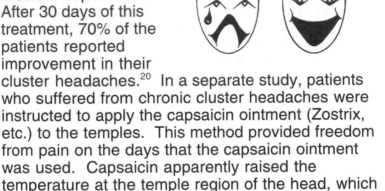 In a separate study, patients who suffered from chronic cluster headaches were instructed to apply the capsaicin ointment (Zostrix, etc.) to the temples. This method provided freedom from pain on the days that the capsaicin ointment was used. Capsaicin apparently raised the temperature at the temple region of the head, which normally experiences a heat loss during these types of headaches. Care should be taken to keep this ointment away from the eyes to prevent stinging.

Heart disease. There are at least two famous medical herbalists, Dr. Richard Schulze[21] and Dr. John Ray Christopher who have written about their lifesaving experiences using cayenne to reverse congenital heart disease. For a particularly potent heart-protective herbal combination, use cayenne, garlic and hawthorne mixed together. See other sections under: fat reduction, high cholesterol, high blood pressure and obesity.

Heart arrhythmia. Irregular heart beat can be somewhere between annoying, frightening and life threatening, depending on how often it happens and for how long. Scientists using capsaicin to treat animals with heart arrhythmias found that capsaicin seemed to work like the prescription drugs, calcium channel blockers, to help regulate the heart beat.[22]

Heat exhaustion. Not to be confused with heat stroke, which can be a fatal condition involving excess exposure to heat, with symptoms of headache, confusion, elevated skin temperature and eventually coma and death. For heat stroke, get medical help immediately. For heat exhaustion, which is characterized by weakness and general dehydration, cayenne, water and electrolytes can help.

For most of the 9000 years that hot peppers have been used, natives in warm climates noticed that chilis make the "dog days" of summer a little bit more bearable. The reason is that capsaicin causes peripheral vasodilation, or expansion of the blood vessels in the skin region.[23] When these blood vessels dilate and the inevitable sweating commences from eating hot chilis, the person is left with all of their natural cooling mechanisms in high gear. Sweating causes evaporation and a cooling effect. Dilating blood vessels in the skin brings the heat from the interior part of the body to the exterior for ventilation, not unlike the radiator on your car. In many different studies, scientists found that capsaicin generated a significant cooling effect.[24] You feel cooler and your body is better able to dissipate the heat buildup during those hot humid days. Drink plenty of pure water and eat hot chilis or take cayenne capsules throughout warm weather.

Herbal augmentor. With the stimulating and vasodilating effects of cayenne, cayenne is used along with other herbs to enhance their value. Hence, whether you are using saw palmetto for enlarged prostate or angelica for female fertility, cayenne improves the efficiency and delivery of nearly all herbal formulas.

High blood pressure (hypertension). Nearly 60 million Americans suffer from hypertension. While there usually are no symptoms from this condition, it slowly wears out the vascular network and the organs connected. Hypertension is called the "silent killer", because the first symptom a person may have is a fatal stroke or heart attack. Cayenne may be able to help.

There is a heavily researched concept, called the calcitonin gene-related peptide or CGRP, which capsaicin can favorably influence to cause dilation of blood vessels. As mentioned above, capsaicin causes peripheral vasodilation, or expansion of the blood vessels in the skin region. High blood pressure can be caused by many factors, including stress, obesity, too much salt or alcohol, not enough calcium, magnesium, or potassium, not enough essential fatty acids and so on. When hypertension is caused by constriction of the blood vessels, which drives up the pressure in this narrower tubes, then cayenne can effectively reduce blood pressure in these people by expanding the diameter of the blood vessels. More room in the vessels means that the pressure goes down and you spare delicate capillaries in the kidney, liver, heart and brain region from the constant pounding of high blood pressure.

High cholesterol. With nearly one million Americans dying each year from heart disease and related disorders, cholesterol in the blood has become a valuable barometer of your overall health. When cholesterol "rusts" or oxidizes in the blood vessels, it creates free radical lipid peroxides that your immune cells gobble up to prevent any more damage from occurring. These immune cells then start stacking up dead in the blood vessel walls and are the beginning of vascular occlusions, which are found in 90% of Americans over age 30. Cholesterol is not as big a problem as "rusted" cholesterol, which is why other researchers have found that the level of vitamin E in the blood may be the most accurate indicator of upcoming heart disease, since vitamin E is the fat soluble antioxidant that protects the cholesterol from "rusting".

Capsaicin reduces the absorption of fats and cholesterol in the intestines, and slows down the making of excess cholesterol in the liver.[25] Whole cayenne powder was more effective at lowering serum fats than pure capsaicin[26], which is just another reason to rely heavily on the whole food more than some isolated extract (like capsaicin) as the only "active ingredient". In one study with animals, capsaicin in the diet was able to substantially drop serum cholesterol levels.[27] In another study with animals fed a high sugar and high fat diet (just like the typical American diet), capsaicin was able to lower the "bad" cholesterol (LDL and VLDL) and raise the "good" cholesterol (HDL).[28] As might be expected, countries that eat more hot peppers have a lower incidence of heart disease.[29]

Libido, sex drive. Most Americans develop measurable "plugged up plumbing", or obstructed arteries, by the time they are in their 30s. In order for erections to occur, the penis must have clean and clear circulation in all the tiny capillaries that are supposed to become engorged with blood. In one study of 440 impotent men ages 40 and above, 92% had at least two major risk factors for heart disease, while 80% were found to have major blockage of the arteries[30], which means that the tiny capillaries in the penis region are likely also blocked. Another common reason for impotence is the use of hypertension medication, which causes a loss of potassium, magnesium and fluid from the body with the resulting inability to develop an erection.

Cayenne can help improve sex drive in several ways:

1) lower blood pressure, for some people possibly to the point where you can discontinue medication

2) dilate and unblock blood vessels to allow the penis to be fully nourished and function as it should

3) stimulate and energize the nervous system.

Malnutrition. Hot chilis are rich in protein, fiber, complex carbohydrates, vitamins, minerals, bioflavonoids, carotenoids, and the magical capsaicin that has numerous benefits. Cayenne improves appetite and digestion. Thus hot peppers provide both direct nourishment and improvement in digestion and absorption of that nourishment. Altogether, hot peppers can help to prevent or reverse malnutriiton when part of an overall balanced diet.

Mouth sores (oral mucositis).   The incidence of cancer in this country has gone from 3% of deaths in 1900 to 22% of deaths in 1990 and climbing. More than 70% of cancer patients receive chemotherapy, which often causes mouth sores, a.k.a. oral mucositis. These painful blisters will stop the cancer patient from eating, which generates severe malnutrition and a compromised immune system. Mouth sores can be the beginning of the end for the cancer patient.

At the Yale Pain Management Center in New Haven, Connecticut, researchers devised an ingenious method of delivering capsaicin to cancer patients with mouth sores. The researchers mixed the cayenne with taffy candy. As reported in the prestigious Journal of the National Cancer Institute, the sugar was able to hide some of the burning sensation and the taffy stayed in the mouth long enough for the capsaicin to do its topical pain control management. All of the 11 patients in the study had signficant decrease in mouth sore pain, with 2 patients reporting complete elimination of pain.[31] To follow this protocol, mix up some taffy from your favorite recipe book and add several capsules of cayenne powder to the mix.

Nausea. Take a teaspoon of cayenne powder mixed in a tablespoon of olive oil before beginning a trip where motion sickness may be a problem. Other herbalists[32] recommend an equal blend of ginger, cayenne, and licorice to prevent and relieve motion sickness and other forms of nausea. For morning sickness in pregnancy, use just the ginger and cayenne mixture.

Neuralgia. This is a pain of a severe throbbing or stabbing nature and can be found anywhere in the body. For relief, see the section "Pain".

Obesity. Although Americans have been in the midst of a "fitness revolution" and rivers of diet soft drinks have been consumed since the FDA approval of aspartame (NutraSweet) in 1982, we now have a 30% increase in the incidence of obesity. Overweight people are more likely to die young of heart disease, diabetes, or various cancers, especially of the breast and colon. Cayenne can help.

There is a region of fatty tissue, called "brown adipose tissue" or BAT, found on the back and buttocks region of people. BAT is so named because it is much more loaded with blood vessels than regular white fatty storage regions. BAT is our body's thermogenic regulator, our internal "wood burning stove", which is supposed to squander excess stored fat in the making of heat. In many people, due to inactivity, wearing too much clothes, keeping the home thermostat set too high and exposure to psychological stress; we end up letting the BAT atrophy. Under ideal conditions, BAT takes excess fat in the body and burns it to maintain the ideal body temperature of 98.6 F. When BAT atrophies, it becomes very difficult for many people to lose weight. Ephedra from the Chinese herb, Ma Huang, along with white willow bark (aspirin) and Gotu Kola (caffeine) have been shown to stimulate BAT into action to help people lose weight. Cayenne also stimulates BAT.[33] One of the simplest things anyone can do to slowly and safely lose weight is to eat cayenne and other hot peppers to gear up the

burning of stored fats in BAT. This simple procedure
requires no change in diet and no exercise. It just
increases the amount of calories being burned while
at rest. Of course, if you do exercise and eat a low fat
diet, the weight will melt away much quicker.

Osteoarthritis. Cartilage tissue normally
cushions the connections between the bones. When
this cartilage deteriorates, osteoarthritis is the result.
This condition is actually bone rubbing against bone,
which is painful and can immobilize people. More
than 50% of men and women over the age of 65
have symptomatic osteoarthritis in at least one joint.[34]
The drug of choice for osteoarthritis for many years
has been NSAIDs, or non-steroidal anti-inflammatory
drugs, like Advil. NSAIDs come with a long grocery
list of complications and side effects, including
stomach upset, ulceration of the small intestine and
colon, kidney failure, liver failure, skin reactions and
interfering with high blood pressure medication.[35]
Other prescription drugs sometimes used for
osteoarthritis include morphine or codeine and
steroid hormones, all of which have a lengthy list of
complications, including addiction.

Cayenne to the rescue. Capsaicin ointments
are sometimes referred to as "rubefacients", since
they are counter-irritants which initially cause
reddening on the skin. Be aware that many
capsaicin "rubefacient" ointments also contain
nicotine (methyl niconate) and aspirin (methyl
salicylate) in small enough quantities to be of little
concern. However, capsaicin ointment alone (no
other therapy, no other ingredients in the ointment)
was able to provide significant relief of osteoarthritis
pain in a 12 week double blind study.[36]

Pain. Here we find one of the many paradoxes regarding cayenne. It seems to cause pain when you eat it or rub it on the skin. Yet, it actually reduces pain by depleting the nerve endings of Substance P (for pain).[37] Researchers also find that capsaicin has some mysterious effect on calcium levels in the nerve endings.[38] Up to 20% of the adult population (50 million Americans) suffer from chronic pain, while half of them are inadequately treated.[39]

Cayenne ointment has been clinically proven to help relieve the pain of:

⇒ shingles (herpes zoster, or postherpetic neuralgia)
⇒ skin diseases
⇒ psoriasis (red scaly lesions on the skin)
⇒ pruritus (itching)
⇒ peripheral neuropathy
⇒ fibromyalgia, which is an arthritis-like condition resembling Chronic Fatigue Syndrome.[40]
⇒ post-mastectomy pain
⇒ stump pain from amputation
⇒ trigeminal neuralgia
⇒ skin cancer

Axsain and Zostrix are capsaicin ointments that are available over-the-counter. Pain relief usually begins after several days of using these ointments.

Researchers have discovered a "mother lode" of healing possibilities in nitric oxide, a substance found throughout the body regulating everything from nerve conduction to the immune system. Capsaicin apparently affects nitric oxide levels.

Patients who undergo a mastectomy for breast cancer often suffer with pain in the surgical region.

Capsaicin creme applied 3 times daily for 2 months produced improvements in post-mastectomy pain syndrome in 68% of the patients.[41]

There is a condition called trigeminal neuralgia, which involves a stabbing pain in the facial region. Topical capsaicin used three times daily provided complete relief of the pain in half (6 of 12) of the subjects and partial relief in a third (4 of 12) of the subjects for an 83% response rate with no addictions, side effects or long term toxicities.[42]

When Substance P is allowed to run amuck, for those willing to tolerate the pain, it can eventually contribute to erosion of the joint endings and result in osteoarthritis. Chronic pain is not something to be endured, since it can lead to even more disabling joint conditions. Capsaicin ointment has become the "drug of choice" to treat many forms of pain, including peripheral neuropathy (tingling numbness in the extremities), local stump pain (from amputation), hyperalgesia (extreme sensitivity to pain response), pain from skin cancer and more.

Parasites. See "worms" below.

Pesticide. Foxes in the Arctic started chewing through important scientific cables. The researchers found that spreading cayenne powder over slightly tacky silicone sealant that was applied to the cables was able to stop the foraging foxes from this costly habit. Other gardeners have found that cayenne can keep out many rabbits, raccoons, deer, insects and other pests. However, birds seem unaffected by the pungency of cayenne. Other animals have developed a penchant for cayenne. Cayenne is an inexpensive and non-toxic pesticide, but I wouldn't "bet the farm on it" as a universal pesticide agent.

Pleurisy. This condition involves the inflammation of the lining of the lungs. Cayenne is a stimulant and vasodilator that may help this condition. Do not inhale cayenne powder, but rather take 2 capsules of cayenne powder (40,000 heat units or higher) with lunch and dinner.

You can also use a time-tested herbalist's favorite rub for speeding the relief of pleurisy. Mix equal parts of powdered cayenne pepper, lobelia herb and slippery elm bark into a small amount of cod liver oil (all found at your health food store). Use just enough cod liver oil to form a thick paste like Vaseline jelly. Apply this paste to the affected region of the chest every 3 hours, then cover with plastic wrap, then a clean flannel cloth. Be sure to wash your hands afterwards.

Psoriasis. Psoriasis is a common, painful and embarrassing skin condition involving red scaly formations throughout the body, usually centered on the elbows, knees and arms. Several studies have shown the impressive results from using capsaicin ointment in psoriasis. In one study, 44 patients with widely distributed psoriasis used a capsaicin ointment on one side of the body and a placebo ointment on the other side of the body. After six weeks, there was considerable improvement in scaling and redness (erythema) on the sides of the body treated with capsaicin.[43] In another much larger study, 197 patients with itching psoriasis were treated in double blind fashion with half of the patients randomly assigned to getting capsaicin ointment and the other half of the patients getting a placebo ointment. The psoriasis was totally or markedly cleared in 82% of the capsaicin treated group versus 33% in the placebo group.[44]

Shingles (herpes zoster). Many children suffer through chicken pox, which is provided to us compliments of the herpes zoster virus. This virus may then lay dormant in the body for decades and re-surface in senior years when the immune system is compromised by poor diet, stress or whatever. The new batch of herpes zoster is often called shingles, and is an extremely painful condition, since the virus attacks the nerves in the skin region. In 7 studies using capsaicin ointment to treat the pain of shingles, ALL showed a substantial decrease in the pain score.[45] In one study, doctors instructed patients suffering from shingles pain (post herpetic neuralgia) to apply capsaicin ointment 4 times a day to the affected painful area. After 8 weeks, 49% of the patients reported improvements In pain, but 13% discontinued the use of the creme due to the burning sensation. Relief was usually noticed within the first 3 weeks and pain relief peaked at 5 weeks.[46]

Sinusitis. One of the more frequent complaints among Americans is sinus problems. This problem is often generated by the common allergies from milk, wheat, ragweed, pollen and the irritation of air pollution. Many Americans develop sinus congestion or continuous sinus flow. Rhinitis is an inflammation of the nasal mucus membranes, which is related to sinusitis and also very common. Cayenne may be able to help. Researchers found that "painting" a capsaicin solution on the nasal membranes in the nose eventually was able to cure chronic rhinitis.[47] This medically supervised procedure may be uncomfortable, but it may also be worth the effort. As an alternative to painting your sinus regions with capsaicin ointment, try taking 2 capsules of cayenne powder with lunch and dinner.

A favorite herbalist's remedy for sinusitis is to mix 1/4 teaspoon each of cayenne powder and garlic powder in with a bowl of hot chicken soup. Drink it down with gusto. Usually relieves the stuffy nose and sneezing.

Skin problems. Since cayenne is such a potent stimulant and vasodilator, it can be very helpful in clearing up minor skin problems, from acne to psoriasis to dry skin. Take 2 capsules of 40,000+ heat unit cayenne with lunch and dinner. Try applying one of the previously mentioned capsaicin ointments on the affected skin region. For the bold readers, mix 1 capsule of cayenne powder with a small amount of pure aloe vera gel. Apply to acne or dry skin at night. Make sure that you do not get any of this solution into your eyes. Wash hands after applying to face. See section for "psoriasis".

Sore throat. With the stimulating effects of cayenne, it has been found to be a valuable component to reduce the severity and duration of sore throats. Mix 1-2 capsules of cayenne powder (40,000 heat units or higher) in 1 cup of warm water. Swish in your mouth and gargle, but do not swallow. If this preparation is too hot to tolerate, then cut the cayenne in half and try again.

Stress reducer. Animals given cayenne have been found to better tolerate physical and psychological stress. Cayenne is a stimulant and encourages the transmission of nerve impulses, therefore it will offer better stress tolerance in regular users.

Stroke. Your body has 60,000 miles of blood vessels which create a complete network of circulation to each and every cell in the human body. In many Americans, due to stress, high fat diet, wrong kind of fat in the diet, sedentary lifestyle, and low intake of vitamin E and fish oil--our blood turns from a thin liquid into a thick sludgy liquid that is unable to feed the distant tissues in the body. This thicker blood is constantly forming clots, or embolisms, in various parts of the body. When these clots form in the brain, a stroke can be the result. Over 155,000 Americans died last year from strokes, or cerebrovascular problems. Those who do survive a stroke often end up with partial paralysis, or a loss of speech or memory. Cayenne to the rescue.

Hot peppers thin the blood by breaking up these clots. People who eat lots of hot chilis have a very low incidence of blood clots (thromboembolism).[48] The people in Thailand, who are world renowned chiliheads, have a full 33% reduction in the clotting tendency of their blood when compared to the typical American. This beneficial effect from cayenne serves many purposes. Obviously, it cuts the risk for stroke or embolism. But more importantly, and not as obviously, cayenne thins the blood to help this "river of life" to circulate throughout the body to feed the distant tissues.

In one study, a scientist placed a sample of chicken heart tissue in a Petri dish full of nutrient solution. Everyday he changed the solution to take away waste products and renew the nutrient supply surrounding this tissue. The tissue basically never aged. When we bring in the right amount of groceries and take out the trash (detoxify the cells), we seem to slow down the aging process and improve our vitality. Cayenne does this and more.

Thyroid problems. Do you suffer from any of the following symptoms: constipation, fatigue, depression, poorly regulated or painful menstrual cycles, hair loss, easy weight gain, allergies, heart disease, and poor tolerance to cold temperatures? If so, then you may have an easily corrected problem: hypothyroidism. According to a huge amount of scientific literature on this subject, up to 40% of the American public suffers from mild to severe hypothyroidism. Stephen Langer, MD[49]; Denis Wilson, MD[50] and Broda Barnes, MD, PhD[51] have been pioneers in alerting the public to this fundamental health problem. If your basal temperature first thing in the morning is below 97.8 F, then you may have hypothyroidism. This simple and easily corrected issue may make a huge difference in your overall health.

Cayenne may be able to help. Herbalists find that a mixture of cayenne (since it is a potent stimulant) along with kelp, gentian root, and Irish moss may be able to stimulate the thyroid back into full action. Otherwise, it may be necessary to find a physician willing to recommend prescription thyroid supplements to gear up the lagging thyroid gland.

Toothache. The earliest report in the medical literature for therapeutic uses of hot peppers comes from an 1850 report in an Irish medical journal which used 1-2 drops of hot pepper extract applied to a cotton swab and then to the toothache gum region.[52] Since capsaicin is easily dissolved in alcohol, one way to make this toothache tincture is to blend 2 capsules of 40,000 heat unit cayenne powder in 4 ounces of gin. Let sit for a day. Strain. Apply a few drops of this tincture to the toothache region.

Toxin protection. Cayenne helps to encourage sweating. The skin is the largest organ in the human body, with about 2000 pores per square inch of surface area. A main function of the skin is to eliminate waste products. You may recall a James Bond film called Gold Finger, in which a young woman model was sprayed completely over with gold paint--and died from having her pores closed up and unable to detoxify. Cayenne encourages sweating and detoxification, which is an extremely important function in toxically burdened Americans.[53]

Ulcers. While it may seem odd that cayenne can actually help to heal a stomach ulcer, scientific evidence points us in that direction. People in Malaysia and India eat much more hot peppers and have fewer stomach ulcers than people in China. Studies since 1937 have shown that people who eat more hot peppers get fewer stomach problems, including ulcers.[54] And while no one will argue that TOO MUCH hot peppers will produce stomach irritation and eventually ulcers, just the right amount will prevent and even cure ulcers. Scientists find that capsaicin may help heal ulcers by:

⇒ dilating blood vessels in the stomach region, which accelerates healing

⇒ increasing the flow of protective mucus over the ulcer

⇒ killing the bacteria, Helicobacter pylori, which causes many case of peptic ulcer.

Dr. D.Y. Graham and colleagues reported in the Journal of the American Medical Association that administering a healthy dose (30 grams or one ounce) of jalapeno alone in the stomach did not cause any gastric erosion based upon their endoscope exams. Yet these researchers did find that taking aspirin with a bland meal caused measurable gastric erosion (the makings of an ulcer) in 11 out of 12 subjects.[55]

One of the most common causes of ulcers in America is the excessive use of aspirin, which provokes microscopic bleeding in the stomach wall. When researchers gave volunteers 20 grams of chilis (less than an ounce) 30 minutes before giving 600 milligrams of aspirin (a routine dose), the damage from the aspirin was substantially reduced.[56]

Another common cause of ulcers in America is alcohol consumption, which irritates the stomach lining. In animal studies, a reasonable amount of chili intake was able to protect the stomach from damage by alcohol, even when the animals were fasted for 24 hours before alcohol was given.[57] If you do drink alcohol, then cayenne may help reduce the damage to the stomach from alcohol.

Urinary tract pain. Medical administration of capsaicin to the bladder has been very effective in reducing pain.[58] Capsaicin supplements taken orally have been helpful in reducing the pain in urination and frequency of urination (micturition).[59] Take 1-2 capsules of cayenne powder with lunch and dinner.

Warming effect. Since cayenne is such a potent vasodilator, it has been used to help speed the sensation of feeling in frostbitten hands and feet. The Denver Broncos professional football team used cayenne rubbed on the feet to keep their feet warm while playing in a blizzard in December of 1987 against the San Diego Chargers.[60] The Broncos won the game. In order to try this, for you snowmobilers out there, sprinkle cayenne pepper in your socks. Or, liquify a small container of petroleum jelly in the microwave, then mix in 3-4 capsules of cayenne powder and let cool before applying to skin. Remember, your feet may "feel" hot, but you may be losing body heat at a faster rate, so watch the possibilities of frostbite.

Worms. Ask any farmer, or veterinarian or pet owner about the need to purge worms and parasites from the colon of ALL animals. Medication, called a vermifuge or anthelmintic, is given often to animals to clean out the inevitable worms and parasites that collect in the digestive tract. These worms and parasites sap us of energy, change the environment in the gut and lower the immune system. Although the sanitation at our dinner table is, no doubt, much better than a dog's dinner bowl or a cow's feeding trough, many humans are afflicted with parasites and worms.[61]

Cayenne can help. At a meeting for the American Society for Microbiology held at Louisiana State University, scientists reported the extraordinary ability of hot sauce to kill microorganisms, including a bacteria (Vibrio vulnificus) that is commonly found in oysters and can cause serious health problems in humans eating the oysters. Hot sauce killed the more common intestinal infections (shigella, E. coli, and salmonella) in one minute flat. Ever notice how "gringos" seem vulnerable to the tap water in many Latin American countries? Maybe all that hot sauce in the local's diet is a major protector against worms, parasites and bacterial food poisoning. Next time someone warns you "don't drink the water", reach for some extra cayenne for that meal.

ENDNOTES

[1] . U.S. Bureau of Census, STATISTICAL ABSTRACT OF THE UNITED STATES, p.94, 116th ed, Washington, DC 1996

[2] . Rubino, A., et al., Cardiovascular Research, vol.31, p.467, 1996

[3] . Quillin, P., HEALING NUTRIENTS, p.314, Random House, NY, 1987

[4] . Cerinic, MM, et al., Journal of Rheumatology, vol.22, no.8, p.1447, 1995

[5] . McCarthy, GM, et al., Journal Rheumatology, vol.19, p.604, 1992

[6] . Colpaert, FC, et al., Life Sciences, vol.32, p.1827, 1983

[7] . Lopez-Carillo, L., et al., American Journal Epidemiology, vol.139, p.263, 1994

[8] . Surh, YJ, et al., Food Chemical Toxicology, vol.34, p.313, 1996

[9] . Unnikrishnan, MC, et al., Cancer Letters, vol.51, p.85, 1990

[10] . Dib, B, Pharmacol Biochem Behav., vol.28, p.65, 1987

[11] . Monsereenusorn, Y., Q.J.Crude Drug Research, vol.18, p.1, 1980

[12] . Emanuele, NV, et al., Comprehensive Therapy, vol.21, no.10, p.579, 1995

[13] . Diabetes Care, vol.15, p.159, 1992

[14] . Tandan, R., et al., Diabetes Care, vol.15, no.1, p.8, 1992

[15] . O'Neil, TP, Respiratory Medicine, vol.85, suppl.A, p.35, 1991

[16] . Roquebert, J., et al., Annales Pharmaceutiques Francaises, vol.36, p.361, 1978

[17] . Bevan, S., et al., British Journal of Pharmacology, p.32, May 1991

[18] . Kawada, T., et al., Journal Nutrition, vol.116, p.1272, 1986

[19] . Wallach, J., INTERPRETATION OF DIAGNOSTIC TESTS, p.465, Little, Brown, Boston, 1996

[20] . Fusco, BM, et al., Pain, vol.59, p.321, 1994

[21]. Biser, S., CURING WITH CAYENNE, Univ.Natural Healing, Charlottesville, VA, 1997

[22] . D'Alonzo, AJ, et al., European Journal Pharmacology, vol.272, p.269, Jan.1995

[23] . Bell, D., et al., Pharmacological Reviews, vol.48, no.2, p.253, 1996

[24] . Govindarajan, VS, et al., Critical Reviews in Food Science & Nutrition, vol.29, no.6, p.435, 1991

[25] . Sambaiah, K., et al., Nutrition Reports International, vol.18, p.521, 1978

[26] . Srinivasan, MR, et al., Nutrition Reports International, vol.21, p.455, 1980

[27] . Ki, P, et al., IRCS Medical Science Library Compendium, vol.10, p.446, 1982

[28] . Srinivasan, MR, et al., Nutrition Reports International, vol.38, no.3, p.571, 1988

[29] . Ki, P, et al., IRCS Medical Science Biochemistry, vol.10, p.446, 1982

[30] . Virag, R., et al., Lancet, p.183, Jan.26, 1985

[31] . Nelson, C., Journal National Cancer Institute, vol.86, p. 1381, 1994

[32] . Mowrey, DB, SCIENTIFIC VALIDATION OF HERBAL MEDICINE, p.197, Keats, New Canaan, CT, 1986

[33] . Yoshida, T., Journal Nutrition Science Vitaminology, vol.34, p.587, 1988

[34] . Griffin, MR, et al., Archives Family Medicine, vol.4, p.1049, Dec.1995

[35] . Berkow, R. (ed), MERCK MANUAL, p.1232, 16th ed.Merck, Rahway, NJ 1992

[36] . Altman, RD, et al., Arthritis Rheumatology, vol.23, suppl.3, p.25, 1994

[37] . Bernstein, JE, Clinics in Dermatology, vol.9, p.497, 1992

[38] . Winter, J., et al., British Journal Anaesthesia, vol.75, p.157, 1995

[39]. Perkins, M., et al., Annals Rheumatic Diseases, vol.55, p.715, 1996
[40]. Markovits, E., International Journal Dermatology, vol.36, p.401, 1997
[41]. Dini, D, et al., Pain, vol.54, p.223, 1993
[42]. Fusco, BM, et al., Anesthesia Analgesics, vol.74, p.375, 1992
[43]. Bernstein, JE, et al., Journal American Academy Dermatology, vol.15, p.504, 1986
[44]. Breberian, B., et al., Journal Investigative Dermatology, vol.94, p.506, 1990
[45]. Palevitch, D., et al., Journal of Herbs, Spices & Medicinal Plants, vol.3, no.2, p.55, 1995
[46]. Peikert, A., et al., Journal Neurology, vol.238, p.452, 1991
[47]. Lacroix, JS, et al., Clinical Experience Allergy, vol.21, p.595, 1991
[48]. Visudhiphan, S., et al., American Journal Clinical Nutrition, vol.35, p.1452, 1982
[49]. Langer, SE, SOLVED THE RIDDLE OF ILLNESS, Keats, New Canaan, CT, 1984
[50]. Wilson, ED, WILSON'S SYNDROME, Cornerstone, Orlando, 1991
[51]. Barnes, BO, et al., HYPOTHYROIDISM, Harper & Row, NY, 1976
[52]. Turnbull, A., Dublin Medical Press, vol.1, p.95, 1850
[53]. Lee, TS, Journal of Physiology, vol.124, p.528, 1954
[54]. Kang, JY, Singapore Medical Journal, vol.33, p.468, 1992
[55]. Graham, DY, et al., Journal American Medical Association, vol.260, p.3473, 1988
[56]. Yeoh, KG, et al., Digestive Disease Science, vol.40, p.580, 1995
[57]. Kang, JY, et al., Gut, vol.36, p.664, 1995
[58]. Barbanti, G, et al., British Journal Urology, vol.71, p.686, 1993
[59]. Maggi, CA, et al., Journal Urology, vol.142, p.150, 1989
[60]. DeWitt, D., et al., HEAT WAVE, p.131, Crossing Press, Freedom, CA, 1995
[61]. Gittleman, AL, GUESS WHAT CAME TO DINNER, Avery, Garden City Park, NY, 1993

CHAPTER THREE
★
COOKING WITH HOT CHILIS

by Noreen Quillin & Patrick Quillin

While using cayenne as a capsule or powder on your food is an effective way of gaining the health benefits, you may want to sample some of the following recipes to see if you can also benefit from the flavor of hot peppers.

How to peel fresh green chilis.
Wash and wipe dry. Arrange peppers close together in a broiler pan; place 1 inch from the heat in a preheated broiler. Turn chilis often until they are blistered and lightly browned all over. As the chilis are done, drop them into a paper bag; then close the bag. When cool enough to handle, peel off loose skin with a knife; leave any small pieces that refuse to come off easily. For a milder flavor; cut the chili open and remove the seeds.

USING CHILIS AS SEASONINGS

Chili Water
2 jalapeno chilis
2 Tbs. minced ginger
2 Tbs. vinegar
1 clove garlic
1/8 tsp. sea salt
2 cups water
Remove the stems and seeds from the chilis. Puree in a blender; the chilis, ginger, vinegar, garlic, salt and 1/2 cup of water. Bring the rest of the water to a boil and add the puree. Bring the mixture to a boil. Remove from the stove and place in a glass jar. Keep it in the refrigerator after it has cooled. Use a few tablespoons as a soup base and in cooking.

Soup or Salad Seasoning
1 tsp. ground chili
2 tsp. onion powder
1 tsp. ground allspice
1 tsp. ground thyme
2 tsp. ground cinnamon
1 tsp. ground cloves
1/4 tsp. ground nutmeg
1/4 tsp. ground mace
1/2 tsp. garlic powder
1/2 tsp. pepper
1/2 tsp. salt
Mix the ingredients together and use in a salt shaker. Use liberally to spice up your food.

Creole Seasoning
12 oz. salt
1/2 oz. black pepper
1 oz. cayenne pepper
1/2 oz. garlic powder
1/2 oz. chili powder
     Blend ingredients and store in a jar with a tight lid. Makes about one and a half cups of seasoning.

Creole Seafood Seasoning
1/6 cup salt
1/6 cup paprika
1/8 cup black pepper
1/8 cup garlic powder
1 1/2 Tbs. onion powder
1 Tbs. cayenne pepper
1 Tbs. oregano
1 Tbs. thyme
     Combine all ingredients and mix. Keeps indefinitely in a tightly sealed glass jar. Makes one cup.

Roasted Nut Meal
1 cup toasted nuts of your choice or combination
1/4 cup toasted sesame or sunflower seeds
1 1/4 tsp. chili powder
1/2 tsp. cumin powder
1/8 tsp. garlic powder
1/8 tsp. onion powder
1/8 tsp. clove powder
2 Tbs. nutritional yeast (opt.)
     Blend all ingredients in blender until nuts make a nut meal. Use to sprinkle on grains, vegetables, or salad dishes.

Hot Bean Paste

6 dried red chilis
1 can (15-16 oz.) red beans
1/2 cup water
1/2 tsp. cornstarch
1 tsp. vinegar
3 cloves garlic, chopped
2 Tbs. onion, minced fine
1 Tbs. vegetable oil
1/4 tsp. salt

Remove stems and seeds from the chilis. Place the chilis in hot water for 15 minutes or until soft. Drain and chop. Strain the beans and puree in a blender until smooth. Use some of the bean liquid if necessary. Mix 1 tablespoon of the water with the cornstarch and vinegar.

Saute the chilis, garlic and onion in the oil. Add the beans, salt and the rest of the water. Cover and simmer for 20 minutes. Stir in the cornstarch and simmer for 12 minutes more. Refrigerate in a glass jar.

USING CHILIS IN SAUCES

Apple Chutney
5 lbs. apples
1/2 cup water
1/4 cup butter
1/2 tsp. crushed chili pepper
1 Tbs. can California diced green chilis
1 tsp. nutmeg
1/2 tsp. allspice
1 tsp. ginger
1 1/2 tsp. cinnamon
dash nutmeg
1 1/2 cups honey

Peel, core, and chop apples into quarters. Steam apples in water until tender. When done, remove lid and cook off excess water, being careful not to burn. In a deep skillet , heat butter and toast spices. Add apples and chilis. Cook away excess liquid on high heat, stirring often. Add honey and cook on medium heat until jamlike, stirring frequently to prevent sticking and burning. Remove from heat, allow to cool, then refrigerate. Can be served warm, but it is better chilled.

Garlic chili
6 dried red New Mexican chilis
1 1/4 tsp. garlic powder
1/8 tsp. onion powder

Remove the stems and seeds from the chilis and cover with water. Boil for 15 minutes. Puree all ingredients together in a blender until smooth. Allow to cool before serving.

Seafood Salsa
2 habanero chilis
2 limes, juiced
2 Tbs. water
1/8 tsp. garlic powder
1/3 head cabbage, grated
1 onion, finely chopped
     Remove stems and seeds from chilis. Mince chilis. Mix the lime juice and water. Pour over rest of the ingredients in a bowl. Mix.

Easy Salsa
5-6 jalapeno chilis
1 large onion, minced
2 medium tomatoes, minced
1 Tbs. cilantro, minced
2 Tbs. parsley, minced
1/4 cup red wine vinegar
1/4 cup olive oil
     Remove stems and seeds from chilis. Mince fine. Mix all the ingredients together. Cover and leave at room temperature for about an hour.

Serrano Salsa
5 serrano chilis
1/2 pound tomatillos, chopped
1/2 cup onion, minced
1 Tbs. cilantro, minced
1 Tbs. parsley, minced
1/4 tsp. salt
     Remove stems and seeds from chilis. Chop. Place all ingredients in a blender and puree. You might need to add a bit of water. You want the sauce to be thick.

Seafood Taco Salsa
5 dried habanero chilis, stems remove
1/4 cup onion, chopped
1 pound mango, peeled and chopped
2 Tbs. golden raisins
1/8 tsp. ground turmeric
1 fresh lime, juiced
     Cover the chilis with water in a saucepan.
Add onions. Simmer until chilis are soft. Add the
mango and raisins and bring to the beginning of a
boil. Remove from heat. Place all the ingredients in
a blender and puree.

Peach Salsa
3 large peaches
1/3 cup fructose
2/3 cup peach juice
2 Tbs. vinegar
3 Tbs. dried red New Mexican chili, crushed
1/4 tsp. cinnamon
1/4 tsp. ground cumin
     Peel and dice the peaches. Dissolve the
fructose in the peach juice and vinegar. Add the
chili, cinnamon, and cumin. Bring to a boil, then
simmer for 20 minutes. Add the peaches and simmer
for 5 minutes. This is great with grilled food.

Relish Salsa
6 cloves garlic, minced
1/4 cup lemon juice
1 1/2 Tbs. olive oil
1 1/2 Tbs. parsley, minced
1 tsp. crushed New Mexican red chili
salt and pepper to taste

Mix the ingredients and place in a nonreactive container. Refrigerate overnight. Let the mixture sit at room temperature for about an hour before serving.

Avocado Chili

1/4 cup serrano chilis
1/4 cup jalapeno chilis
1/4 cup onion, chopped
1/2 cup lime juice
1/4 tsp. sea salt
3 tomatoes, chopped fine, keep juice
1/4 cup parsley, minced
1 large avocado, chopped fine

Place the first 5 ingredients in a nonreactive bowl. Mix. Refrigerate for 1 hour. Drain off the lime juice. Add the rest of the ingredients. Serve.

Green Chili Sauce

12 green chilis, finely chopped
2 tomatoes, finely chopped
2-3 cloves garlic, minced
1 onion, diced
salt, optional

Place all the ingredients in a saucepan. Add enough water to just cover. Simmer over medium low heat for 10 minutes. Add salt to taste.

Chili Wine Sauce

6 green chilis, roasted and peeled
1 onion, minced
3 cloves garlic, minced
1 Tbs. canola oil
1 Tbs. whole wheat flour
1 tomato, chopped
1 cup water

2/3 cup white wine (or water)

Chop the chilis. Saute the onion and garlic in the oil. Add the flour. Toast the flour lightly. Add all of the ingredients and bring to a boil. Reduce the heat and simmer for 30 minutes.

Hot Hot Chili Sauce
12 chili de arbols
2 1/2 Tbs. apple cider vinegar
3 cloves garlic
1/2 tsp. dried oregano
1/2 tsp. salt
1/2 tsp. dry parsley
1/4 tsp. ground cumin
1/2 tsp. salt
1/2 cup water

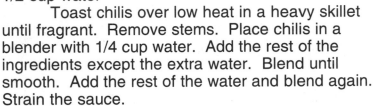

Toast chilis over low heat in a heavy skillet until fragrant. Remove stems. Place chilis in a blender with 1/4 cup water. Add the rest of the ingredients except the extra water. Blend until smooth. Add the rest of the water and blend again. Strain the sauce.

Enchilada Sauce
10 dried New Mexican chilis
1 large onion, chopped
4 cloves garlic, chopped
1 Tbs. canola oil
1 Tbs. dried parsley
2 2/3 cups water
1/2 tsp. dried oregano

Bake chilis on a baking pan in a preheated 240 degree oven for about 10 minutes until chilis smell like they are toasted.

Saute the onion and garlic in the oil in a sauce pan until soft. Remove stems and seeds from the chilis and crumble into the sauce pan. Add the rest of the ingredients and simmer for 25 minutes. Puree in a blender until smooth. Strain.

USING CHILIS IN APPETIZERS

Spicy Peanuts
10 small dried red chilis
3 cloves garlic, minced fine
1/2 Tbs. olive oil
1 pound salted peanuts
1/2 tsp. chili powder

Fry chilis, garlic and oil for 1 minute. Stir the full minute. Mix in the nuts and fry until lightly brown. Sprinkle on the chili powder. Mix well. Cool. Make this snack up the day before.

Chili Cheese Dip
6 fresh California green chilis
1/2 Tbs. canola oil
1 onion, chopped
1 clove garlic, minced fine
1/2 tsp. salt
2 1/2 oz. evaporated milk
pinch cumin (opt.)
2/3 cup shredded cheddar cheese
Baked corn chips

Wash and dry the chilis. Peel the chilis as directed in the beginning of this section. Remove seeds if you want it more mild. Chop the chilis.

Saute onions and garlic in the oil. Add the chilis and salt and cook for about 5 minutes. Add the evaporated milk and optional cumin and cook gently for 4 minutes. Remove from heat. After one minute,

add cheese and cover. Stir after the cheese melts.
Serve hot with chips.

Stuffed Hot Chilis
1/2 pound lean ground beef
1 onion, diced
2 cloves garlic, crushed
1/4 cup raisins
10 black olives, sliced
1 cup cooked brown rice,
measured after cooking
2 ounces grated gouda cheese
12 large yellow chilis

 Brown the beef, onion and garlic. Remove
from heat. Add the rest of the ingredients. Cut stems
out of each chili and remove the seeds. Keep the
top. Stuff the chilis with the mixture. Seal the hole
with the top of the chili. Bake in a preheated 350
degree oven, covered, for 20 minutes.

Stuffed Mushrooms
8 large mushrooms
1 Tbs. butter
1 spring onion, finely chopped
1 clove garlic, minced
1 Tbs. parsley, finely chopped
1 tsp. chili powder
1/4 cup dry whole wheat cracker crumbs
1/4 cup feta cheese, crumbled fine

 Twist the stems off the mushrooms. Finely
chop the stems. Saute the onion, stems and garlic in
the butter. Remove from heat. Add the rest of the
ingredients. Mix well. Stuff the mushrooms with the
filling. Make a mound of the filling. Place
mushrooms, filling side up, in a baking dish sprayed

with vegetable oil. Bake in a preheated 350 degree oven for 20 minutes.

Raw Fish Appetizer
1 1/2 pounds sole (or other mild-flavored fish)
1 cup lemon juice
2 canned California green chilis, seeded and chopped
1/2 cup onion, minced
1 clove garlic, minced (opt.)
2 tomatoes, chopped
1 tsp. salt
1/4 tsp. oregano leaves, crushed
1 tsp. dry parsley, crushed
1/4 cup olive oil
      Cut fish in small, thin slices. Place in a bowl with the lemon juice and refrigerate for 2 hours. Stir in the rest of the ingredients. Serve in chilled cups.

USING CHILIS IN SOUPS AND SALADS

Yogurt Dressing
1 can (4 oz.) diced California green chilis
1 cup plain yogurt
2 Tbs. minced onion
1 tsp. Dijon mustard
1/4 tsp. garlic salt
pepper
   Mix all of the ingredients and refrigerate for at least an hour.

Gazpacho
2 medium tomatoes, chopped
1 small onion, diced
1/2 cucumber, peeled
and diced
1/2 avocado, chopped
2 Tbs. canned mild green
diced chilis
1/2 tsp. oregano leaves,
crumbled
1/2 Tbs. parsley,
chopped
2 Tbs. wine vinegar
2 Tbs. olive oil
4 cups canned tomato juice
2 limes

   Put the first 9 ingredients into a serving bowl. Stir in the tomato juice. Chill. Serve with lime juice to taste.

Black Bean Soup

2 cups dried black beans
2 quarts water
8 cups chicken broth
1 pound ham hocks, cracked
1/4 tsp. allspice or cumin
6 jalapeno chilis, stems & seeds removed, chopped
2 medium onions, chopped
1 Tbs. parsley, chopped
1 Tbs. cilantro, chopped (opt.)
2 cloves garlic, minced
1 can (8 oz.) tomato sauce
1/2 cup dry red wine or 3 Tbs. lemon juice

Rinse and sort beans, discarding any foreign material. Combine beans and water in a 5-quart pot and bring to a boil for 2 minutes. Cover and set aside for 1 hour. Drain off water and add the chicken broth, ham, allspice, chilis, onion, parsley, optional cilantro and garlic. Bring to a boil and reduce to a simmer. Cook for about 1 1/2 hours. Add the tomato sauce and simmer for 1/2 hour. Remove the ham and shred the meat. Puree the bean mixture, if desired, and add back to the pot. Add the ham and wine and reheat soup.

Salad of Swordfish

1 1/2 cups chicken stock
2 tsp. vinegar
3/4 pound swordfish, crosscut into 1/4-inch strips
1/2 cup celery, julienne
1/2 cup carrots, julienne
1/2 cup spring onions, sliced
1 Tbs. California diced green chilis (canned)
4 olives, sliced
1 Tbs. olive oil

1 Tbs. lemon juice
1 Tbs. orange juice
cayenne pepper
alfalfa sprouts or spinach leaves

Combine the chicken stock and vinegar in a large nonstick skillet. Bring to a boil, then simmer. Drop in fish and poach for 3 to 5 minutes. Remove fish and set aside. Now poach celery and carrots for 3 to 5 minutes. Drain and add the vegetables to the fish. Chill for 30 minutes.

Combine the rest of the ingredients except the cayenne and sprouts and add to the chilled fish. Coat evenly. Serve on the sprouts. Sprinkle with the cayenne pepper.

Tangy Crab Salad
Salad:
Mixed salad greens
1 small onion, thinly sliced
1 carrot, peeled and grated
3/4 pound cooked crabmeat
1 tomato, chopped
8 black olives, sliced
Dressing:
4 green Mexican chilis, roasted, peeled, seeded and chopped.
1/2 cup plain yogurt
2 Tbs. lime juice
1 tsp. horseradish sauce (opt.)

Combine the ingredients for the dressing. Refrigerate for an hour. Arrange the salad greens on 4 individual plates and arrange the onions and carrots on top. Next add the crab. Top with the tomatoes and olives. Serve the dressing on the side.

USING CHILIS WITH EGGS

Huevos Rancheros
Eggs, fried
corn or flour tortillas
mild salsa, warmed
avocado slices
chopped green
onion
grated cheese

    Fry eggs and
place on warmed tortillas. Pour 1/8 to 1/4 cup salsa
over eggs and garnish with the avocado and onion.
Sprinkle with cheese.

Mexican Omelet
butter or spray vegetable oil
2 eggs, beaten
1Tbs. olives, chopped
1 Tbs. canned green chilis
1/2 Tbs. onion, minced
    Melt a bit of butter or spray a frying pan with
oil. Add all the ingredients into the frying pan. As
soon as the bottom begins to set, lift edges to let
uncooked portion flow into contact with center of the
pan. When eggs are set, turn omelet out of pan.

Potato Omelet
2 potatoes, peeled and diced
1 onion, diced
2 tsp. ground chili
1 tsp. butter
1 Tbs. canola oil
1 4 oz. can diced green chili
6 eggs

2 Tbs. water
1 tsp. parsley
1/2 tsp. salt

Saute potatoes, onion and chili powder in the butter and oil over medium heat. Cover and cook for fifteen minutes or until potatoes are tender. Add the green chilis. Combine the eggs, water, parsley and salt in a bowl and beat with a fork. Pour over the potato mixture in the skillet and cook over low heat until eggs are set.

Egg Burrito
1 medium onion, diced
1 clove garlic, minced
1 Tbs. canola oil
6 eggs, beaten
1/2 cup salsa
warmed flour tortillas
6 olives, sliced
2/3 cup grated cheese
1 small tomato, diced
1 small avocado, diced
sour cream
salt to taste

Saute onion and garlic in the oil until soft. Add the eggs and salsa. Scramble until done. Place some of the egg mixture in a tortilla and add some of the rest of the ingredients to taste. Roll into a burrito.

USING CHILIS IN ENTREES

Jambalaya
1 Tbs. canola oil
1/2 pound chicken, diced
1 onion, diced
1/2 pound smoked sausage
3 cloves garlic, minced
1 bay leaf
1 Tbs. parsley, minced
1/4 tsp. dried thyme
1/4 tsp. dried basil
1/4 tsp. ground cloves
1/4 tsp. ground anise, (opt.)
1/4 tsp. Cajun powder
1 1/2 cups chicken broth
3/4 cup rice
3 small hot red chilis, crushed
1/2 tsp. Louisiana hot sauce
Salt and pepper to taste

In a large pot, saute the onion and chicken in oil until the onion is soft. Add the next 9 ingredients in oil and cook for an additional 5 minutes. Add the broth and bring to a boil. Boil for 5 minutes, then add the rest of the ingredients. Boil, then simmer, uncovered, until rice absorbs the liquid and is soft, about 15 to 20 minutes.

Casserole Enchilada
8 corn tortillas
canola oil
1 can (7 oz.) green chili salsa, heated
4 eggs, separated
1 Tbs. whole wheat flour
6 oz. shredded jack cheese

3 canned California green chilis, seeds removed and chopped

Fry the tortillas in a frying pan brushed with oil and dip in heated chili salsa. Put 1 tortilla in bottom of a 7 or 8-inch baking dish (2 inches deep at least) that has been lightly sprayed with vegetable oil. Arrange remaining tortillas, overlapping, around sides and slightly over bottom center tortilla. Beat egg whites until stiff. With same beater whip egg yolks until slightly thickened. Beat in the flour. Stir in 2/3 of the cheese, chilis and egg white. Pour into dish with tortillas. Fold tortillas down over filling. Spoon remaining salsa over tortillas, then sprinkle with cheese. Bake uncovered in a 375 degree oven for 30 minutes.

Indian Spice Chicken
4 spring onions, sliced
1 Tbs. canola oil
10 whole cardamon pods, crushed
1/4 tsp. ground cumin
1/4 tsp. lemon peel, diced fine
1/4 tsp. ground cloves
1/4 tsp. cinnamon
1 tsp. ginger, minced
3 dried red chilis, stems & seeds removed, crushed
1 tsp. honey
2 cups water
1 whole chicken, cleaned
salt to taste

Saute the onion in oil in a pot and add the cardamon and toast for one minute. Stir in all the seasonings and add the water. Stir and bring to a boil. Add the chicken and cover. Simmer for 45 minutes, turning the chicken 3 times. Remove the cover and cook until the the chicken is done, turning often to coat the chicken with the spices.

Apricot Chicken
2 tsp. cornstarch
2 tsp. apple juice or water
1/2 pound chicken breast, cut into strips
1 tsp. ginger, minced
2 tsp. garlic, minced
1 Tbs. white wine
2 Tbs. soy sauce
1 Tbs. hot bean sauce
5 dried apricots,cut in pieces and soaked in the wine
1 1/2 tsp. honey
1 Tbs. canola oil
5 small dried hot chilis
  Combine the cornstarch and apple juice. Toss with the chicken in a zip lock bag and marinate for 15 minutes. Mix together the rest of the ingredients except the oil and chilis, then set aside. This will be the sauce. Heat a wok until hot and add the oil. As soon as the oil is hot, add the chilis and chicken. Stir-fry until chicken is almost done and add the sauce. Cook for another 45 seconds. Serve on top of cooked brown rice.

Turkey Treat
1/2 medium size onion, finely chopped
2 tsp. finely chopped almonds
1 Tbs. olive oil
1 can (10 oz.) tomatillos
1/2 Tbs. cilantro, minced

1 1/2 Tbs. minced
canned California
green chilis, seeds
removed
1 cup chicken broth
1 pound sliced cooked
turkey
3 cups hot cooked wild
rice or brown rice

Combine the
onion, almonds, and oil in a pan over medium heat
and cook, stirring, until onion is limp. Whirl tomatillos
and their liquid in a blender until mixture is fairly
smooth (or rub through wire strainer, using all liquid
and pulp). Add to the onion mixture. Stir in cilantro
and chilis. Add the chicken broth and boil rapidly,
uncovered, until reduced to about 1 1/4 cups. Stir
occasionally.

Arrange meat in a wide frying pan. Pour
sauce over the meat and cover. Warm over low heat
until mixture begins to bubble slightly. Simmer for 5
to 10 minutes. Add salt to taste and serve on top of
the rice.

Chilis Rellenos
8 fresh California chilis, peeled or
1 can (7 oz) California green chilis
1/4 cup almonds, slivered
1/2 Tbs. butter
1/2 pound lean ground beef
1 Tbs. onion, minced fine
1 clove garlic, minced fine
1/4 cup tomato puree
1/4 cup raisins
2 Tbs. dry sherry
1 tsp. ground cinnamon

1/2 tsp. salt
1/4 tsp. ground
cloves
1/8 tsp. allspice
1 Tbs. vinegar
1 Tbs. dry sherry
1 tsp. fructose
4 eggs
4 Tbs. whole wheat
flour
1 Tbs. water
1/4 tsp. salt
butter

Drain the can chilis and slit down the side of each. Remove the seeds. Do the same for fresh chilis after peeling them.

Make the filling by lightly toasting the almond in the butter in a frying pan. Remove the almonds and brown the beef and onion. Add the garlic, tomato, raisins, sherry, the spices, vinegar, sherry and fructose. Cook, uncovered, until liquid is almost all gone.

Stuff the chilis. Fold the edges over each other to hold in the filling, which includes almonds. Roll each chili in flour to coat all over.

Separate the eggs. Beat whites until they form soft peaks. Beat yolks with the 4 Tbs. flour, water and salt. Fold into whites.

Over medium heat, melt enough butter to coat bottom of frying pan. Make an oval mound of about 1/2 cup of the egg mixture. Quickly lay a stuffed chili in the center of the mound and spoon about 1/3 cup mixture over top of chili. Cook for 2 to 3 minutes; gently turn and cook for 3 minutes longer or until golden brown.

You can use a cheese filling by stuffing each chili with a piece of jack cheese one inch shorter than the chili.

Enchilada Pie
1 pound lean ground beef
1 onion, chopped
1 clove garlic, minced
1 tsp. salt
1/4 tsp. cumin powder
1 Tbs. chili powder
1 can (8 oz.) tomato sauce
6 corn tortillas
olive oil
1 can (4 1/2 oz.) black olives, chopped
1 cup Cheddar cheese, grated
1/3 cup water

Brown beef and onion in a frying pan. Add the garlic, salt, cumin powder, chili powder, and tomato sauce. Spread each tortilla with a touch of oil and alternate layers of tortillas, meat sauce, olives and cheese in a 2-quart casserole dish. Add water. Cover and bake in a 400 degree oven for 20 minutes.

Green Chili Stew
2 pounds boneless beef chuck, cut in 1-inch cubes
2 Tbs. olive oil
1 bell pepper diced
1 medium onion, diced
2 cloves garlic, minced
2 cans (1 lb. 12 oz. each) tomatoes
1 can (7 oz.) California green chilis, seeded and chopped
1/4 cup parsley, chopped
1/2 tsp. honey

1/4 tsp. ground cloves
2 tsp. ground cumin
1 tsp. lemon juice
1 cup red wine or beef broth
Salt to taste

Brown the meat in 2 Tbs olive oil on all sides in a large frying pan. Remove meat with a slotted spoon and set aside. Throw away drippings, add the olive oil and cook the bell pepper, onion, and garlic until soft. In a large pot, pour in the tomatoes with the liquid. Break up tomatoes with a spoon. Add the chilis, parsley, honey, cloves, cumin, lemon juice and wine. Bring to a boil, then reduce heat to a simmer. Add all of the ingredients together, cover, and cook over low heat for 1 1/2 hours, stirring occasionally. Remove cover and simmer for 1 more hour or until meat is tender.

Chili
1 large onion, diced
1 celery stock, diced
3 cloves garlic, minced
2 jalapenos, stemmed & seeded, minced
1 1/2 pounds lean ground beef
1/2 Tbs. canola oil
1 (7-ounce) can diced green chilis
2 to 3 Tbs. chili powder
1 can (16 ounces) whole tomatoes
3 Tbs. tomato paste
2 tsp. ground cumin
1 1/2 cups water
1 bay leaf
1/2 tsp. Worcester sauce (opt.)

1 tsp. sugar
6 ounces beer
salt and pepper to taste

In a large pot, saute the onions, celery, garlic and jalapeno in the oil. Add the beef and cook until meat is brown. Add remaining ingredients. Mash the tomatoes in the sauce. Simmer for 1 1/2 to 2 hours, stirring occasionally.

Stuffed Beef Steaks
5 Anaheim chilis
4 jalapeno chilis
1 medium onion, chopped
3 cloves garlic, minced
1 Tbs. olive oil
1/2 Tbs. parsley, minced
1/2 grated Monterey Jack cheese
2 pounds trimmed filet of beef, cut in 4 thick steaks
fresh ground pepper (opt.)

Remove the stems and seeds, then chop the chilis. Saute the onion, chilis, and garlic in the oil until slightly soft. Remove, cool and mix in the cheese and parsley. Refrigerate this a day before using it.

Slice into the steaks from the edge, creating a pocket for the stuffing. Stuff with the chili mixture and close the opening with a toothpick. You can season the outside of the steaks with the black pepper. Grill over hot charcoal or gas barbecue.

Hot Time Halibut
1/4 cup hot pepper sauce
1/4 cup red wine vinegar
1 Tbs. olive oil
1/2 Tbs. Worcestershire sauce
1/4 tsp. garlic powder

2 Tbs. smoke-flavor BBQ sauce
4 halibut steaks
  In a small bowl, blend the first 6 ingredients.
Place this marinade in a zip lock bag with the fish
and gently coat the fish with the marinade.
Refrigerate for several hours. Place the fish on a
nonstick baking sheet and bake in a 425 degree
oven for 10-15 minutes until done.

Tuna Cakes
2 slices whole wheat bread (crusts removed)
1 can (6 1/2 ounces) tuna, drained
1 egg
1 pimiento, chopped
1/4 tsp. celery salt
1/8 tsp. cayenne pepper
1/4 tsp. lemon juice
1 Tbs. canned California diced green chilis
  Tear the bread into small pieces. Mix all the
ingredients together in a bowl. Shape the mixture
into 3 firm patties about 1/2 inch thick. Fry the patties
in oil over medium heat until golden brown on both
sides, 4 to 5 minutes.

Scallops in a Blanket
1/4 cup spring onions, sliced
1/4 cup olives, sliced
1 clove garlic, minced
1 tsp. chili peppers, minced
1/8 tsp. ground cumin
1 pound scallops
4 flour tortillas (9 or 10 inch)
1/2 cup chunky salsa
1/2 cup no-fat sour cream
  Saute the onions, olives, garlic and chili in oil
in a frying pan for 2 minutes over medium heat. Add

the cumin and scallops and saute for 3 minutes.
Warm the tortillas in a cloth napkin in the microwave
for 20-25 seconds. Spoon the scallop mixture onto
the tortillas, then roll to wrap and fold under ends.
Serve with the salsa and sour cream.

Hog Heaven
16 dried New Mexican chilis, stems removed
2 1/2 cups water
4 cloves garlic
1 tsp. dried oregano
1/2 tsp. dried basil
1 tsp. dried parsley
1/2 cup light white wine
3 pounds lean pork, cut into strips
Cover the chilis with the water and simmer for
10 minutes or until softened. Place the drained chilis
and seasonings in a blender and puree with just
enough of the wine to make a thick sauce. Marinate
the pork in the sauce overnight.
In a 300 degree preheated oven, bake the
pork in the marinade, covered, for a couple of hours
or until the meat is very tender and starts to fall apart.
Uncover during the last 30 minutes of cooking to
slowly bake off excess liquid.

Chipotle Tenderloin
3 dried or canned chipotle chilis
6 cloves garlic
1 small onion, chopped
1/2 tsp. ground allspice
1/2 tsp. ground mace
1/2 tsp. ground cloves
1/4 cup vinegar
1/2 cup orange juice
1/4 cup lime juice

1/4 cup sucanat or brown sugar
1/2 tsp. black pepper
1 cup olive oil
2 pork tenderloins, trimmed of excess fat

If using dried chipotles, cover with hot water for 15 minutes to soften. Remove the stems. Place all ingredients except the oil and meat in a blender and puree while slowly drizzling in the oil. Place the meat and this marinate in a ziplock bag for at least an hour.

Bake in a 400 degree oven for about 8 minutes, turning every 2 minutes. Slice the tenderloins into 1/2 inch pieces and serve.

APPENDIX
★
WHERE TO FIND HOT CHILI PRODUCTS

Mail-Order Catalogs

Blazing Chile Bros.
(800) 473-8840

Calido Chile Traders
5360 Merriam Drive
Merriam, KS 66203
(800) 568-8468

Chile Pepper Magazine
 (800) 359-1483

Chile Today, Hot Tamale
919 Highway 33, Suite 47
Freehold, NJ 07728
(800) 468-7377

Colorado Spice Company
5030 Nome Street, Unit A
Denver CO 80239
(800) 866-HOWL

Dean and DeLuca
560 Broadway
New York, NY 10012
(212) 431-1691

Don Alfonso Foods
P.O. Box 201988
Austin, TX 78720
(800) 456-6100

Enchanted Seeds
P.O. Box 6087
Las Cruces, NM 88006
(505) 233-3033

Flamingo Flats
Box 441
St. Michael's, MD 21663
(800) 468-8841

Frieda's, Inc.
P.O. Box 584888
Los Angeles, CA 90058
(800) 421-9477

GMB Specialty Foods, Inc.
Norma Bishop Mustard & Sauces
Scottsdale Mustard Co.
Gourmet Mustard Co.
P.O. Box 962
San Juan Capistrano, CA 92693-0962
(714) 240-3053

Gourmet Gallery
320 North Highway 89A
Singua Plaza
Sedona, AZ 86336
(800) 888-3484

Hell's Kitchen Inc.
216 Lippincott Avenue
Riverside, NJ 08075
(609) 764-1487

Hot Sauce Club of America
P.O. Box 687
Indian Rocks Beach
FL 34635-0687
(800) SAUCE-2-U

Hot Sauce Harry's
3422 Flair Drive
Dallas TX 75229
(214) 902-8552

Le Saucier
Faneuil Hall Marketplace
Boston, MA 02109
(617) 227-9649

Lotta Hotta
3150 Mercier, Suite 516
Kansas City, MO 64111
(816) 931-6700

Melissa's World Variety
P.O. Box 21127
Los Angeles, CA 90021
(800) 468-7111

Nancy's Specialty Market
P.O. Box 327
Wye Mills, MD 21679
(800) 462-6291

Old Southwest Trading
Company
P.O. Box 7545
Albuquerque, NM 87194
(505) 836-0168

Pendery's
304 East Belknap
Fort Worth, TX 76102
(800) 533-1879

The Pepper Gal
P.O. Box 23006
Ft. Lauderdale, FL 33307
(305) 537-5540

Pepper Joe's, Inc.
7 Tyburn Court
Timonium, MD 21093
(410) 561-8158

Santa Fe School of Cooking
116 W. San Francisco Street
Santa Fe, NM 87501
(505) 983-4511

Shepherd's Garden Seeds
6116 Highway 9
Felton, CA 95018
(408) 335-6910

South Side Pepper Co.
320 N. Walnut Street
Mechanicsburg, PA 17055
(717) 691-7132

Salsa Express
100 N. Tower Rd.
Alamo, TX 78516
800-437-2572

Retail Shops

Calido Chile Traders
5360 Merriam Drive
Merriam, KS 66203
(913) 384-0019; (800) 568-8468

Caribbean Spice Company
2 South Church Street
Fairhope, AL 36532
(800) 990-6088

Central Market
4001 North Lamar
Austin, TX 78756
(512) 206-1000

Chile Hill Emporium
Box 9100
Bernalillo, NM 87004
(505) 867-3294

The Chile Shop
109 East Water Street
Santa Fe, NM 87501
(505) 983-6080

Chili Patch U.S.A.
204 San Felipe N.W.
Albuquerque, NM 87104
(505) 242-4454; (800) 458-0646

Chili Pepper Emporium
328 San Felipe N.W.
Albuquerque, NM 87104
(505) 242-7538

Chili Pepper Mania
1709-F Airline Hwy., P.O. Box 232
Hollister, CA 95023
(408) 636-8259

Chutney's
143 Delaware Street
Lexington, OH 44904
(419) 884-2853

Colorado Spice Company
5030 Nome Street, Unit A
Denver, CO 80239
(303) 373-0141; (800) 67-SPICE

Coyote Cafe General Store
132 West Water Street
Santa Fe, NM 87501
(505) 982-2454; (800) 866-HOWL

Dat'l Do-It Hot Shop
P.O. Box 4019
St. Augustine, FL 32085
(904) 824-5303; (800) HOT-DATL

Dat'l Do-It Hot Shop
Dadeland Mall
7535 North Kendall Drive
Miami, FL 37211
(305) 253-0248

Down Island Ventures
P.O. Box 37
Cruz Bay
St. John, U.S. Virgin Islands
00832
(809) 693-7200

Eagle Mountain Gifts
634 South China Lake
Boulevard
Ridgecrest, CA 93555
(619) 375-3071

Fiery Foods
909 20th Avenue South
Nashville, TN 37212
(615) 320-5475

Free Spirit
420 South Mill Avenue
Tempe, AZ 85281
(602) 966-4339

Garden Gate Gift Shop
Tucson Botanical Gardens
2150 North Alvernon Way
Tucson, AZ 85712
(602) 326-9686

GMB Specialty Foods, Inc.
P.O. Box 962
San Juan Capistrano, CA
92693-0962
(714) 240-3053

Gourmet Gallery
320 North Highway 89A
Singua Plaza
Sedona, AZ 86336
(520) 282-2682

Hatch Chile Express
P.O. Box 350
Hatch, NM 87937
(505) 267-3226

Hell's Kitchen Inc.
Route 130 at Route 73
Haddonfield Road
Pennsauken, NJ 08010
~~(609) 663-6606~~

Hot Hot Hot
56 South Delacey Avenue
Pasadena, CA 91105
(818) 564-1090; 800) 959-
7742

Hot Kicks
4349 Raymir Place
Wauwatosa, WI 53222
(414) 536-7808

Hot Licks
P.O. Box 7854
Hollywood, FL 33081
(305) 987-7105

Hot Lovers Fiery Foods
1282 Wolseley Avenue
Winnipeg, Manitoba R3G
1H4, Canada
~~(204) 772-8418~~ *not in service*

Hot Papa's Fiery Flavors
11121 Weeden Road
Randolph, NY 14772
(716) 358-4302

The Hot Spot
5777 South Lakeshore Dr
Shreveport, LA 71119
(318) 635-3581

The Hot Spot
1 Riverfront Plaza #300
Lawrence, KS 66044
(913) 841-7200

Hot Stuff
288 Argonne Avenue
Long Beach, CA 90803
(310) 438-1118

Hot Stuff
227 Sullivan Street
New York, NY 10012
(212) 254-6120; (800) 466-8206

Hots for You—
Chili Pepper Emporium
8843 Shady Meadow Drive
Sandy, UT 84093
(801) 255-7800

Jones and Bones
621 Capitola Avenue
Capitola, CA 95010
(408) 462-0521

Le Saucier
Faneuil Hall Marketplace
Boston, MA 02109
(617) 227-9649

Lotta Hotta
3150 Mercier, Suite 516
Kansas City, MO 64111
(816) 931-6700

The Original Hot Sauce
Company
Avenue of Shops
1421-C Larimer Street

Denver, CO 80202
(303) 615-5812

New Orleans
School of Cooking
620 Decatur Street
New Orleans, LA 70130
(504) 482-3632

Pampered Pirate
4 Norre Gade
St. Thomas, U.S. Virgin
Islands 00802
(809) 775-5450
Mailing address: P.O. Box
590
St. Thomas, U.S. Virgin
Islands 00804

Peppers
2009 Highway 1
Dewey Beach, DE 19971
(302) 227-1958; (800) 998-3473

Pepperhead Hot Shoppe
7036 Kristi Court
Garner, NC 27529
(919) 553-4576

Pepper Joe's, Inc.
7 Tyburn Court
Timonium, MD 21093
(410) 561-8158

Potpourri
303 Romero NW
Plaza Don Luis, Old Town
Albuquerque, NM 87104
(505) 243-4087

Pungent Pod
25 Haviland Road
Queensbury, NY 12804
(518) 793-3180

Rivera's Chile Shop
109 1/2 Concho Street
San Antonio, TX 78207
(210) 226-9106

Salsas, Etc.!
3693 Tunis Avenue
San Jose, CA 95132
(408) 263-6392

Salsas, Etc.!
374 Eastridge Mall
San Jose, CA 95122
(408) 223-9020

Sambet's Cajun Store
8644 Spicewood Springs
RD, #F, Austin, TX 78759
(800) 472-6238

Santa Fe Emporium
104 West San Francisco St
Santa Fe, NM 87501
(505) 984-1966

Santa Fe School of Cooking
116 West San Francisco St
Santa Fe, NM 87501
(505) 983-4511

Santa Fe Trading Company
7 Main Street
Tarrytown, NY 10591
(914) 332-1730

Señor Chile's at Rawhide
23020 North Scottsdale RD
Scottsdale, AZ 85255
(602) 563-5600

Sherwood's Lotsa Hotsa
P.O. Box 2106
Lakeside, CA 92040
(619) 443-7982

Some Like It Hot
3208 Scott Street
San Francisco, CA 94123
(415) 441-7HOT

Some Like It Hot
301 South Light St
Baltimore, MD 21202
(410) 547-2HOT

Southern Season
P.O. Box 2678
Chapel Hill, NC 27515
(800) 253-3663

Stonewall Chili Pepper
P.O. Box 241
Stonewall, TX 78671
(210) 644-2667; (800) 232-
2995

Sunbelt Shows
P.O. Box 4980
Albuquerque, NM 87196
(505) 873-9103

Sunny Caribbee Spice
P.O. Box 3237
St. Thomas, U.S. Virgin
Islands 00803
(809) 494-2178

Tabasco Country Store
Avery Island, LA 70513
(318) 365-8173

Tabasco Country Store
1 Poydras Street
New Orleans, LA 70130
(504) 523-1711

Uncle Bill's Hot Sauce
311 N. Higgins Avenue
Missoula, MT 59801
(406) 543-5627

The Whole Earth Grainery
111 Ivinson Avenue
Laramie, WY 82070
(307) 745-4268

Seed Companies

The Cook's Garden
P.O. Box 535
Londonderry, VT 05148
(802) 824-3400

Enchanted Seeds
P.O. Box 6087
Las Cruces, NM 88006
(505) 233-3033

Native Seeds/SEARCH
2509 Campbell Ave#325
Tucson, AZ 85719

Old Southwest Trading
P.O. Box 7545
Albuquerque, NM 87194
(505) 836-0168

The Pepper Gal
P.O. Box 12534
Lake Park, FL 33403
(305) 537-5540

Plants of the Southwest
Agua Fria Route 6, Box 11A
Santa Fe, NM 87501
(505) 438-8888

Redwood City Seed Co.
P.O. Box 361
Redwood City, CA 94064
(415) 325-SEED

Seed Savers Exchange
Route 3, Box 239
Decorah, LA 52101

Seeds of Change
1364 Rufina Circle #5
Santa Fe, NM 87501
(505) 983-8956

Seeds West
P.O. Box 1739
El Prado, NM 87529
(505) 758-7268

Shepherd's Garden Seeds
6116 Highway 9
Felton, CA 95018
(408) 335-6910

Twilley Seed Co.
P.O. Box 65
Trevose, PA 19053
(800) 622-SEED

Honey, Garlic and Vinegar Better Than Prescription Drugs?

(SPECIAL) We know from scholars that ancient civilizations relied on their healing power for a wide variety of ailments. In fact, honey was so prized by the Romans for its medicinal properties that it was used instead of gold to pay taxes. Egyptian doctors believed garlic was the ultimate cure-all. And vinegar is said to have been used for everything from arthritis to obesity for thousands of years.

Today doctors and researchers hail the healing abilities of honey, garlic and vinegar as much more than folklore. Hundreds of scientific studies have been conducted on this dream team of healers. The results are conclusive on their amazing power to prevent and cure many common health problems.

These studies prove that this trio from nature's pharmacy can help **reduce blood pressure, lower cholesterol, improve circulation, lower blood sugar levels and help fight cancer.** Scientific evidence also indicates that they can be of medicinal value in the treatment of: **arthritis, athlete's foot, bronchitis, burns, colds and flu, cold sores, constipation, cramps, diarrhea, eczema, earaches, fatigue, fungus, heart problems, muscle aches, prostatitis, rheumatism, ringworm, sinus congestion, sore throat, urinary infections, virus and yeast infections and more.**

A new book called *Honey, Garlic & Vinegar Home Remedies* is now available to the general public. It shows you exactly how to make hundreds of remedies using honey, garlic and vinegar separately and in unique combinations. Each preparation is carefully described along with the health condition for which it is formulated .

Learn how to prepare ointments, tonics, lotions, poultices, syrups and compresses in your own kitchen. Whip up a batch to treat:
- **ARTHRITIS:** Doctor reports that this remedy helps relieve the pain with no side effects
- **AGE SPOTS:** Watch them fade with this mixture
- **CORNS & CALLOUSES:** Get rid of them fast with this natural method
- **HEADACHE:** Enjoy fast relief without drugs
- **HEMORRHOIDS:** Don't suffer another day without this proven recipe
- **LEG CRAMPS:** Try this simple way to quick relief
- **MUSCLE ACHES:** Just mix up a batch of this and rub it on
- **STINGS & BITES:** Medical journals recommend this remedy to reduce pain and swelling fast
- **STOMACH PROBLEMS:** This remedy calms upset stomach and is noted in medical journals for ulcers
- **TOOTHACHE:** This remedy gives instant relief until you can get to the dentist
- **WEIGHT LOSS:** Secret remedy speeds fat burn and flushes stubborn fat from hiding places

Discover all these health tips and more. You'll find: ***Dozens of easy-to-make beauty preparations for hair and skin, including a wrinkle smoother that really works. *Loads of delicious recipes using these health-giving super foods. *Tons of money-saving cleaning compounds to keep your home, car and clothing sparkling.**

Right now, as part of a special introductory offer, you can receive a special press run of the book *Honey, Garlic & Vinegar Home Remedies* for only $8.95 plus $1.00 postage and handling. Your satisfaction is 100% guaranteed. You must be completely satisfied, or simply return it in 90 days for a full refund — no questions asked.

HERE'S HOW TO ORDER: Simply print your name and address and the word "Remedies" on a piece of paper and mail it along with a check or money order for only $9.95 to: THE LEADER CO., INC., Publishing Division, Dept. HG554, P.O. Box 8347, Canton, Ohio 44711. (Make checks payable to The Leader Co., Inc.) VISA or MasterCard send card number and expiration date. Act now. Orders are filled on a first-come, first-served basis. ©1997 The Leader Co., Inc.